An Introduction To The Devout Life

François De Sales

Nihil Obstat:

P. J. TYNAN, S. T. D.

Imprimatur:

✠ EDUARDUS CARD. MACCABE
ARCHIEPISCOPUS DUBLINENSIS,
HIBERNIÆ PRIMAS.

DEDICATORY PRAYER.

O SWEET JESUS, my Lord, my Saviour, and my God, behold me here prostrate before thy majesty, devoting and consecrating this book to thy glory; give life to its words by thy blessing, that those souls for which I have written it, may receive from it the sacred inspirations which I desire for them. And particularly that of imploring for me thy immense mercy; to the end that, whilst showing others the way of devotion in this world, I may not myself be eternally rejected and confounded in the other; but that, with them, I may for ever sing, as a canticle of triumph, the words which, with my whole heart I pronounce, in testimony of my fidelity amidst the dangers of this mortal life: LIVE JESUS, LIVE JESUS; *yea, Lord Jesus, live and reign in our hearts for ever and ever. Amen.*

PREFACE

OF

St. Francis de Sales.

◆

Dear reader, I pray you to read this Preface for your satisfaction and for mine.

THE bouquet-maker, Glycera, was so skilful in diversifying the arrangement and mixture of the flowers which she used, that with the same flowers she made a great variety of bouquets: so much so that the painter, Pansias, failed when he endea-voured to copy so great a diversity, for he could not change his painting so many ways as Glycera did her bouquets. Thus the Holy Ghost disposes and arranges with such variety the instructions regarding devotion which He gives by the tongues

and pens of his servants, that, although the doctrine is always one and the same, the discourses
which are held on it are, nevertheless, very different, according to the various methods in which
they are composed. I certainly cannot, neither do
I wish, nor ought I to write in this Introduction
but what has been written by our predecessors on
this subject.   They are the same flowers which I
present to you, my reader; but the bouquet which
I have formed from them will be different from
theirs, on account of the difference of the method
of making it.

Almost all those who have hitherto treated of
devotion have had the instruction of persons wholly
retired from the world in view, or have taught a
kind of devotion leading to this absolute retire-
ment: whereas my intention is to instruct such as
live in towns, in households, or in courts, and who,
by their condition, are obliged to lead, as to the
exterior, an ordinary life, and who frequently,
under the pretext of a pretended impossibility,
will not even think of undertaking a *devout life*,
believing, that as no animal dares to taste the seed
of the herb called *Palma Christi*, so no man ought
to aspire to the palm of Christian piety so long as
he lives in the turmoil of worldly affairs.   Now,

to such persons I shall make it appear that, as the mother-of-pearl oyster lives in the sea without taking in a drop of salt-water; and as, near the Chelidonian islands, springs of fresh water may be found in the midst of the sea; and as the fire-fly moves through the flames without singeing its wings; even so, a vigorous and resolute soul may live in the world without being infected by any of its contaminations, may discover sweet springs of piety amidst its bitter waters, and may fly through the flames of earthly concupiscences without burning the wings of the holy desires of a devout life. This, it is true, is a difficult task, and therefore I could wish that many would endeavour to accomplish it with more ardour than has been hitherto used; and I, weak as I am, shall endeavour by this treatise to contribute some kind of help to those who, with a generous heart, undertake so worthy an enterprise.

Yet it was neither by my own choice nor inclination that this Introduction now appears in public. A truly honourable and virtuous soul, having some time since received of God the grace of aspiring to a devout life, desired my particular assistance for that purpose; and I, being in many ways obliged to her, and having long before discovered in her a warm disposition for this design, and, having conducted her through all the exercises suitable to her desires and condition, I left her certain instructions, in writing, to make use of, and she afterwards communicated those to a great, learned, and devout religious man; who, believing that many might profit from their perusal, earnestly requested me to publish them. I readily acquiesced, from a conviction that his judgment was superior to mine, and because his friendship had great power over my will.

Now that the whole may be more profitable and agreeable, I have revised and arranged it into a kind of method, adding several advices and instructions which appeared suited to my intention. But all this I have done, having scarcely any leisure; for which reason you will find nothing in this treatise exact or in order, but only a heap of good admonitions, delivered in plain and intelligible words, without my having bestowed as much as a thought on the ornaments of language, having business of more consequence on my hands.

I address my discourse to Philothea, because, desiring to reduce what I at first had written for one only, to the common advantage of many souls, I make use of a name applicable to all such as aspire to devotion; for the Greek word, Philothea, signifies a soul loving, or in love with, God. Regarding, then, throughout this work, a soul which, by the desire of devotion, aspires to the love of God, I have divided it into five parts. In the *first*, I endeavour, by remonstrances and exercises, to convert the simple desire of Philothea into an absolute resolution, which she at last makes, by a firm protestation, after her general confession, followed by the most Holy Communion; in which, giving herself up to her Saviour, she happily enters into his holy love. Then, in the *second part*, I try to lead her farther on; I show her the two great means whereby she may unite herself more and more to his Divine Majesty, viz., the use of the sacraments, whereby God comes to us, and holy prayer, by which He attracts us to Himself In the *third*, I show her how she ought to exercise herself in the virtues most proper for her advancement; not stopping, except at some particular advices, which she could hardly have received elsewhere, or discovered herself. In the *fourth part*, I expose some of the ambushes of her enemies to her view, showing her how she may escape them, and proceed forward in her laudable undertaking. In the *fifth, and last*, I make her retire a little to refresh herself, recover breath, and repair her strength, that she may afterwards more happily gain ground, and advance in a devout life.

In this capricious age I foresee that many will say: "It belongs only to religious to give particular directions concerning piety, since they have more leisure than a bishop can have, who is charged with a diocese so heavy as mine is; that such an undertaking too much distracts the understanding, which should be employed in affairs of importance." But I say to thee, dear reader, with the great St. Denis, that it belongs principally to bishops to conduct souls to perfection, since their order is as supreme among men as that of the seraphim is among the angels; so that their leisure cannot be better employed. The ancient bishops and fathers of the Church, it must be granted, were at least as careful of their charge as we are; yet they did not decline to superintend the particular conduct of several souls who had recourse to their assistance, as appears by their epistles; in this they imitated the apostles, who, amidst the general harvest of the world, picked up certain remarkable ears of corn with a special and particular affection. Who is ignorant that Timothy, Titus, Philemon, Onesimus, St. Thecla,

woman whom he loved the most in the world: in which action, saith Pliny, he showed the greatness of his mind, as much as he could have by the most signal victory.

Now I am of opinion, beloved reader, that it is the will of God that I, being a bishop, should paint upon the hearts of his people, not only *common virtues*, but also his most dear and *well-beloved devotion*. And I willingly undertake the office, as well in obedience to Him, and to discharge my duty, as with the hope that by engraving it on the minds of others, my own may become holily enamoured with its beauty. Now, if ever the Divine Majesty shall see me passionately in love with it, He will give it to me in an eternal marriage. The fair and chaste Rebecca, watering Isaac's camels, was destined to be his wife, and received, on his part, golden ear-rings and bracelets. Thus do I flatter myself, through the infinite goodness of God, that, in conducting his dear sheep to the wholesome waters of devotion, He will make my soul his spouse, putting in my ears the golden words of his holy love, and on my arms the strength to practise good works, in which consists the essence of true devotion; which I humbly beseech his Majesty to grant to me and to all the children of his Church, to which I for ever submit my writings, my actions, my words, my thoughts, and my inclinations.

At Annecy, this day of
    St. Mary Magdalen, 1609.

———————

CONTENTS.

—◆—

PART I.

PART II.

PART III.

Contents.

PART IV.

PART V.

Contents.

Introduction to the Devout Life.

PART THE FIRST.

INSTRUCTIONS AND EXERCISES FOR CONDUCTING THE SOUL FROM HER FIRST DESIRE FOR A DEVOUT LIFE TILL SHE IS BROUGHT TO A FULL RESOLUTION OF EMBRACING IT.

CHAPTER I.
Description of True Devotion.

You aspire to Devotion, Philothea, because, being a Christian, you know it to be a virtue extremely pleasing to the Divine Majesty. But since small faults, committed in the beginning of any business, grow in the progress much greater, and become in the end almost irreparable, you must first know what the virtue of devotion is; for, since there is but one true kind, and many vain and counterfeit, if you cannot distinguish that which is true, you may easily be deceived, and attach yourself to some imprudent and superstitious devotion.

As Aurelius painted all the faces of his pictures to the air and resemblance of the woman he loved, so everyone paints devotion according to his own passion and fancy. He that is addicted to fasting thinks himself very devout if he fasts, even though his heart be at the same time full of rancour; and scrupling to moisten his tongue with wine, or even with water, through sobriety, he makes no difficulty of drinking deep of his neighbour's blood by detraction and calumny. Another accounts himself devout if he recites daily a multiplicity of prayers, though he immediately afterwards utters the most disagreeable, arrogant, and injurious words amongst his domestics and neighbours. Another cheerfully draws an alms out of his purse to relieve the poor, but cannot draw meekness out of his heart to forgive his enemies. Another readily forgives his enemies, but by some means, never satisfies his creditors but by constraint. These are esteemed devout, when, in reality, they are by no means so.

As Saul's servants sought David in his house, Michol laid a statue in his bed, and covering it with David's clothes, made them believe it was David himself; so many persons, by covering themselves with certain external actions belonging to devotion, make the world believe that they are truly devout, whereas they are actually nothing but statues and phantoms of devotion.

True devotion, Philothea, presupposes, not a partial, but a thorough love of God. For inasmuch as divine love adorns the soul, it is called grace, making us pleasing to the Divine Majesty : inasmuch as it gives us the strength to do good, it is called charity; but when it has arrived at that degree of perfection, by which it not only makes us act well, but also work diligently, frequently, and readily, then it is called devotion.

As ostriches never fly; as hens fly low, heavily, and but seldom ; and as eagles, doves, and swallows fly aloft, swiftly and frequently, so sinners fly, not towards God, but direct all their courses on the earth, and towards worldly objects : and good people who have not as yet attained to devotion fly towards God by their good works, but rarely, slowly, and heavily; whereas devout souls fly up to Him by more frequent, prompt, and lofty flights. In short, devotion is nothing but that spiritual agility and vivacity, by ᵇⁱᶜʰ charity works in us, or we by her, with alacrity and affection ; and as it is the business of charity to make us observe all God's commandments generally and without exception, so it is the part of devotion to make us observe them cheerfully and with diligence. Wherefore, he who observes not all the commandments of God, cannot be esteemed either good or devout ; since to be good, he must be possessed of charity, and to be devout, besides charity, he must show cheerfulness and alacrity in the performance of charitable actions.

As devotion, then, consists in a certain excellent degree of charity, it makes us not only active and diligent in the observance of God's commandments, but it also excites us to the performance of every good work with an affectionate alacrity, not commanded, indeed, but only counselled. For as a man newly recovered from any infirmity walks as much as is necessary for him, but slowly and at his leisure, so a sinner, just healed of his iniquities, walks as fast as God commands him, yet slowly and heavily, till such time as he attains to devotion ; for then, like a man in sound health, he not only walks, but runs and springs forward in the way of God's commandments, and, moreover, advances with rapidity in the paths of his heavenly counsels and inspirations.

To conclude: charity and devotion differ no more one from another than the fire does from the flame ; for charity is a spiritual fire which, when inflamed, is called devotion. Hence it appears that devotion adds nothing to the fire of charity, but the flame, which makes it ready, active, and diligent, not only in the observance of the commandments of God, but also in the execution of his heavenly counsels and inspirations.

CHAPTER II.
The Properties and Excellence of Devotion.

They who discouraged the Israelites from going into

the Land of Promise told them it was a country which destroyed its inhabitants, that is, that it had an air so contagious, that it was impossible to live long there : and further, that the natives were such monsters that they ate up other men like locusts. So the world, Philothea, defames holy Devotion, representing devout persons with angry, sad, and grim countenances; pretending that Devotion engenders melancholy and unsociableness. But as Josue and Caleb protested that the Promised Land was not only good and fair, but also that the acquisition and possession of it would be easy and pleasant, so the Holy Ghost, by the mouths of all the saints, and our Saviour, by his own, assure us that a devout life is pleasant, happy, and amiable.

The world sees that devout people pray often, suffer injuries, serve the sick, give to the poor, watch, moderate their hunger, restrain their passions, deprive themselves of sensual pleasures, and such other acts as are in themselves severe and rigorous; but the world does not see the inward cordial devotion which render all these actions agreeable, pleasant, and easy. Consider the bees upon the thyme : they find there very bitter juice, yet in sucking it they turn it into honey. O worldlings! it is true devout souls find much bitterness in these exercises of mortification, but, in performing them they convert them into sweetness and delight. The fire, the flames, the racks, the swords, seemed flowers and perfumes to the martyrs, because they were devout. If, then, Devotion can give a sweetness to the cruellest torments, and even to death itself, what will it not do to the actions of virtue ? Sugar sweetens green fruits, and tempers the crudity and unwholesomeness of those which are ripe. Now, devotion is the spiritual sugar, which takes away bitterness from mortification, and offensiveness from consolation; it takes away discontent from the poor man, and solicitude from the rich—desolation from the oppressed, and insolence from the exalted—sadness from the solitary, and dissoluteness from those who must live in society; it serves for fire in winter, and dew in summer; it shows us how to live in abundance, and how to suffer want; it renders alike profitable honour and contempt; it entertains pleasure and pain almost with the same cheerfulness; and it replenishes our soul with admirable sweetness.

Contemplate Jacob's ladder, for it is the true emblem of a devout life. The two sides between which we ascend, and in which the rounds are fastened, represent prayer, which obtains the love of God, and the sacraments which confer it; the rounds are nothing but divers degrees of charity, by which we advance from virtue to virtue, either descending, by action, to the help and support of our neighbour, or ascending, by contemplation, to a blessed union with God. Now, look upon those who are on this ladder: they are either men who have angelical hearts, or angels who have human bodies. They are not young, yet they seem so, because they are full of vigour and spiritual activity. They have wings to fly, and soar up to God in holy prayer; but they have feet also to walk with men, by holy and friendly conversation. Their faces are fair and pleasant, because they receive all things with sweetness and content; their legs, arms, and heads are all uncovered, because their thoughts, affections, and actions have no other design nor motive but to please God; the rest of their bodies are covered only with a fair and light robe, to show that they make use indeed of the world and worldly things, yet in a most pure and sincere manner, not touching more of them than is necessary for their condition. Such are devout persons. Believe me, Philothea, Devotion is the pleasure of pleasures the queen of virtues, and the perfection of charity. If charity be milk, devotion is the cream; if charity be a plant, devotion is its flowers; if charity be a precious stone, devotion is its lustre; if charity be a rich balm, devotion is its odour: yea, the odour of sweetness, which comforts men and rejoices angels.

CHAPTER III.

Devotion is suitable to all sorts of vocations and professions.

In the creation God commanded the plants to bring forth their fruits, each one according to its kind; even so He commands all Christians, who are living plants of the Church, to bring forth their fruits of devotion, each one according to his quality and vocation Devotion ought to be differently exercised by the prince, by the gentleman, by the tradesman, by the servant, by the widow, by the maid, and by the married person: and not only so, but the practice also of devotion must be accommodated to the health, the capacity, the employment, and the obligations of each one in particular. For, I pray thee, would it be fit for a bishop to be as retired as a Carthusian; and if the married people should store up no more than Capuchins, if the tradesman should be all day in the church like a monk, and the religious continually exposed to all exterior exercises of charity for the service of his neighbour as the bishop, would not this devotion be ridiculous, preposterous, and insupportable? This fault, nevertheless, happens very often, and the world, which does not, or will not discern any difference between real devotion and the indiscretion of those who pretend to be devout, blames and murmurs at it, which cannot remedy such disorders.

No, Philothea, devotion prejudices nothing, when

it is true, but rather makes all things perfect; and when it is not suitable to the lawful vocation of any person, then without doubt it is not safe. The bee, says Aristotle, draws honey from flowers without hurting them, leaving them as entire and fresh as it found them; but true devotion goes yet farther, for it does not prejudice any calling or employment, but, on the contrary, adorns and beautifies all.

All sorts of precious stones cast into honey become more glittering, each one according to its colour; and all persons become more acceptable in their vocation when they join devotion to it. The care of the family is thereby rendered less burdensome, the love of the husband and wife more sincere, the service to the prince more faithful, and all sorts of business more easy and supportable.

It is an error, or rather a heresy, to endeavour to banish a devout life from the camps of soldiers, the shops of tradesmen, the courts of princes, or the affairs of married people. It is true, Philothea, that devotion, merely contemplative, monastical, and religious, cannot be exercised in these vocations; but besides these three sorts of devotion there are divers others proper to make those perfect who live in secular conditions. Abraham, Isaac, and Jacob, David, Job, Tobias, Sarah, Rebecca, and Judith, bear witness to this in the Old Testament. In the New, St. Joseph, Lydia, and St. Crispin were perfectly devout in their shops; St. Anne, St. Martha, St. Monica, Aquila, Priscilla, in their families; Cornelius, St. Sebastian, St. Maurice in the wars; Constantine, Helena, St. Lewis, St. Anne, and St. Edward, on their thrones. Nay, it has happened that many have lost perfection in solitude, which, notwithstanding, is so much to be desired for perfection, and have preserved it in society, which seems so little favourable to it. Lot, says St. Gregory,

who was so chaste in the city, sinned against chastity
in solitude. Wheresoever we are, we may and ought
to aspire to a perfect life.

CHAPTER IV.

*The necessity of a Guide to conduct us on the way of
Devotion.*

Young Tobias, being commanded to go to Rages,
answered : "I know not the way." "Go, then," replied his father, "and seek some man to conduct
thee." I say the same to you, Philothea ; if you
would, in good earnest, walk towards devotion, seek
some good man who may guide and conduct you: this
is the advice of advices. Though you search, says
the devout Avila, you shall never so assuredly find
the will of God as by means of this humble obedience,
so much recommended and practised by the ancient
saints. The blessed mother Teresa, seeing the lady
Catherine of Cordova perform such great penances,
desired much to imitate her, against the advice of
her confessor, who had forbidden her. She was much
tempted to disobey in that particular ; but God said
to her : "Daughter, thou art in a good and secure
way: thou esteemest much her penances ; but I value
more thy obedience." And hence she so highly esteemed this virtue, that besides the obedience due
to her superiors, she vowed a particular one to a
man of excellent perfection, obliging herself to follow his direction and conduct, by which she was
infinitely comforted, as well as many devout souls
before and after her, who, for the more entire resignation of themselves to God, have submitted their
will to that of their servants, which St. Catherine of
Sienna highly applauds in her dialogues. The devout
princess, St. Elizabeth, submitted herself with an
exemplary obedience to Conradus. And one of the

advices given by the great St. Louis to his son, a
little before his death, was this: "Confess often,
choose an able and upright confessor who can instruct
thee to do those things which are necessary."

"A faithful friend," says the Holy Scripture, "is a
strong protection; he that has found him has found a
treasure. A faithful friend is a medicine which gives
life and immortality; those who fear God find Him."
These divine words point chiefly, as you may see, at
immortality, for which it is principally necessary to
have this faithful friend, who by his directions and
counsels may watch over our actions, and by this
means save us from the ambushes and wiles of our
ghostly enemy. He will be to us a treasure of wisdom in our afflictions, discontents, and relapses; he
will serve us as a cordial to refresh and comfort our
hearts in spiritual diseases : he will preserve us from
evil, and make what is good better : and when any
infirmity shall befall us, he will hinder it from being
mortal, for he will heal us.

But who shall find this man ? The wise men answer, "They that fear God:" that is, the humble, who
earnestly desire their spiritual advancement. Since,
then, it concerns you so much, Philothea, to go with
a good guide on this holy voyage of devotion, beseech
God with great fervency to grant you one that may
be according to his heart; and doubt not, for he
will rather send you an angel from heaven, as He did
to young Tobias, than fail to give you a good and
faithful guide.

Now, he ought always to be an angel to you: that
is to say, when you have found him, consider him
not simply as a man; neither confide in him, nor in
his human knowledge, but in God, who will favour
you by the ministry of this man, and make him think
and speak whatsoever shall be requisite for your
happiness; so you ought to hear him as an ange'

descending from heaven to conduct you thither. Treat him with an open heart, in all sincerity and fidelity, manifesting clearly to him the good and the ill which is in you without fear or dissimulation : and by this means your good shall be tried and more assured, and your ill shall be corrected and amended ; you shall be relieved and strengthened in your afflictions, and moderate and even-tempered in your consolations. Place in him an entire confidence ; mixed with holy reverence, in such a way as that the reverence may not diminish the confidence, nor the confidence prejudice the reverence due to him. Confide in him with the respect of a daughter to-wards her father ; respect him with the confidence of a son towards his mother. In a word, this friend-ship ought to be firm and sweet, all holy, all sancti-fied, all divine, and all spiritual.

To this end, choose one amongst a thousand, saith Avila, and I say one amongst ten thousand ; for there are fewer than can be imagined who are capable of this office. He must be full of charity, knowledge, and prudence. If any one of these three qualities is wanting in him there is danger ; and therefore, I say again, ask him of God, and having obtained him, bless the Divine Majesty, remain constant, and seek no others, but rather go on with him innocently, humbly, and confidently, for so you will make a most happy voyage.

———

CHAPTER V.

We must begin by purifying our Souls.

" When flowers appear in our land," says the Divine Spouse, " the time of cleansing and pruning is come." What are the flowers of our hearts, Philothea, but good desires. Now, as soon as they appear, the hand must be put to the knife, to prune off from our consciences all dead and superfluous works. A foreign maid, when about to marry an Israelite, was to put off the robe of her captivity, to cut short her nails, and shave her hair; thus the soul that aspires to the honour of being spouse to the Son of God, ought to put off the old man, and clothe herself with the new; to cast off sin, and then cut and shave away all manner of impediments which may divert her from the love of God. The beginning of our health is to be purged from offensive humours. St. Paul, in a moment, was cleansed in a perfect manner; so were St. Catherine of Genoa, St. M. Magdalen, St. Pelagia, and some other saints; but this sort of purgation is wholly miraculous and extraordinary in grace, as is the resurrection of the dead in nature, and therefore we must not pretend to it. The ordinary purifying and healing, be it of the body or the soul, is only effected little and little, going on by degrees, with pain and labour.

The angels upon Jacob's ladder have wings, yet they fly not, but ascend and descend from step to step. The soul which rises from sin to devotion is compared to the dawning of morning, which drives not away the darkness instantaneously, but by degrees. "The cure," says a proverb, "which is made leisurely is ever the most assured." The diseases of the soul, as well as those of the body, come posting on horseback, but depart leisurely on foot. Courage and patience, then, Philothea, are necessary in this enterprise. Alas! how much are those souls to be pitied who, seeing themselves subject to so many imperfections, having exercised themselves a little in devotion, begin to be troubled, disquieted, and discouraged, suffering their hearts almost to yield to the temptation of forsaking all, and returning back! But, on the other side, is it not also exceedingly dangerous for those others, who, by a contrary temptation, make themselves believe that they are cleansed from their imperfections the first day of their purgation, and esteeming themselves perfect, though scarce as yet roughly moulded, endeavour to fly without wings.

O Philothea, in what danger are they of relapsing, having been taken too soon out of the physician's hands? "Rise not before it is light," says the prophet: "rise after you have rested;" and he himself practising this lesson, and having been already washed and purified, yet desires to be cleansed again.

The exercise of cleansing the soul neither can nor ought to end but with our lives. Let us not, then, afflict ourselves with our imperfections, for our perfection consists in resisting them; and we cannot resist them without seeing them, nor vanquish them without encountering them. Our victory lies not in feeling them, but in not consenting to them. But to be disturbed by them is not to consent to them: nay, it is necessary, for the exercise of our humility, that we should be sometimes wounded in this spiritual combat; but we are never to be considered conquered, unless we either lose our life or our courage. Now, imperfections or venial sins cannot deprive us of spiritual life, for that is only lost by mortal sin. It then remains only that they deprive us not of our courage. "Deliver me, O Lord," said David, "from cowardice and faint-heartedness." It is a happy condition for us in this war if by always fighting we can be always conquerors.

CHAPTER VI.

The first Purification, which is from mortal sin.

The first purification which ought to be made is from sin; the means to make it is the sacrament of penance. Seek the most worthy confessor you can:

read one of the little books which have been composed in order to help us to make an entire and good confession ; read it carefully, and observe from point to point in what you have offended, beginning from the time you had the use of reason, and on to the present hour. If you distrust your memory, write down what you have thought of ; and, having so prepared and gathered together the offensive humours of your conscience, abhor and reject them with the greatest grief and contrition that your heart can conceive, well meditating on these four things : That by sin you have lost the grace of God, forsaken your part of heaven, deserved the perpetual pains of hell, and renounced the eternal love of God.

You see, Philothea, that I speak of a general confession of your whole life, which, though I confess that it is not always absolutely necessary, yet I consider that it will be exceedingly profitable to you in this beginning, and therefore I earnestly advise it. It often happens that the ordinary confessions of those who live a common and vulgar life are full of great defects, for many times they do not prepare themselves at all, or very little ; neither have they sufficient contrition ; nay, it so frequently happens that they confess with a tacit desire to return to sin, because they are not willing to avoid the occasions of sinning, nor make use of the means necessary to amendment of life ; and in all these cases a general confession is requisite to secure the soul. But, besides, a general confession brings us back to the knowledge of ourselves ; it stirs us up to a wholesome shame and sorrow for our past life ; causes us to admire the mercy of God, who has so long and so patiently expected us : it quiets our hearts, refreshes our spirits, excites in us good resolutions, gives occasion to our spiritual father to

give advice more suitable to our condition; **and**
opens our hearts, that we may with more confidence
express ourselves in our future confessions. Speaking, then, of a general renewing of our hearts, and of
an entire conversion of our souls to God, by means of
a devout life, it seems reasonable to me, Philothea,
that I recommend this general confession.

CHAPTER VII.

*The second Purification, which is that from affection
to sin.*

All the Israelites departed, indeed, out of the land
of Egypt, but they did not all depart heartily and
willingly; wherefore, in the wilderness, many of
them repined that they had not the onions and
flesh-pots of Egypt. Thus there are penitents who,
in effect, forsake sin, but not from their hearts: that
is, they purpose to sin no more; but it is with a certain reluctance of heart to abstain from the mis-
chievous delights of sin. Their hearts renounce sin,
and avoid it, but they cease not to look back often
that way, as Lot's wife did towards Sodom. They
abstain from sin, as sick men do from melons, which
they abstain from because the physician threatens
them with death if they eat them; but it is troublesome to them to refrain: they talk of them and are
unwilling to believe them hurtful; they would at
least smell them, and account those happy who
may eat them. Thus those weak and faint-hearted
penitents abstain from sin for a time, but to their
grief: they would like to sin without running the
risk of damnation; they speak of sin with a kind of
satisfaction and relish, and think those happy who
deliver themselves up to it.

A man resolved to revenge himself will renounce
the desire in confession; but soon after he will be

found among his friends, taking pleasure in speaking of his quarrel, and saying, *had it not been for fear of God he would have done this or that. Oh, how strict is God's law on this point of forgiving!* Ah! who does not see that, although this poor man is without sin he is embarrassed with the passion of sin; and, being out of Egypt in effect, he is yet there in desire, longing for the garlic and onions he was wont to eat. Alas! in how great danger are such penitents!

Since you are willing, Philothea, to undertake a devout life, you must not only forsake sin itself, but also cleanse your heart from all affections to sin. For, besides the danger of relapsing, these wretched passions will perpetually weigh on and deject your soul, so that you will not be able to do good works, cheerfully, diligently, and frequently: in this, nevertheless, consists the very essence of devotion. Souls that have quitted sin itself, but do not avoid propensities to sin, may, in my opinion, be compared to delicate girls, not exactly sick, yet having all their actions languid and depressed: they eat without relish, sleep without rest, laugh without delight, and rather drag themselves along than walk. In such a way these souls do good, but with so great spiritual weariness, that it takes away all the grace from their good works, which are few in number and small in effect.

CHAPTER VIII.

The means to arrive at this second Purification.

Now the first means and foundation of this second purification is a lively and strong apprehension of the great injury sin does us, which causes us to enter into a deep and lively contrition. For as contrition (so it be true, be it ever so little, especially being joined

with the virtue of the sacraments), cleanses us sufficiently from sin, so when it is great and fervent, it
cleanses us from all affections which depend upon
sin.   A weak hatred makes us loathe and avoid the
company of him we hate; but if it be mortal and
violent hatred, we not only fly and abhor him, but
we detest the conversation even of his friends and
kindred; yea, we hate his very picture, and whatsoever belongs to him. So, when the penitent hates
his sin, but only with a light, though true contrition, he resolves indeed to sin no more; but when he
abhors it with a powerful and vigorous contrition,
he then not only detests the sin, but all the affections, tendencies, and occasions of it.

We must then, Philothea, increase our contrition
and repentance, as much as possible, to the end
that it may extend to the least and remotest consequences of sin.   St. Mary Magdalen, in her conversion, so utterly lost the contentment and pleasure
she had found in sin, that she never more thought
of it.   And David protested not only that he ab-
horred sin, but also all the ways and paths of it.
In this point consists the renewing of the soul,
which the same prophet compares to the growing
young of an eagle.

Now, to gain this apprehension and contrition,
you must diligently employ yourself in these following meditations, which, being well practised, will, by
the help of God's grace, root out from your heart all
sin with its principal affections: and indeed it is
to this end that I have framed them. You shall
use them in order, as I have placed them, taking
but one for each day, and that, if possible, in the
morning, which is the most proper time for all spiritual exercises, to the end that you may think and
meditate on them during the day. But if you are
not yet accustomed to meditation observe that
which will be said in the Second Part.

CHAPTER IX.

First Meditation.—The Creation.

PREPARATION.

1. Place yourself in the presence of God.
2. Beseech Him to inspire you.

CONSIDERATIONS.

1. Consider that not many years ago you were not yet in the world, and that your being was a mere nothing. Where were we, O my soul, at that time?—the world had then lasted so many ages, and yet we existed not.

2. God has formed you out of nothing, to make you what you are: purely of his own goodness, having no need whatsoever of you.

3. Consider the being that God has given you, for it is the highest in the visible world, capable of eternal life, and of being perfectly united to his Divine Majesty.

AFFECTIONS AND RESOLUTIONS.

1. Humble yourself exceedingly in the presence of God, saying in your heart with the Psalmist: O Lord, I am in thy sight as a mere nothing, and how hast Thou thought of me to create me? Alas! my soul, thou wert lost in that ancient nothing, and hadst yet been there had not God drawn thee from thence: and what couldst thou have done remaining there?

2. Give thanks to God: O my great and good Creator, how am I indebted to Thee, since Thou hast vouchsafed to make me out of nothing, and by thy great mercy to make me what I am. What can I do to bless thy holy name as I ought, and to render due thanks to thy inestimable goodness?

3. Confound yourself: But, alas! my Creator, instead of uniting myself to Thee. by love and service,

I have become rebellious by my inordinate affections, wandering and straying from Thee, to unite myself to sin: valuing thy goodness no more than if Thou hadst not been my Creator.

4. Prostrate yourself before God: O my soul, know that the Lord is thy God: it is He that has made thee, and not thou thyself. O God, I am the work of thy hand.

I will not, henceforth, take pleasure in myself, since of myself I am nothing. Why dost thou magnify thyself, O dust and ashes! yea, rather, O mere nothing, why dost thou exalt thyself? To humble myself, therefore, I resolve to do such-and-such things, to suffer such-and-such disgraces. I will change my life, henceforth follow my Creator, and esteem myself honoured with that condition and being which He has given me, employing it entirely in obedience to his will, by such means as shall be taught me, and as I shall learn from my spiritual father.

CONCLUSION.

1. Give thanks to God: Bless thy God, O my soul, and let all my being praise his holy name, for his goodness has drawn me, and his mercy has created me out of nothing.

2. Offering: O my God, I offer to Thee the being which Thou hast given me; from my heart I dedicate and consecrate it to Thee.

3. Prayer: O God, strengthen me in these affections and resolutions. O holy Virgin, recommend them to the mercy of thy Son, with all for whom I ought to pray, &c. *Pater, Ave, Credo.*

After your prayer, out of these considerations which you have made, make a little spiritual nosegay to smell all the rest of the day.

CHAPTER X.

Second Meditation.—On the end for which we were created.

PREPARATION.

1. Place yourself before God.
2. Beseech Him to inspire you.

CONSIDERATIONS.

1. God has not placed us in this world for any need He has of us, who are altogether unprofitable to Him, but only in order to exercise his goodness in us, by giving us his grace and glory. And to that end He has enriched us with an understanding to know Him, with a memory to be mindful of Him, a will to love Him, an imagination to represent to ourselves his benefits, eyes to behold his wonderful works, a tongue to praise Him, and so of our other faculties.

2. Being created, and put into the world with this intention, all actions contrary to it are to be avoided and rejected; and those which do not conduce to this end should be despised as vain and superfluous.

3. Consider the wretchedness of worldlings who never think of this, but live as though they believed themselves created to no other end but to build houses, plant trees, hoard up riches, and such like follies!

AFFECTIONS AND RESOLUTIONS.

1. Confound yourself, reproaching your soul with her misery, and for having forgotten these truths: Alas! you shall say, how did I employ my thoughts, O God, when I placed them not upon Thee? What did I remember when I forgot Thee? What did I love, when I loved not Thee? Alas! I ought to have nourished myself upon truth, and I have glutted

myself with vanity : slave of the world, I have served·that which was created only to serve me.

2. Detest your past life : I renounce you, O vain thoughts and unprofitable fancies. I abhor you, O frivolous and hateful remembrances : O unfaithful and disloyal friendships, impure and wretched slaveries, ungrateful contentments and irksome pleasures, I abhor you.

3. Return to God : And Thou, O my God, my Saviour, Thou shalt be from henceforth the sole object of my thoughts : I will no more apply my mind to such as are displeasing to Thee. My memory shall entertain itself all the days of my life with the greatness of thy clemency, so mercifully exercised on me : Thou shalt be the delight of my heart and the sweetness of my whole being.

4. Ah ! such-and-such vanities and amusements, to which I applied myself ; such-and-such unprofitable employments, in which I wasted my days ; such-and-such affections which captivated my heart, shall henceforth be objects of horror to me : and to this end I will use such-and-such good remedies.

CONCLUSION.

1. Thank God, who made you for so excellent an end : Thou hast created me, O Lord for thyself, and for the eternal enjoyment of thy incomprehensible glory : Oh, when shall I be worthy of it ! When shall I bless Thee as I ought?

2. Offering : I offer Thee, O my dear Creator, all these affections and resolutions, with all my heart and soul.

3. Prayer : I beseech Thee, O God, to accept these my desires and vows, and to give thy holy benediction to my soul, to the end that it may accomplish them, through the merits of thy blessed Son's blood, shed upon the cross for me. *Pater. Ave, Credo.* [Make here a little spiritual nosegay.]

CHAPTER XI.

Third Meditation.—On the Benefits of God.

PREPARATION.

1. Place yourself in the presence of God.
2. Beseech Him to inspire you.

CONSIDERATIONS.

1. Consider the bodily advantages which God has given you : what a perfect body, and what means to maintain it; what health and lawful recreations to entertain it; what friends and assistances. But consider all this with respect to many other persons, much more worthy than yourself, who are destitute of all these blessings : some defective in their bodies, health, and members; others abandoned to the stings of reproaches, contempt, and dishonour; others oppressed with poverty, and God has not suffered you to become so miserable.

2. Consider the gifts of mind: How many are there in the world stupid, frantic, and mad—and why are not you of this number ? God has favoured you. How many are there who have been brought up in coarse habits and extreme ignorance? And by God's providence you have been educated well and honourably.

3. Consider the spiritual graces : You are a child of the Catholic Church. God has taught you to know Him even from your youth. How often has He given you his sacraments ? How many inspirations, interior illuminations, and reproaches of conscience for your amendment? How frequently has He pardoned you your faults ? How often has He delivered you from the occasions of losing your soul, to which you are exposed ? And was there not for years given you leisure and opportunity to advance the good of your soul ? Consider in particular how good and gracious God has been to you:

AFFECTIONS AND CONSIDERATIONS.

1. Admire the goodness of God: Oh, how good is God to me! Oh, how gracious is He! How rich is thy Heart, O Lord, in mercy, and how liberal in clemency? O my soul, let us publish for ever the many favours He has done us.

2. Repent of your ingratitude: But what am I, O Lord, that Thou art so mindful of me! Ah, how great is my unworthiness! Alas! I have even trampled thy blessings under foot; I have dishonoured thy graces, converting them into abuse and contempt of thy sovereign goodness. I have opposed the depth of my ingratitude to the height of thy grace and favour.

3. Stir yourself up to great thankfulness: Well, then, my heart, be now no longer unfaithful, ungrateful, and disloyal to so great a Benefactor And how shall not my soul henceforth be wholly subject to God, who has wrought so many wonders and favours in me and for me?

Ah! withdraw, then, your body, Philothea, from such-and-such sensualities, and consecrate it to the service of God, who has done so much for it. Apply your soul to know and acknowledge Him by such exercises as shall be requisite for that purpose. Employ diligently the means which the Church affords you to save yourself and love Almighty God. Yes, O my God, I will pray frequently. I will hear your holy word, and put in practice your inspirations and counsels.

CONCLUSIONS.

1. Thank God for the knowledge He has now given you of your duty, and for the benefits hitherto received.

2. Offer Him your heart with all your resolutions.

3. Pray Him to enable you to practise them faithfully, through the merits of his Son's death; im-

plore the intercession of the Blessed Virgin, and of the saints. *Pater, Ave Credo.* [Here make a little spiritual nosegay.]

CHAPTER XII.

Fourth Meditation.—On Sin.

PREPARATION.

1. Place yourself in the presence of God.
2. Beseech Him to inspire you.

CONSIDERATIONS.

1. Call to mind how long it is since you began to sin, and examine to how great an extent, since that beginning sins have been multiplied in your heart. How every day you have increased and multiplied your sins against God, against yourself, and against your neighbour, by word, by deed, by desire.

2. Consider, in particular, the sin of ingratitude towards God, which is a general sin, and extends itself over all the rest, making them infinitely more enormous. Consider, then, how many benefits God has bestowed on you, and how you have abused them, turning them against Him, to dishonour Him. And, in particular, how many inspirations you have made unprofitable. But above all, how many times you have received the sacraments, and where are the fruits of them? What is become of all those precious jewels, with which your dear Spouse adorned you? They have all been buried under your iniquities. With what preparation have you received them? Think on your ingratitude; that God having run so far after you, you have fled from Him to lose yourself.

AFFECTIONS AND RESOLUTIONS.

Be humiliated at the thought of your misery. O my God, how dare I appear before thine eyes? Alas! I am nothing but corruption, and a mere sink of sin and ingratitude. Is it possible that I have been so disloyal as not to have left any one of my senses, not any one of the powers of my soul, which I have not corrupted, violated, and defiled?—and that not so much as one day of my life has passed in which I have not brought forth such bad fruits. Is this the use I should have made of the benefits of my Creator, and the Precious Blood of my Redeemer?

2. Ask pardon, and cast yourself at the feet of your Lord, like a prodigal child, like St. Mary Magdalen, or like the woman taken in adultery, at the feet of Jesus, her Judge. Have mercy, O Lord, on this poor sinner! Alas! O Living Fountain of Compassion, have pity on this wretch.

3. Resolve to live better: No, O Lord, never more, with the help of thy grace, never more will I abandon myself to sin. Alas! I have loved it too much; now I detest it, and embrace Thee, O Father of Mercy. I live and die in Thee.

To expiate my past sins I will accuse myself of them courageously, and will not leave one unbanished from my heart.

I will use all possible endeavours to extirpate all the roots of sin from my heart, and, in particular, such-and-such vices, which chiefly cause me remorse.

To accomplish this, I will constantly embrace the means which shall be recommended to me, and think I have never done enough to repair such grievous offences.

CONCLUSIONS.

1. Give God thanks for awaiting your amendment to this hour, and bless Him that He has given you such good dispositions.

2. Offer Him your heart, that you may put them in execution.

3. Pray that He may give you grace, strength,

&c. *Pater, Ave, Credo.* [Here make a spiritual nosegay.]

CHAPTER XIII.
Fifth Meditation.—On Death.

PREPARATION.
1. Place yourself in the presence of God.
2. Beseech Him to grant you his grace.

Imagine yourself to be in extremity of sickness, on your death-bed, without any hope of recovery.

CONSIDERATIONS.

1. Consider the uncertainty as to the time of your death: O my soul, thou must one day quit this body; but when shall that day be? Shall it be in winter or in summer? Shall it be suddenly or after notice given thee? By sickness or by accident? Shalt thou have leisure to confess thy sins? Shalt thou have the assistance of thy spiritual father? Alas! of all this we know nothing: certain only is it that we shall die, and that always sooner than we expect.

2. Consider, that when the world shall end in regard to you—for this world will be no longer for you—it will perish before your eyes; for then the pleasures, the vanities, the worldly joys and fond affections of our lives will seem to us mere shadows and airy clouds. Ah, wretch! for what toys and trifles have I offended God? You shall then see that for a mere nothing you have forsaken Him. On the contrary, devotion and good works will then seem to you sweet and delightful. Oh, why did I not follow this fair and pleasant path? Then sins, which seemed but little, will appear as huge as mountains, and your devotion very small.

3. Consider the long, languishing farewell your soul must then give this world; she will then take

her leave of its riches and vanities, and of all idle company; of pleasures, pastimes, friends, and neighbours; of kindred and children; of husband and wife; in short, of every creature; and, finally, of her very body, which she must leave pale, hideous, and loathsome.

4. Consider with what haste they will carry away that body, to hide it under the earth; which done, the world will think no more of you than you thought of others who died; "God's peace be with him," they will say, and that is all. O Death, how void art thou of regard or pity!

5. Consider how the soul, having departed from the body, takes her way to the right or to the left! Alas! whither shall yours go? What way shall it take for eternity? No other than that which it begun here in this world.

AFFECTIONS AND RESOLUTIONS.

1. Pray to God, and cast yourself into his arms: Alas! O my God, receive me under thy protection on that dreadful day; make that hour happy and favourable to me; rather than it should not be so, let all the other days of my life be sad and sorrowful.

2. Despise the world: Seeing that I know not the hour at which I must leave thee, O wretched world, I will no more fix my love upon thee. O my dear friends and relations, pardon me if I love you only in future with a holy friendship, which may last eternally; for why should I unite myself to you in such a way as to be forced to break and dissolve the knot afterwards?

3. I will, then, prepare myself for that hour, and take all requisite precautions to end this journey happily: I will secure the state of my conscience to the utmost of my ability, and take immediate care to repair the defects to which I am subject.

CONCLUSION.

Give thanks to God for all those resolutions which He has given you: offer them to his Divine Majesty. Beseech of Him to give you a happy death, by the merits of his dearly-beloved Son. Implore the assistance of the Blessed Virgin, and of the saints. *Pater, Ave, Credo.* [Here make a spiritual nosegay.]

CHAPTER XIV.

Sixth Meditation.—On Judgment.

PREPARATION.
1. Place yourself before God.
2. Beseech Him to inspire you.

CONSIDERATIONS.

1. After the time that God prescribed for the continuance of this world, after the many signs and horrible presages, which will cause men to faint away with fear and anguish, a deluge of fire shall burn and reduce to ashes everything upon the face of the earth. Nothing which we see there shall be spared.

2. After these flames and thunderbolts, all men shall arise, and at the sound of the trumpet of the Archangel they shall appear in the Valley of Josaphat; but, alas! in what different conditions! for the good shall rise with glorified and resplendent bodies, the bad with bodies most frightful and horrid.

3. Consider the majesty with which the Sovereign Judge will appear, environed with all his angels and saints; his cross, shining much brighter than the sun, shall be carried before Him as a sign of mercy to the good, and of justice to the wicked.

4. This Sovereign Judge, by his dreadful command, which shall be instantly obeyed, will separate the good from the bad, placing the one at his right hand,

and the other at his left.   Oh, everlasting separation ! after this they shall never meet again.

5. This separation being made, and the books of consciences opened, all men shall see clearly the malice of the wicked, and their contempt of God ; and on the other side, the penances of the good, and the effects of God's grace which they have received. Nothing shall lie hid. O God ! what a confusion will this be to the reprobate, and what consolation to the saved.

6. Consider the last sentence pronounced against the wicked: "Go, ye accursed, into everlasting fire, prepared for the devil and his angels." Ponder well on these mighty words. "Go!" saith He, a word of eternal banishment against those miserable wretches, excluding them eternally from his glorious presence. He calls them accursed. O my soul ! how dreadful a malediction—a general curse, including all manner of woes; an irrevocable curse, comprehending all times and all eternity. He adds, " into everlasting fire." Behold, O my soul, this miserable eternity. O eternal eternity of pains, how dreadful art thou !

7. Consider the contrary sentence on the good. "Come !" saith the Judge. O sweet word of salvation, by which God draws us to Himself, and receives us into the arms of his goodness. "Blessed of my Father!" O dear blessing, which comprehends all happiness ! "Possess the kingdom which is prepared for you from the beginning of the world." O God, what an excess of bounty! for this kingdom shall never have an end.

AFFECTIONS AND RESOLUTIONS.

1. Tremble, O my soul, at the remembrance of these things. O my God, what security shall there be for me on that day, when even the pillars of heaven shall tremble for fear ?

2. Detest your sins, which alone can condemn you on that dreadful day.

3. Ah, wretched heart ! resolve to amend. O Lord,

I will judge myself now, that I may not be judged then. I will examine my conscience, and condemn myself. I will accuse and chastise myself, so that the eternal Judge may not condemn me on that dreadful day. I will therefore confess, and accept of all necessary advice, &c.

CONCLUSIONS.

1. Thank God, who has given you means to provide for that day, and time to do penance.

2. Offer Him your heart, that He may make good fruits grow from it.

3. Pray of Him to give you his grace.

Pater, Ave, Credo. [Here make a spiritual nosegay.]

CHAPTER XV.
Seventh Meditation.---On Hell.

PREPARATION.

1. Place yourself in the presence of God.
2. Humble yourself and implore the assistance of his grace.
3. Represent to yourself a city covered with darkness, all burning with brimstone and stinking pitch, and full of inhabitants who cannot escape from it.

CONSIDERATIONS.

1. The damned are in the depths of hell, within this woeful city, where they suffer unspeakable torments in all their senses and members; because, as they have employed all their senses and members in sinning, so shall they suffer in them all the pains which are due to sin. The eyes, for having indulged in lascivious looks, shall be afflicted with the vision of hell and devils. The ears, for having delighted in vicious discourses, shall hear nothing but wailings, lamentations, and desperate howlings; and so of all the rest.

2. In addition to all these torments there is yet another even greater, that is the loss and privation of God's glory, from the sight of which they are

excluded for ever. Now, if Absalom found it more grievous to be deprived of the loving face of his father David than to be banished, O God, what grief would it not be for me to be for ever excluded from beholding thy most sweet and gracious countenance!

3. Consider principally the eternity of those pains, which above all things make hell intolerable. Alas! if an insect in the ear, or the heat of a slight fever, makes one short night seem so long and tedious, how terrible will the night of eternity be, accompanied with so many torments? From this eternity proceeds everlasting despair, infinite rage, blasphemy, &c.

AFFECTIONS AND RESOLUTIONS.

1. Terrify your soul with the words of Job: O my soul, art thou able to live for ever in everlasting flames, and amidst a devouring fire? Wilt thou renounce the sight of thy God for ever?

2. Confess that you have deserved it, yea, oftentimes: From this time forward I will adopt a new course; for why should I descend into that bottomless pit? I will therefore endeavour to my utmost to avoid sin, which alone can condemn me to this eternal death.

Give thanks; make an offering; pray. *Pater, Ave, Credo.*

CHAPTER XVI.

Eighth Meditation.—On Heaven.

PREPARATION.

1. Place yourself in the presence of God.
2. Beseech Him to inspire you with his grace.

CONSIDERATIONS.

1. Imagine a beautiful and clear night, and think how pleasant it is to behold the sky, all spangled with such a multitude and variety of stars. Add

now to this exquisite beauty the delights of just as lovely a day, so that the brightness of the sun may no ways hinder the lustre of the stars or moon: and then say boldly that all this put together is nothing in comparison with the radiant beauty of that great Paradise. Oh, how this lovely place is to be desired! Oh, how precious is this city?

2. Consider the glory, beauty, and multitude of the inhabitants in that blessed country; those millions of millions of angels, cherubim, and seraphim; armies of apostles, prophets, martyrs, confessors, virgins, and holy matrons: their number is innumerable. How blessed is this company! the meanest of them is more beautiful to behold than all the world;—what a sight then will it be to see them all! But, O my God, how happy are they!—they sing continually harmonious songs of eternal love; they enjoy for ever a constant mirth; they interchange one with another unspeakable delights, and live in the comfort of a happy and indissoluble society.

3. In fine, to consider how blessed they are in enjoying God, who rewards them for ever with his glorious aspect, and by it infuses into their hearts such treasures of delight; how great a happiness is it to be united everlastingly to their Maker? They are like happy birds flying and singing perpetually in the atmosphere of his divinity, which encompasses them on all sides with inconceivable pleasure. There everyone does his best, and, without envy, sings the Creator's praise. Blessed be Thou for ever, O sweet and sovereign Creator and Redeemer, who art so bountiful to us, and dost communicate to us so liberally the everlasting treasures of thy glory. Blessed be ye for ever, says He, my beloved creatures, who have so faithfully served me, and who now shall praise me everlastingly with so great love and courage.

AFFECTIONS AND RESOLUTIONS.

1. Admire and praise his heavenly country : O how beautiful art thou, heavenly Jerusalem, and how happy are thy inhabitants.

2. Reproach your heart with the little courage it has had hitherto, in wandering so far from the road that leads to this glorious habitation: Oh, why have I so far strayed from my Sovereign Good? Ah! wretch that I am, for these foolish and trivial pleasures I have a thousand times forsaken eternal and infinite delights! was I mad to despise such precious blessings, for such vain, contemptible affections?

3. Aspire, notwithstanding, with fervour to this delicious habitation: O my gracious God, since it has pleased Thee at length to direct my wandering steps into the right way, never hereafter will I turn back. Let us go, my soul, let us go to this eternal repose; let us walk towards this blessed land, which is promised us. Why should we remain in this Egypt? I will therefore disburden myself of all such things as may divert me from or retard me in so happy a journey; I will perform all things that may conduct me to it.

Give thanks ; make an offering; pray. *Pater, Ave, Credo.*

CHAPTER XVII.
Ninth Meditation.—On the choice of Heaven.

PREPARATION.

1. Place yourself in the presence of God.
2. Humble yourself before Him, and beseech Him to inspire you with his grace.
3. Imagine yourself to be in an open plain, alone with your Angel Guardian, like young Tobias on his journey with the glorious Archangel Raphael, and that then he shows you hell open beneath, with all the torments described in the meditation on hell; you being thus situated, in imagination, and kneeling before your good angel.

CONSIDERATIONS.

1. Consider that it is most true that you are be-

killing one another; others wasted with greed and anxiety to heap up riches; others devoted to vanity, without any pleasure but that which is unprofitable and vain; others wallowing, buried and putrefied in their brutish passions. Behold how they are all without rest, order, and decency; behold how they despise, hate, and persecute one another, and love but in outward show. In a word, you see a pitiful commonwealth so miserably tyrannised over by its accursed king, that it must move you to compassion.

2. On the other side, behold Jesus Christ crucified, who, with a mighty love, prays for these poor enslaved people, that they may be freed from this tyranny, and who calls them to Himself. Behold around Him a troop of devout persons with their angels. Contemplate the beauty of this kingdom of devotion. Oh! what a sight it is to see this troop of virgins, men and women, whiter than the lilies; that assembly of widows full of holy mortification and humility; those ranks of married people, living peaceably together, with mutual respect and love. Consider how these devout souls join the care of their households with the care of their souls; the love of husband or wife with that of the celestial Bridegroom. Consider them all in general, and you shall see them in a sweet, holy, and lovely method, observing our Saviour, whom everyone would willingly plant in the midst of his heart. They are full of joy, charitable and well-ordered; they love one another, but their love is pure and sacred. Such as suffer afflictions amongst this devout company torment not themselves much, nor do they lose courage. Lastly, behold the eyes of our Saviour, who comforts them; and how they altogether aspire to Him.

3. You have already shaken off Satan, with all his accursed and execrable troop, by the good affections you have conceived; but you have not yet arrived to

Jesus, nor united with his blessed and holy company of devout people, but have hitherto kept yourself between the one and the other.

4. The Blessed Virgin, with St. Joseph, St. Louis, St. Monica, and a hundred thousand others, who formed the kingdom of God in the world, invite and encourage you. The crucified King calls you: "Come, my well-beloved, come, that I may crown thee."

ELECTION.

1. O world! O abominable troop! never shall you see me under your banner. I have for ever renounced your follies and vanities. O king of pride, O accursed king, infernal spirit, I renounce thee with all thy vain pomps, I detest thee with all thy works.

2. And turning to Thee, dear Jesus, King of felicity and immortal glory, I embrace Thee with all the powers of my soul; I adore Thee with all my heart; I choose Thee, now and for ever, for my King; and with all that I am I pay Thee irrevocable homage, and submit myself to faithfully obey all thy holy laws and commandments.

3. O holy Virgin, I choose thee for my guide, I place myself under thy standard. I offer thee a particular respect and special devotion.

4. O my good angel, present me to this sacred assembly, and forsake me not till I join this blessed company, with whom I will say for ever, in testimony of my choice: "Live Jesus, live Jesus." *Pater, Ave, Credo.*

CHAPTER XIX.

How to make a General Confession.

1. Behold here, Philothea, the meditations most requisite for our purpose, which, when you have made, go on courageously, in the spirit of humility, to make your general confession; but, I beseech you,

do not suffer yourself to be troubled with any kind of apprehension. The scorpion which has stung us is venomous in stinging, but, being reduced into oil, becomes a sovereign remedy against his own sting. Thus confession of sin is a sovereign remedy against sin itself. Contrition and confession are so precious, and have so sweet an odour, that they deface the ugliness and destroy the infection of sin. Simon the Pharisee pronounced St. Mary Magdalen a sinner; but our Saviour denied it, and speaks of nothing but of the sweet perfumes she poured on Him, and of the greatness of her charity. If we be truly humble, Philothea, our sins will infinitely displease us, because God is offended by them; but the confession of our sins will be sweet and pleasant to us, because God is honoured thereby. It is a kind of consolation to us to inform the physician correctly of the disease that torments us.

When you are in the presence of your spiritual Father, imagine yourself on Mount Calvary, kneeling at the feet of Jesus Christ crucified, whose Precious Blood streams down on all sides, to wash away your iniquities. For though it is not the very blood of our Saviour, yet it is the merits of his blood shed for us which abundantly flows on the souls of penitents in every confessional. Open, then, your heart freely to cleanse yourself from your sins by confession; for as fast as they go from your soul the precious merits of his divine passion will enter into it, to replenish it with blessings.

But be sure to declare all, simply and plainly. Satisfy fully your conscience in this, now once for all; which done, then pay attention to the admonitions and instructions of your spiritual father, and say in your heart: "Speak, Lord, for thy servant hearkeneth unto thee." Yea, Philothea, it is God whom you hear, since He has said to his ministers, "He that heareth you heareth Me."

After that read again the following protestation, which serves as a conclusion of all your contrition, and which you ought first to have meditated on and considered. Read it attentively, and with the greatest care you possibly can.

CHAPTER XX.

Protestation from the soul to God to strengthen it in a firm resolution to serve Him, and to conclude the Acts of Penance.

I, the undersigned, placed in the presence of the Eternal God, and of all the court of heaven, having considered the exceeding mercy of his divine goodness towards me, most unworthy and wretched creature, whom He has created out of nothing; preserved, sustained, and delivered from so many dangers, and loaded with so many benefits; but, above all, having considered the incomprehensible sweetness and clemency wherewith this most good God has so graciously spared me in my iniquities; so frequently inspired me, inviting me to amendment, and so patiently awaited my repentance and conversion until this (*N.*) year of my age, notwithstanding all my ingratitude, disloyalty, and infidelity : on which account, deferring my conversion, and despising his graces, I have so unadvisedly offended Him. Having, moreover, considered that on the day of my holy baptism I was happily and holily given up and dedicated to my God, to be his child, and that, contrary to the profession then made in my name, I have so often, so execrably and detestably profaned and violated my understanding, applying and employing it against his Divine Majesty. At length, returning to myself, prostrate in heart and mind before the throne of Divine Justice, I acknowledge, confess, and avow myself lawfully attainted and convicted of high treason against his Divine Majesty, and guilty of the

able sacrament, as a sacred seal upon your renewed heart.

Thus I hope, Philothea, that your soul will be purged from sin, and from all sinful affections. Yet, because these affections return easily to the soul through our frailty and concupiscence, which may indeed be mortified, but which can never die while we live here on earth, I will give you some instructions which, being well practised, shall preserve you from mortal sin, and from all inclinations thereto, so that it shall never take root in your heart. And as the same instructions serve also towards a greater degree of purification, before I deliver them I will say something more of that more perfect purity to which I desire to conduct you.

CHAPTER XXII.
We must purify ourselves from all affection to venial sins.

As the daylight increases, we see more clearly in a mirror the spots and blemishes on our face; even so, as the inward light of the Holy Ghost more and more illumines our consciences, we see more plainly and distinctly the sins, the inclinations, and imperfections, which hinder us from attaining to true devotion; and the very same light which causes us to discover those spots and deformities, inflames us likewise with a desire to cleanse ourselves from them.

Thou shalt then discover, Philothea, that besides mortal sins, and the affections to them, from which, by the aforementioned exercises, you have been purged, there remain yet in your soul various inclinations and affections to venial sins. I do not say you shall discover in it many venial sins, but affections and inclinations to them. Now the one is far different from the other; for we can never be free

altogether from venial sins for any long time, but
we may, by the grace of God, destroy within us all
affection for venial sins; for it is one thing to lie
once or twice in matters of small importance, and
another thing to take pleasure in lying, and to have
a liking for that sin.

I say, then, that it is necessary to purge the soul
from all affections and inclinations to venial sins,
that is to say, we must not nourish voluntarily a will
to continue and persevere in any kind of venial sin :
for it would be a great want of fidelity and most cul-
pable cowardice to keep willingly in our conscience a
thing so hateful to God as the will to displease Him.
Venial sin, be it ever so little, displeases God, though
not to so great a degree that He will reject or damn
us for it. If, then, venial sin displeases Him, the will
to commit it is no other than a resolution to displease his divine majesty : and is it possible that a
generous soul should not only displease its God, but
even take pleasure in displeasing Him?

Such affections, Philothea, are as directly contrary
to devotion as affections to mortal sins are to charity;
they weaken the strength of the spirit, hinder the
course of divine consolations, open a gate to temptations, and though they do not kill the soul, yet they
make it exceedingly sick. "Dying flies," says the wise
man, "mar the sweetness of and remove all its virtue
from a precious ointment." He means that flies, staying
not long upon the ointment, but eating it and flying
away, spoil no more than they take, the rest remaining good ; but when they die in the ointment, they
deprive it of its virtue, and leave it worth nothing. So,
venial sins entering into a devout soul, and staying
not long there, do not prejudice it much ; but if the
same sins remain in the soul, by the affection she con-
ceives for them, they make her without doubt lose the
-eetness of the ointment—that is, holy devotion.

CHAPTER XXIV.

We must purify ourselves from our natural imperfections.

We have besides, Philothea, certain natural inclinations, which, because they do not proceed from our particular sins, are not properly sins, neither mortal nor venial, but are called imperfections, and their acts are termed faults or omissions. For example, St. Paula, as St. Jerome relates, had a great natural tendency to grief and sadness; so that, at the death of her children and husband, she ran a risk of dying of sorrow;—this was a great imperfection, but not a sin, since she had it against her will.

There are some naturally cheerful, others moody; some annoyed at being given advice, others inclined to indignation and anger; others to human affections: and, in fine, there are few persons in whom some such imperfections may not be observed. Now, although they are, as it were, common and natural to everyone, yet, by care and contrary affections, they may be corrected and moderated, and we may even purify and free our souls from them. And I tell thee, Philothea, we ought to do so. Men have succeeded in changing the bitter almond-tree into the sweet by piercing it near the root, so as to let out the juice; and why may not we let out our perverse inclinations and become better? There is no nature so good that it may not be corrupted by vicious customs; nor so perverse that it may not, first by the grace of God, and next by proper diligence, be reduced and overcome.

I will, therefore, now give you the instructions, and propose the exercises, by which you may purge your soul from dangerous affections to venial sins, and secure your conscience also, more and more, against all mortal sin. May God give you the grace to practise them well!

PART THE SECOND.

INSTRUCTIONS FOR ELEVATING THE SOUL TO GOD
BY PRAYER AND BY THE SACRAMENTS.

CHAPTER I.
The Necessity of Prayer.

PRAYER places our mind in the brightness and light of God, and exposes our will to the heat of heavenly love. There is nothing that so effectually frees our understanding from its ignorance, or our will from its depraved affections, as prayer. It is the water of benediction which causes the plants of our good desires to grow green and flourish. It cleanses our souls from their imperfections, and quenches the thirst of passion in our hearts.

But, above all, I recommend to you mental and heartfelt prayer, and particularly that which has the life and passion of our Lord for its object. By making Him the frequent subject of your meditation, your whole soul will be replenished with Him; you shall learn his carriage, and you will conform your interior and exterior conduct to his. As He is the light of the world, it is then in Him, by Him, and for Him, that we ought to acquire lustre, and become enlightened. He is the tree of desire, under whose shadow we ought to refresh ourselves. He is the living fountain of Jacob, in which we may wash away all our stains. In fine, as little children, by hearing their mothers talk, lisp at first, and learn at length to speak their language; so we, by keeping close to our Saviour by meditation, and observing his words, actions, and affections, shall, by the help of his grace, learn to speak, to act, and to will like Him. Here we must stop, Philothea, as we cannot find access to God the Father but through this gate; for as the glass of a mirror could never stop our view if its back were not tinned or leaded, so we could never contemplate the Divinity in this world had we not been united to the sacred humanity of our Saviour, whose life and death is the most fit, delightful, sweet, and profitable object we can choose for our ordinary meditation. It is not without reason that our Saviour called Himself the bread that came down from heaven, for, as bread ought to be eaten with all sorts of meat, so our Saviour ought to be the subject of our meditation, consideration, and imitation in all our prayers and actions. His life, passion, and death have been, for this purpose, arranged into distinct points by several authors: those whom I recommend to you are St. Bonaventure, Bellitani, Bruno, Capiglia, Grenada, and Dupont.

Employ an hour every day before dinner in this spiritual exercise, or, if convenient, early in the morning, when your mind will be less distracted and more fresh, after the repose of the night: but see that you extend it not beyond an hour, except with the advice of your spiritual director.

If you could perform this exercise in the church, it would be the best and most convenient place possible; because neither father nor mother, wife nor husband, nor any other person whatsoever, could well prevent you from staying one hour in the church; whereas, being perhaps under subjection, you could not promise yourself so much leisure at home.

Begin all your prayers, whether mental or vocal, by placing yourself in the presence of God. By attending strictly to this rule, you will soon becr sensible of its salutary effects.

Would you be advised by me, Philothea, say your *Pater, Ave,* and *Credo* in Latin; but, at the same time, learn perfectly to comprehend the meaning of the words in your own native tongue, so that whilst you unite with the faithful in prayer, in the language of the Church, you may, at the same time, relish the delicious sense of those holy and admirable prayers. Pray with your attention fixed, and your affections excited by what the words signify; pray deliberately, and from your heart; for, believe me, one *Our Father* said with feeling and affection is of infinitely more value than ever so many repetitions of it run over in haste.

The Rosary is a most profitable way of praying, provided you know how to say it properly: to this end, procure one of those little books which teach the way of reciting it. It is good also to say the Litanies of our Lord Jesus, of Our Lady, and of the Saints, and of such other vocal prayers as may be found in approved manuals of devotion; yet with this caution, that if you have the gift of mental prayer you should always give it the preference. So that if, either through pressure of business, or some other cause, you cannot say your vocal prayers, you must not be troubled on that account, but rest contented with saying, either before or after your meditation, the *Pater, Ave,* and *Credo.*

If whilst at vocal prayer you feel your heart inclined to mental prayer, do not refuse the invitation, but let your mind turn gently to it, without being concerned at not finishing the vocal prayers you purposed to say; for the choice you have made is more pleasing to God and more profitable to your soul; with this exception, however, that if you are bound to say the Office of the Church you must fulfil your obligation.

ld it happen that, through pressure of busi-
ome accidental cause, your morning should

pass away without allowing you leisure for the exercise of mental prayer, endeavour to repair that loss some time after dinner, as much after it as possible, because by doing it immediately after, before digestion is advanced, besides being heavy and drowsy, your health would be prejudiced thereby.

But if, during the course of the day, you should find no leisure for this heavenly exercise, you may in some measure make amends, by multiplying your ejaculatory prayers, reading some book of devotion, or by performing some penance, which may prevent the ill consequences of this omission, making the firm resolution to repair your loss the day following.

CHAPTER II.

Short Method of Meditation : and, first, of the Presence of God, which is the first point of the preparation.

But perhaps, Philothea, you know not how to pray *mentally*, for it is a thing with which few in our age are so happy as to be acquainted ; for which reason I present you with the following short and plain method, till by practice or by reading some of the good books composed on the subject, you may be more fully instructed.

I shall begin with the preparation, which consists in placing yourself in the presence of God, and in imploring his assistance. Now, to assist you to place yourself in the presence of God, I shall set before you four principal means. The first consists of a lively and attentive comprehension that He is present in all things and in all places : for there is neither place nor thing in the world in which He is not most truly present, so that, as birds, wheresoever they fly, always meet with the air, so we, wheresoever we go or happen to be, always find Go

Everyone acknowledges this truth, but few con·sider it with a lively attention. Blind men, who do not see their prince, though present among them, behave themselves, nevertheless, with respect when they are told of his presence; but the fact is, be-cause they do not see him, they easily forget that he is present, and having forgot it, they still more easily lose their respect for him. Alas, Philothea, we do not see God, who is present amongst us; and, though faith assures us of his presence, yet not beholding Him with our eyes, we too often forget Him, and behave ourselves as though He were at a far distance from us; for although we well know that He is present in all things, yet, not reflecting on it, we act as if we knew it not. Therefore, before prayer, we must always excite in our souls an attentive apprehension of the presence of God, such as David apprehended, when he exclaimed: "If I ascend into heaven, O my God, Thou art there : if I descend into hell, Thou art there !" (Ps. cxxxviii.) And thus we should use the words of Jacob, who, having seen the sacred ladder, said: "O how terrible is this place! Indeed the Lord is in this place, and I knew it not " (Gen. xxxviii.): meaning that he did not reflect on his presence; for he could not be ignorant that God was in all, and through all. When, therefore, you come to prayer, you must say with your whole heart, and to your heart: "Oh, be attentive, for God is truly here !"

The second means to place yourself in his sacred presence is, to reflect that God is not only in the place where you are, but that He is, after a most particular manner, in your heart, nay, in the very centre of your soul, which He enlivens and animates by his divine presence, being there as the heart of your heart, and the spirit of your spirit; for as the soul, being diffused through the whole body, is pre-

sent in every part thereof, and yet resides in a
special manner in the heart, so likewise God, being
present to all things, yet He resides in a more particular manner in our soul, for which reason David
calls him "the God of his heart." (Ps. lxxii.) And
St. Paul says that it is in God "we live, and move,
and have our being." (Acts, xvii.) In consideration, therefore, of this truth, excite in your heart a
profound reverence for God, who is there so inti-
mately present.

A third means is to consider our Saviour in his
humanity, looking down from heaven on all mankind, but especially on Christians, who are his
children, and more particularly on such as are at
prayer, whose good and bad actions He minutely
observes. This is by no means a mere flight of the
imagination, but a most certain truth; for, although
we see Him not, yet He beholds us from above. It
was thus that St. Stephen saw Him at the time of
his martyrdom. So that we may truly say with the
Spouse (Cantic. ii.), "Behold! He stands behind
our wall, looking through the windows—looking
through the lattice."

A fourth method consists in imagining to ourselves that Jesus Christ is, in his sacred humanity,
just at hand, as we sometimes imagine some friend
to be present, saying, "It seems as if I saw him, or
someone very like him." But if the Blessed Sacrament be present, then his presence would be actual
and not imaginary; since we must consider the
species and appearance of bread only as a tapestry,
behind which our Lord, being really present, observes us, though we cannot actually see Him. Use,
then, some of these four means of placing yourself
in the presence of God before prayer, not all at
once, but one at a time, in as concise and simple
manner as possible.

CHAPTER III.

Invocation, the second point of the Preparation.

Being sensible that you are in the presence of God, prostrate yourself with the most profound reverence, acknowledging yourself unworthy to appear before so sovereign a Majesty; yet, knowing that his goodness so wills it, humbly beg the grace to serve and worship Him in this meditation. To this end you may use these short and inflamed words of David: "Cast me not, O God, away from thy face, and take not thy holy spirit from me. Make thy face to shine upon thy servant, and I will consider the wondrous things of thy law. Give me understanding, and I will search out thy law, and I will keep it with all my heart. I am thy servant; give me understanding." (Ps. cxvii.) It would also be advisable to invoke your guardian angel, as well as the saints who had some part in the mysteries on which you meditate; as, for example, in meditating on the death of our Lord, you may invoke our Blessed Lady, St. John, St. Mary Magdalen, and other saints, begging that the inward affections and emotions which they at that time conceived, may be communicated to you. Also, in meditating on your own death, you may invoke your good angel, who will then be present with you, beseeching him to inspire you with proper considerations; and so of other mysteries.

CHAPTER IV.

The third point of Preparation, consisting in the proposition of the Mystery.

After these two general points of the meditation, there remains a third, not common to all sorts of meditation, which some call the arrangement of the

of God; and sincere sorrow for the sins of our past life. In these affections your spirit should extend itself as much as possible, and if you desire to aid yourself with books of devotion, read the preface to the first volume of the Meditations of Dom Andrew Capiglia, where he shows the manner of exercising yourself in this practice, as Father Arias does more at large in the second part of his treatise on prayer.

Yet you must not dwell, Philothea, upon these general affections, without resolving to reduce them to specific and particular resolutions. For example: the first word our Lord spoke on the cross will doubtless excite in your soul a desire to pardon and to love your enemies; but this will be to little purpose if you do not add to it a particular resolution, saying: "Well, then, I will not hereafter be offended at what this or that particular person may say of me, nor resent any affront he may put on me; but, on the contrary, I will embrace every opportunity to gain his heart, and appease him." By this means you will correct your faults in a short time; whereas, by affections only, your amendment will be but slow, and attended with greater difficulty.

CHAPTER VII.

The conclusion, and the Spiritual Nosegay.

Last of all, we must conclude our meditation by three acts, which require the utmost humility. The first consists in giving thanks to God for the good affections and resolutions wherewith He has inspired us, and for his goodness and mercy, manifested to us in the mystery of the meditation. The second is, to unite our affections and resolutions to his goodness and mercy, and make an offering of them union with the death, blood, and virtues of his Son. The third should be an humble petition, whereby we implore God to communicate to us the graces and virtues of his Son, and grant his blessing on our affections and resolutions, in order that we may faithfully put them in practice. We then pray for the Church, our pastors, relatives, friends, and others; imploring, to that end, the intercession of our Blessed Lady and of the angels and saints; and lastly, as I have already observed, we conclude with saying Our Father, Hail Mary, &c., which are the common and necessary prayers of all the faithful.

From all this, as I have already advised, gather a little nosegay of devotion; for as those who walk in a beautiful garden do not willingly depart from it without gathering a few flowers to smell during the whole day, even so ought we, when our spirit has entertained itself by meditating on some mystery, to select one, two, or three of those points which we most relish, and which are most proper for our advancement, in order to think frequently on them, and to smell them, as it were, spiritually during the course of the day. This is to be done in the same place where we have been meditating, or whilst walking in solitude for some time after.

CHAPTER VIII.

Profitable advice on the practice of Meditation.

Above all things, Philothea, when you rise from meditation, remember the resolutions you have made, and, as occasion presents itself, carefully reduce them to practice that very day. This is the great fruit of meditation, without which it is not only unprofitable, but frequently hurtful: for virtues meditated upon, and not practised often puff up the spirit, and make

us imagine ourselves to be such as we have resolved
to be.   This, doubtless, would be true if our resolutions were strong and solid ; but how can they be
really such, but rather vain and dangerous, if not reduced to practice ? We must, therefore, by all means,
endeavour to practise them, and seek every occasion,
little or great, to put them into execution.   For example : if I have resolved, by mildness, to become re-
conciled with such as offend me, I will seek this very
day an opportunity to meet them, and kindly salute
them ; or, if I should not meet them, at least speak
well of them, and pray to God for them.

After prayer, be careful not to cause violent agita-
tion to your heart, lest the precious balm it has received thereby should fall from it.   My meaning is,
that you must, for some time, if possible, remain in
silence, and gently remove your heart from prayer to
your other employments, retaining as long as you
can, a feeling of the affections you have conceived.
As a man that has received some precious liquor in
a dish, in carrying it walks home gently, not looking
aside, but straight before him, for fear of stumbling,
and sometimes on his dish, lest he should spill the
liquor, even so ought you to act when you finish
your meditation ; suffer nothing to distract you, but
look forward with caution ; or, to speak more plainly,
should you meet with anyone with whom you are
obliged to enter into conversation, there is no other
remedy but to watch over your heart, so that as
little of the liquor of holy prayer as possible may be
spilt on the occasion.

Nay, you must even accustom yourself to know
how to pass from prayer to those occupations which
your state of life lawfully requires, though ever so
distant from the affections you have received in
prayer : for example, let the lawyer learn to pas-
from prayer to pleading, the merchant to his

mercial transactions, and the married woman to the care of her family, with so much ease and tranquillity that their spirits may not be disturbed ; for, since all of them are in positions according to the will of God, they must learn to pass from the one to the other in the spirit of humility and devotion.

You must also know that it may sometimes happen that immediately after preparation your affection will feel itself aspiring to God. In such a case, Philothea, you must lay aside the method I have before given; for although, generally speaking, the exercise of the understanding should precede that of the will, yet when the Holy Ghost gives you the latter before the former, you must not then seek the former, since it is used for no other purpose but to excite the latter. In a word, whenever affections present themselves, we must expand our hearts to make room for them, whether they come before or after ; and, although I have placed them after the considerations, I have done so merely to distinguish more plainly the parts of prayer ; for, otherwise, it is a general rule never to restrain the affections, but always to let them have their free course when they present themselves; and this I say, not only with regard to the other affections, but also with respect to the thanksgiving, oblation, and petition which may likewise be used in the midst of the considerations, for they must no more be restrained than the other affections, though afterwards, for the conclusion of the meditation, they must be repeated and taken up again. But as for resolutions, they are always to be made after the affections, and at the end, before the conclusion of the whole meditation; because as in these we represent to ourselves particular and familiar objects, they would put us in danger of distractions, should we mix up our affections with them.

Amidst our affections and resolutions, it is advisable to use conversations and to speak sometimes to our Lord, sometimes to the angels, the saints, and the persons represented in the mysteries; to ourselves, to our own hearts, to sinners, and even to insensible creatures, after the example of David in his Psalms, and of other saints, in their prayers and meditations.

CHAPTER IX.

The dryness which we sometimes experience in Meditation.

Should it happen, Philothea, that you feel no relish or comfort in meditation, I conjure you not to disturb yourself on that account, but repeat some of the prayers which are most dear to your heart. Complaining of yourself to our Lord, confess your unworthiness, and beseech Him to assist you. Kiss his picture if you have it at hand, addressing to Him those words of Jacob: "I will not let Thee go, O Lord, till Thou hast given me thy blessing" (Gen. xxxii.); or those of the Canaanean woman: "Yea, Lord, I am a dog; but yet the dogs eat of the crumbs that fall from their master's table." (Matt. xv.)

At other times take up some spiritual book, and read it with attention, till your spirit is awakened, and returns to you. Or stir up your heart by some exterior act of devotion, such as prostrating yourself on the ground, crossing your hands before your breast, or embracing a crucifix—provided you be alone or in some private place. But if you should, after all, receive no comfort, do not disturb yourself, be the dryness ever so excessive, but continue to keep yourself in a devout posture. How many courtiers go a hundred times a year into the prince's presence-chamber, without hope of speaking to him, but only to be seen by him, and to pay their court to him ? So ought we come to prayer purely and solely to pay our homage, and testify our fidelity to God ; and should it please his Divine Majesty to speak, and entertain Himself with us by his holy aspirations and interior consolations, it would doubtless be to us a great honour, and most delightful pleasure ; but should it not please Him to grant us this favour, but leave us, without taking any more notice of us, than if we were not in his presence, we must not therefore depart, but remain before his Sovereign Goodness with a devout and respectful deportment : and then observing our diligence, our patience, and perseverance, He will, when we again come before Him, favour us with his consolations, and make us experience the sweetness of holy prayer. Yet, if He should not do so, let us rest content, Philothea, for it is an exceeding great honour for us to come before Him and be admitted into his presence.

CHAPTER X.

On Morning Exercise.

Besides mental and vocal prayer there are other kinds, which are, as it were, slips and twigs of the principal prayer : the first is morning prayer, intended as a general preparation to all the actions of the day, and it may be made in the following manner :

1. Adore God most profoundly, and return Him thanks for having preserved you from the dangers of the past night ; and if, during the course thereof, you have committed any sin, beseech his pardon.

2. Consider that the present day is given you in order that you may gain the future day of eternity : make a firm resolution, therefore, to employ it well, and with that intention.

3. Bring before your mind the occupations with which you are likely to be engaged during the day; what opportunities to serve God, what temptations to offend Him, either through anger, or vanity, or any other irregularity, and prepare yourself with a firm resolution to make the best use of the means which shall be offered to you, to serve God and advance in devotion; so also, on the other hand, dispose yourself carefully to avoid, resist, and overcome whatever may present itself that is prejudicial to your salvation and to the glory of God. Now, it is not sufficient to make this resolution unless you also prepare the means to put it effectually into execution. For example : if you foresee that you are to negotiate any business with a person who is passionate and easily provoked to anger, you will not only resolve to refrain from giving him any offence, but you will also prepare words of meekness to prevent his anger, or use the assistance of some person to keep him in temper. If you foresee that you shall have an opportunity of visiting some sick person, you will forecast the time, with the comforts and assistance you may afford him : and so of the rest.

4. This done, humble yourself in the presence of God. Acknowledge that, of yourself, you can do nothing of all that you have resolved, either as to the avoiding evil or doing good ; and, as if you held your heart in your hands, offer it, together with all your good intentions, to the Divine Majesty, beseeching Him to take it under his protection, and to strengthen it, that it may proceed prosperously in his service, using these or similar words interiorly : "Behold, O Lord, this poor miserable heart of mine, which, through thy goodness, has conceived many good affections, but which, alas! is of itself too weak and wretched to execute the good which it desires, unless Thou shouldst impart to it

thy heavenly blessing, which for this end I humbly beg of Thee, O merciful Father, through the merits of the Passion of thy Son, to whose honour and glory I consecrate this and all the remaining days of my life." Then invoke our Blessed Lady, your good angel, and the saints, in order that they may all assist you by their intercession.

But all these spiritual acts must be made briefly and fervently, and before you depart from your chamber, if it be possible, that by means of this exercise all that you may have to do throughout the day may be watered with the blessing of God: and I beg of you, Philothea, never to fail herein.

CHAPTER XI.

The Evening Exercise and Examination of Conscience.

As you have nourished your soul in the morning with the heavenly bread of meditation so you must also make a devout supper. Take, then, some little opportunity, before supper, to prostrate yourself before God, and recollect yourself in the presence of Jesus Christ crucified, whom you may represent to yourself by a single consideration, and an interior glance of the eye, and kindle again in your heart the fire of your morning meditation, by several lively aspirations, humiliations, and loving efforts, which you shall make to this Divine Saviour of your soul; or else, by repeating portions of your morning meditation, which you relished most, or by stirring yourself up to devotion, by some new spiritual subject, as you may like best.

As to the examination of conscience, which must always be made before bedtime, everyone knows how it is to be performed. 1. We give thanks to God for having preserved us during the day. 2. We

When the father or mother of St. Catherine of Siena had deprived her of a place and leisure to pray and meditate, our Lord inspired her to make a little oratory within her soul, into which, retiring mentally, she might, amidst her everyday affairs, attend to this holy mental solitude; and when the world afterwards assaulted her, she received no inconvenience from it, because, as she said, she had shut herself up in her interior closet, where she comforted herself with her heavenly Spouse. From her own experience of this exercise, she afterwards counselled her spiritual children to make a room within their hearts, and to abide therein.

Withdraw yourself, therefore, from time to time, into your heart, where, separated from all men, you may familiarly treat on the affairs of your soul and of your salvation with God. Say with David (Ps. ci.) : "I watched and am become like a pelican in the wilderness, like the night raven within the house. I have watched and am become as a sparrow all alone on the house-top." Which words, besides their literal meaning, namely, that this great king spent some solitary hours in the contemplation of spiritual things, also point out, in a mystical sense, three excellent retreats or hermitages, wherein we may imitate the solitude of our Saviour, who on Mount Calvary was likened to the pelican of the wilderness, which nourishes and gives life to her young ones with her own blood; in his Nativity, in a desolate state, to the night raven in a ruinous building, mourning and weeping over our offences and sins; and at his Ascension, to the sparrow flying up to heaven, which is, as it were, the house-top of the world. In these three solitudes we may make our spiritual retreats, even amidst the turmoils of our worldly employments. Blessed Elzear, Count of Arian in Provence, having been long absent from his devout and chaste

Delphina, she sent a courier to him to inform herself of his health, by whom he sent back this answer: "I am very well, my dear wife, but if you desire to see me, seek me in the wound of the side of our sweet Saviour; for, as it is there only that I dwell, it is there you shall find me; if you seek for me elsewhere, you will search in vain." This was a Christian gentleman indeed

---

CHAPTER XIII.

Aspirations, ejaculatory prayers, and good thoughts.

We retire into God, because we aspire to Him; and we aspire to Him that we may retire into Him: so that the aspiring to God, and the spiritual retiring into Him, are the mutual supports of each other, and both proceed from the same source, namely, from devout and pious thoughts.

Aspire then frequently to God, Philothea, by short but ardent dartings of your heart; admire his beauty, invoke his assistance; cast yourself in spirit at the foot of the cross; adore his goodness; converse with Him frequently on the business of your salvation; give your soul to Him a thousand times a day; contemplate his clemency and his sweetness; stretch out your hand to Him as a little child does to his father, that He may conduct you; place Him in your bosom like a delicious nosegay; plant him in your soul like a standard; and move your heart a thousand times to enkindle and excite within you a passionate and tender affection for your Divine Spouse. The making of ejaculatory prayer was strongly recommended by the great St. Augustin to the devout Lady Proba. Our spirit. Philothea, by habituating itself thus privately to the company and familiarity of God, will be altogether perfumed with his perfections. Now, there is no difficulty in this exercise, as it is not incompatible with our occupations, without any inconvenience whatever, since, in these spiritual and interior aspirations, we only take short diversions, which, instead of preventing, rather assist us in the pursuit of what we are seeking. The pilgrim, though he may stop to take a little wine to strengthen his heart and cool his mouth, does not delay his journey by so doing, but rather acquires strength to finish it with more ease and expedition, resting only that he may afterwards proceed with greater speed.

Many have formed collections of ejaculatory prayers, which may be very profitable; but I would advise you not to conform yourself to any set form of words, but to pronounce, either from your heart or mouth, such as love may suddenly suggest to you; for it will furnish you with as many as you could wish. It is, indeed, true there are certain words which have a peculiar force to satisfy the heart in this respect. Such are the aspirations interspersed so copiously throughout the Psalms of David; the frequent invocation of the name of Jesus; the ejaculations of love expressed in the Canticles, &c. Spiritual songs will also answer the same purpose, when sung with attention.

In fine, as they that love, in a human and natural manner, have their thoughts and hearts incessantly occupied with the object of their affection, and their mouth ever employed in its praise, in its absence they lose no opportunity to testify that affection by letters, and by cutting the name of their beloved on the bark of trees; even so, such as truly love God can never cease to think on Him, breathe for Him, aspire to Him, and speak of Him; and, were it possible, they would engrave the sacred name of Jesus on the breasts of all mankind.

To this all things invite them, as there is no creature that does not declare to them the praises of their beloved. Yes, says St. Augustin, after St. Anthony, everything in the world addresses them in a most intelligible, yet dumb kind of language, in favour of their love: all things excite them to good thoughts, which give birth to many animated emotions and aspirations of the soul to God. The following are some examples :—

St. Gregory Nazianzen, walking on the sea shore, remarked how the waves, advancing upon the beach, left on it shells, sea-weeds, star-fishes, and such like things, and then, other waves returning, took part of them back, and swallowed them up again, whilst the adjoining rocks continued firm and immovable, though the billows beat against them with ever so much violence. Upon which he made the salutary reflection, that feeble souls, like shells and weeds, suffer themselves to be borne away, sometimes by affliction, and at other times by consolation, at the mercy of the inconstant billows of fortune, but that courageous souls continue firm and unmoved amid all kinds of storms. From this thought he proceeded to those aspirations of David (Ps. lxviii.) : "Save me, O God, for the waters are come in even to my very soul. O Lord, deliver me out of those deep waters; I am come into the depth of the sea, and a tempest has overwhelmed me." At the time he was in affliction on account of the unhappy usurpation attempted by Maximus on his bishopric.

St. Fulgentius, Bishop of Ruspa, being present at a general assembly of the Roman nobility, when Theodoric, King of the Goths, made an oration to them, and beholding the splendour of so many great lords, each ranked according to his quality, exclaimed : "O God, how glorious and beautiful must the heavenly Jerusalem be, since earthly Rome appears in so much pomp ! for, if in this world the lovers of vanity are permitted to shine so brightly, what must not that glory be which is reserved, in the next world, for those who love truth !"

St. Anselm, Archbishop of Canterbury, by whose birth our mountains have been highly honoured, was admirable in the application of good thoughts. A hare, pressed by hounds, as this holy prelate was proceeding on a journey, fearing death, took refuge under his horse; whilst the hounds, barking around, did not attempt to violate the sanctuary to which their prey had fled. A sight so very extraordinary made the whole company burst into a fit of laughter, whilst the saint, weeping and sighing, cried out: "Alas! you laugh, but the poor beast does not laugh; the enemies of the soul, having hunted, and driven her on, by divers turnings and windings, through all sorts of sins, lie in wait for her at the narrow passage of death, to catch and devour her, and she, being in so dreadful a plight, looks for succour and refuge on every side ; and, if she does not find it, she is mocked and derided by her enemies." When the saint had said this, he rode on sighing.

Constantine the Great, having written with great respect to St. Anthony, the religious about him were greatly astonished. "Why," said he, "do you feel astonished that a king should write to a man? Be astonished, rather, that the Eternal God should have written down his law to mortal men; yea, more, should have spoken to them by word of mouth in the person of his Son."

St. Francis, seeing a sheep alone amidst a flock of goats: "Observe," said he to his companion, "the poor sheep, how mild it is amidst the goats ; our blessed Lord walked thus meekly and humbly among the Pharisees." At another time, seeing a lamb devoured by a wild boar: "Ah! little lamb," said he, weeping, "how strikingly dost thou represent the death of my Saviour !"

An illustrious person of our age, St. Francis Borgia, whilst yet Duke of Candia, whilst engaged in the chase, used to make to himself a thousand devout reflections. "I admired," said he afterwards, "how the falcons come to hand, suffer themselves to be hooded, and to be tied to the perch ; and, on the other hand, how rebellious men are to the voice of God."

The great St. Basil said, that the rose in the midst of thorns affords this beautiful instruction to men : "That which is most agreeable in this world, O ye mortals, is mingled with sorrow ; nothing here is pure ; regret is always at the side of mirth ; widowhood at that of marriage ; care at that of maturity ; and ignominy at that of glory ; expense follows honour ; loathing comes after delight, and sickness after health. "The rose is a beautiful flower," said this holy man, "yet it makes me sorrowful, putting me in mind of sin, on account of which the earth has been condemned to bring forth thorns."

A devout soul, standing over a brook on a very clear night, and seeing the heavens and stars reflected therein, exclaimed : "O my God, these very stars which I now behold shall be one day beneath my feet, when Thou shalt have received me into thy celestial tabernacles ; and as the stars of heaven are thus represented on earth, even so are the men of this earth represented in heaven in the living fountain of divine charity." Another, seeing a river flow swiftly along, cried out : "My soul shall never be at rest till she is swallowed up in the sea of the divinity, her original source." St. Francisca, contemplating a pleasant brook, upon the bank of which she was kneeling at her prayers, being in an ecstasy, often repeated these words : "The grace of my God flows thus gently and sweetly, like this little stream." Another, looking n the tree in bloom, sighed and said : "Ah ! why am

I alone without blossom in the garden of the Church?" Another, seeing little chickens gathered together under a hen, said: "Preserve us, O Lord, continually, under the shadow of thy wings." Another, looking upon the flower called heliotrope, which turns to the sun, exclaimed: "When shall the time come, O my God, that my soul shall faithfully follow the attractions of thy goodness?" And seeing the flowers called pansies, fair to the eye, but having no smell: "Ah," said he, "such are my thoughts, fair in appearance, but good for nothing."

Behold, Philothea, how we may extract good thoughts and holy aspirations from everything that presents itself amidst the variety of this mortal life. Unhappy they who use creatures differently from what their Creator intended, and make them the instruments of sin; and thrice happy they that turn creatures to the glory of their Creator, and employ them to the honour of his Sovereign Majesty; as St. Gregory Nazianzen says: "I am wont to refer all things to my spiritual profit." Read the devout epitaph composed by St. Jerome for St. Paula; how agreeable to behold it sprinkled all over with those aspirations and holy thoughts which he was wont to draw from all sorts of occurrences.

Now, as the great work of devotion consists in the exercise of spiritual recollection and ejaculatory prayers, the want of all other prayers may be supplied by them: but failing in them, the loss can scarcely be made good by any other means. Without them we cannot lead a good active life, much less a contemplative one. Then repose would be but idleness, and labour vexation. Wherefore I conjure you to embrace it with your whole heart, without ever desisting from its practice.

CHAPTER XIV.

The most Holy Mass, and how we ought to hear it.

Hitherto I have said nothing of the most holy, sacred, and august sacrifice and sacrament of the Altar, the sun of spiritual exercises, the centre of the Christian religion, the heart of devotion, and the soul of piety; a mystery so ineffable as to comprise within itself that abyss of divine charity from whence God communicates Himself really to us; and, in a special manner, replenishes our souls with spiritual graces and favours.

When prayer, Philothea, is united with this divine sacrifice, it becomes so efficacious as to cause the soul to overflow, as it were, with heavenly consolations. Here she reclines upon her Well-beloved, who fills her with so much spiritual sweetness that she resembles, as is said in the Canticles, a pillar of smoke proceeding from a fire of aromatic wood, from myrrh and frankincense, and from all the most exquisite perfumes.

Endeavour therefore to assist at Mass every day, that you may, jointly with the priest, offer up the holy sacrifice of your Redeemer to God his Father, for yourself and for the whole Church. The angels, says St. John Chrysostom, always attend in great numbers to honour this adorable mystery; and we, by associating ourselves with them, having one and the same intention, cannot but receive many favourable influences from such a holy society. The choirs of the triumphant church, and those of the church militant, unite themselves to our Lord in this divine action, that with Him, in Him, and through Him, they may gain the heart of God the Father, and make his mercy all our own. Oh, what a happiness is it to a soul to devoutly contribute her affections for obtaining so precious and desirable a treasure !

Should some indispensable business prevent you from assisting in person at the celebration of this great sacrifice, endeavour at least to send your heart thither, to assist thereat by a spiritual presence, uniting your intention with that of all the faithful, and using the same acts of devotion in your closet which you would use were you actually present at Mass.

Now, to hear Mass in a proper manner, either really or mentally, you must—1. From the beginning till the priest goes up to the altar, make with him your preparation, which consists in placing yourself in the presence of God, acknowledging your unworthiness, and asking pardon for your sins. 2. From the time he goes up to the altar to the Gospel, consider the nativity of our Lord and his life in this world by presenting a simple and general idea of them to your mind. 3. From the Gospel till after the Creed, consider the preaching of our Saviour, and promise that you resolve to live and die in faith and obedience to his holy word, and in the communion of the holy Catholic Church. 4. From the Creed to the Pater Noster, apply your heart to the mysteries of the death and passion of our Redeemer, essentially represented in this holy sacrifice, and which, with the priest and the rest of the people, you must offer to God the Father, for his glory and your salvation. 5. From the Pater Noster to the Communion, strive to excite a thousand desires in your heart, wishing ardently to be for ever united to your Saviour by everlasting love. 6. From the Communion to the end, return thanks to Jesus Christ for his incarnation, life, passion, and death; as well as for the love He testifies to us in this holy sacrifice, beseeching Him to be for ever merciful his whole Church ; and, finally, humbling yourself, receive devoutly, with your whole heart, the benediction of God, which our Lord gives you by the ministry of the officiating priest.

But should you choose during the Mass to meditate on the mystery you proposed for your consideration on that day, it is not necessary that you should divert your thoughts to perform all these particular acts, but that at the beginning you direct your attention to adore, and offer up this holy sacrifice by the exercise of your meditation and prayer; for in all meditations the aforesaid acts may be found either expressly or tacitly, and in an equivalent manner.

CHAPTER XV.

Other public and common exercises of Devotion.

Besides hearing Mass on Sundays and holidays, you ought also, Philothea, to be present at vespers and other portions of the divine office, as far as your convenience will permit. For, as these days are dedicated to God, we ought to perform more acts to his honour and glory on them than on other days. By this means you shall feel a thousand spiritual consolations, as St. Augustin did, who testifies, in his Confessions, that, hearing the divine office in the beginning of his conversion, his heart melted into tenderness, and his eyes into tears of devotion. And indeed, to speak once for all, there is always more benefit and comfort in the public offices of the Church than in private evotion, God having so ordained, that the communion of the faithful should be preferred to all kinds of devotion practised privately.

Enter, then, willingly into the confraternities of ᵔlace wherein you reside, and especially those whose exercises are most productive of fruit and edification, as in so doing you practise a sort of obedience acceptable to God; for, although these confraternities are not commanded, they are, nevertheless, recommended by the Church, which, to testify her approbation of them, grants indulgences and other privileges to such as enter them. Besides, it is always very laudable to concur and co-operate with many in their good designs, for, although we might perform quite as good exercises alone as in the company of a confraternity, and perhaps take more pleasure in performing them in private, yet God is more glorified when we unite our good works with those of our brethren and neighbours.

I say the same of all public prayers and devotions, which we should countenance as much as possible by our good example, for the glory of God, for the edification of our neighbour, and for the common end which we propose to ourselves when we take part in them.

CHAPTER XVI.

We must honour and invoke the Saints.

Since God often sends us inspirations by his angels, we ought also frequently to send back our inspirations to Him by similar messengers. The holy souls of the deceased, who dwell in heaven with the angels, and are, as our Saviour says (Luke, xv. 36), equal and like to the angels, perform also the same office of inspiring us, and interceding for us by their prayers. Let us then join our hearts with these heavenly spirits and happy souls; and as the young nightingales learn to sing in the company of the old ones, so, by the holy association we make with the saints, we shall learn to pray, and to sing the div praises in a much better manner: " I will sir

Thee, O Lord," says David, "in the sight of thy angels" (Ps. cxxxvii. 2).

Honour, reverence, love, and respect in a special manner the sacred and glorious Virgin Mary, as she was the Mother of our sovereign Lord, so is she consequently our Mother. Let us run, then, to her, and, as her little children, cast ourselves into her bosom with perfect confidence, at all times and in all circumstances. Let us call upon this sweet Mother, let us invoke her motherly love; and, endeavouring to imitate her virtues, let us feel true filial affection for her.

Make yourself familiar with the angels, and behold them frequently in spirit; for, without being seen, they are present with you. Have always a particular love and reverence for the Guardian Angels of the diocese wherein you dwell, and of the persons with whom you live, but especially your own. Address yourself often to them, bless God for having given them, and beg for their assistance in all your affairs, spiritual or temporal, that they may co-operate with your intentions.

The great Peter Faber, first priest, first preacher, and first professor of theology of the Holy Society of Jesus, and the companion of St. Ignatius, its founder, returning from Germany, where he had done great service for the glory of our Lord, and travelling through this diocese, the place of his birth, related, that having passed through many heretical places, he had received innumerable consolations from the Guardian Angels of the several parishes, of whose protection, on repeated occasions, he had received the most sensible and convincing proofs: sometimes by preserving him from the ambushes of heretics, at other times by rendering numerous souls more mild and tractable to receive from him the doctrine of salvation. This he related with so much earnestness, that a gentlewomen, then very young.

who heard it from his own mouth, related it but a few years ago, that is to say, about threescore years after he had told it, with extraordinary feeling. I had the consolation last year to consecrate an altar on the spot where God was pleased that this blessed man should be born, in a little village called Villaret, amidst our most inaccessible mountains.

Choose some particular saint or saints whose lives you may most desire to imitate, and in whose intercession you may have great confidence. The saints whose names you bear are already assigned to you from your baptism.

CHAPTER XVII.

How we ought to hear and read the Word of God.

Listen with devotion to the word of God, whether you hear it in familiar conversation or at a sermon. Extract all the profit from it you possibly can, and suffer it not to fall to the ground, but receive it into your heart as a precious balm; imitating the most Holy Virgin, who preserved carefully in her heart all the words which were spoken by her Son. Remember that our Lord hears our prayers favourably only in proportion to the attention with which we listen to and profit by his words when we hear sermons.

Have always at hand some approved book of devotion: such as the spiritual works of St. Bonaventure, of Gerson, of Denis the Carthusian, of Louis de Blois of Grenada, of Stella, of Arias, of Pinelli, of Dupont, of Avila, the Spiritual Combat, St. Augustin's Confessions, St. Jerome's Epistles, &c., and read a little of them every day with as much devotion as if you were reading a letter which those saints had sent you from heaven to show you the way to it, and encourage you to come. Read also the h tories and lives of the saints, in which, as in a looking-glass, you may behold the portraiture of a Christian's life, and accommodate their actions to your state of life; for, although several actions of the saints cannot absolutely be imitated by such as live in the world, yet they may be in some degree followed; for example, you may imitate the solitude of St. Paul, the first hermit, by the spiritual solitude of your heart, and by retreats which you can make, of which we shall hereafter speak, and have already spoken; the extreme poverty of St. Francis, by the practices of poverty; and so of the rest. It is true that there are some of their histories which give more light for the conduct of our lives than others, such as the life of the blessed mother Teresa, the lives of the first Jesuits, that of St. Charles Borromeus, Archbishop of Milan, of St. Louis, of Bernard, the Chronicles of St. Francis, and several others.

There are others, again, which contain more subjects for admiration than imitation, such as the life of St. Mary of Egypt, of St. Simon Stylites, of St. Catherine of Sienna, and of St. Catherine of Genoa, of St. Angela, and others; which, nevertheless, do not fail in general to give us a great relish for the holy love of God.

CHAPTER XVIII.

How we ought to receive Inspirations.

By inspirations are meant all attractions of grace, good movements of our hearts, reproaches and remorses of conscience, lights and conceptions which God excites in us, presenting our souls with his blessings, through his fatherly care and love, in order to awaken, stimulate, urge, and attract us to the practice of every virtue, to heavenly love, to good resolutions, and in a word, to everything that may help us on our way to eternal happiness. This is what the Spouse of the Canticles calls, in mysterious language, knocking at the door, and speaking to the heart of his Spouse, awaking her when she sleeps, calling after her when she is absent, inviting her to gather fruits and flowers in his garden, to sing, and cause her sweet voice to sound in his ears.

That you may the more perfectly comprehend me, I must use a comparison. For the conclusion of a marriage three things are necessary : First, the intended husband is proposed to the lady ; secondly, she entertains the proposition ; thirdly, she gives her consent. In like manner, when God intends doing in, by, or with us, some great act of grace, at first He proposes it by inspiration ; secondly, we are pleased with it ; and, thirdly, we give our full consent to it. For, as there are three steps whereby we descend to the commission of sin—temptation, delectation, and consent—so there are also three steps whereby we ascend to the practice of virtue—inspiration, which is the opposite of temptation; the pleasure conceived in the inspiration, which is the opposite of the delectation in the temptation ; and the consent of the inspiration, which is the opposite of the consent given to the temptation.

Now, though the inspiration should continue during our whole life, yet we could not render ourselves pleasing to God if we took no pleasure in it: on the contrary, He would be offended with us, as He was with the Israelites, whose conversion He had been soliciting very nearly forty years (Ps. xlv.), during which time they would give no ear to Him ; whereupon He swore in his wrath that they should never enter into his rest.

By the pleasure we take in inspirations, we not only show a disposition to glorify God, but begin already to please his Divine Majesty ; for although this delight may not be a complete consent, yet it is a certain disposition towards it ; and if it be a good sign to take pleasure in hearing the word of God, which is, as it were, an exterior inspiration, it must also, no doubt, be a good thing, and pleasing to God, to take delight in his internal inspiration. Of this kind of pleasure the sacred Spouse speaks (Cant. v. 6) : "My soul was melted when my beloved spoke ; " but she did not open the door to Him, and excused herself with some frivolous pretext. The Spouse therefore indignantly quitted her.

Resolve, then, Philothea, to accept with cordiality all the inspirations it shall please God to send you, and, when they come, receive them as ambassadors sent by the King of Heaven, who desires to enter into a contract of marriage with you. Attend calmly to his propositions ; think of the love with which you are inspired, and cherish the holy inspirations ; consent to them, but with an entire. loving, and permanent consent; for by this means God, who cannot be under any obligation to us, will, nevertheless, be greatly pleased with this faithful correspondence to his love. But before you consent to inspirations in things that are of great importance, or that are out of the ordinary way, always consult your spiritual guide, lest you should be deceived; because the enemy, seeing a soul ready to consent to the inspirations, often proposes false ones to deceive her, which he can never do so long as she, with humility, obeys her director.

The consent being given, you must diligently procure the effects, and hasten to put the inspiration into execution, which is the height of true virtue : for, to have the consent within the heart, without producing effects, would be like planting a vine, and not intending that it should bring forth fruit.

Now, what contributes wonderfully to all this, is the practice of the morning exercise, and those spiritual retreats of the heart above recommended, as by these means we prepare ourselves to do what is good, not only by a general, but also by a particular preparation.

CHAPTER XIX.
On Holy Confession.

Our Saviour has left the holy sacrament of penance and confession to his Church, that in it we may cleanse ourselves from all our iniquities, as often as we should be defiled by them. Never suffer your heart, then, Philothea, to remain long affected with sin, since you have so easy a remedy at hand. A soul which has consented to sin ought to conceive a horror of herself, and cleanse herself as quickly as possible, out of the respect she ought to bear to the Divine Majesty, who incessantly beholds her. Alas! why should we die a spiritual death, when we have so sovereign a remedy at hand?

Confess yourself humbly and devoutly once every week, and always, if possible, before you communicate, even though your conscience should not reproach you with the guilt of mortal sin : for by confession you not only receive absolution from the venial sins you confess, but likewise strength to avoid them, light to discern them well, and grace to repair all the damage you may have sustained by them. You will also practise the virtues of humility, obedience, sincerity, charity ; nay, in a word, in this one act of confession you can exercise more virtues than in any other whatsoever.

Conceive always a sincere sorrow for the sins you confess, be they ever so small, with a firm resolution never to commit them for the time to come. Many who confess their venial sins merely out of custom,

7

and for the sake of order, without any thought of
amendment, continue, on that account, during their
whole lifetime under the guilt of them, and thus
lose several spiritual advantages. If, then, you confess that you have told a small falsehood, spoken
some disorderly words, or have played excessively,
repent, and form a determined resolution to amend;
for it is an abuse to confess any kind of sin, whether √
mortal or venial, without a will to be delivered therefrom, since confession was instituted for no other end.

Make none of those superfluous accusations, viz.,
I have not loved God so much as I ought; I have
not prayed with as much devotion as I ought; I
have not cherished my neighbour as I ought; I have
not received the sacraments with as great reverence
as I ought, &c. &c.; for in speaking thus you will
say nothing that can make your confessor understand the state of your conscience; since all the
saints in heaven and on earth might say the same
thing if they came to confession Examine, then,
what particular reason you may have to make these
accusations; and when you have discovered it, accuse yourself sincerely and distinctly. For example,
you accuse yourself that you have not loved your
neighbour so much as you ought; perhaps, because
having seen some poor person in distress, whom
you might easily have assisted, you took no notice
of him. In such a case you should have said,
" Having seen a poor man in necessity, I did not
assist him as l ought to have done ;" through negligence, hard-heartedness, contempt, or whatever you
may discover to have been the cause of this fault.
In like manner, do not accuse yourself of not having
prayed to God with as much devotion as you ought;
but if you have admitted any voluntary distraction,
or neglected to choose a proper place, time, or posture necessary for proper attention in prayer, accuse

with assurance that the distance between the days for communicating for such as desire to serve God devoutly should not exceed a month.

If you act with prudence, neither father, mother, husband, nor wife, will prevent you from communicating often, for if, on the day of your communion, you are not less diligent in the discharge of your duties, and even acquit yourself of them with more cheerfulness and alacrity, be they ever so irksome, there can be no likelihood that they should seek to prevent you from an exercise in which they find no kind of inconvenience, except they should be of a spirit extremely narrow and unreasonable; and in that case, as I have said already, your director will advise you to yield somewhat to them.

As for bodily diseases, there are none which can be a lawful impediment to this holy devotion, excepting those which provoke to frequent vomiting.

To communicate every eight days, it is requisite that one should be free from mortal sin, and without any affection to mortal sin, and to have, moreover, a great desire of communicating; but to communicate every day, it is necessary we should overcome the greatest part of our evil inclinations, and that it should be by the advice of our spiritual director.

CHAPTER XXI.
How we ought to communicate.

Prepare yourself for the holy Communion the evening before, by many ejaculations of love, retiring earlier, that you may rise sooner in the morning. Should you awake in the night, sanctify your heart and mouth with some devout aspirations, in order to prepare your soul for the reception of her spouse, who being awake whilst you were asleep, prepares a thousand graces and favours for you, if on your part you are disposed to receive them. In the morning.

rise up with alacrity to enjoy the happiness you hope for; and go with a great but humble confidence, to receive this heavenly meat, which nourishes your soul to immortality; and after repeating thrice, " Lord, I am not worthy," &c., cease to move your head or lips, either to pray or to sigh, but opening your mouth gently and moderately, and lifting up your head as much as is necessary, so that the priest may see what he is about, full of faith, hope, and charity, receive Him in whom, by whom, and for whom you believe, hope, and love. Represent to yourself, Philothea, that as the bee, after gathering from the flowers the dew of heaven, and their choicest juices, and reducing them into honey, carries them into her hive, so the priest, having taken from the altar the Saviour of the world, the true Son of God, who, as the dew descended from heaven, and the true Son of the Virgin, who, as a flower sprung from the earth of our humanity, he puts Him as delicious food into your mouth.

Having received Him into your breast, excite your heart to do homage to the King of your salvation, treat with Him concerning your internal affairs; consider that He has taken up his abode within you for your happiness: make Him, then, as welcome as you possibly can, and conduct yourself in such a manner as to make it appear by all your actions that God is with you.

But when you cannot enjoy the benefit of communicating really at the holy Mass, communicate at least spiritually, uniting yourself by an ardent desire to this life-giving flesh of your Saviour.

Your principal intention in communicating should be to advance, comfort, and strengthen yourself in the love of God; for you must receive through love that which love alone caused to be given to you. You cannot consider your Saviour in an action either ᵗore full of love, or more tender than this, in which

cence ; but meekness, temperance, modesty, and humility are virtues wherewith all the actions of our life ought to be tempered. It is true there are other virtues more excellent, but the use of these is more necessary. Sugar is more excellent than salt, but the use of salt is more necessary and general. We must always, therefore, have a good store of these general virtues in readiness, since we stand in need of them almost continually.

In the exercise of the virtues we should always prefer that which is most conformable to our duty, not that which is most agreeable to our imagination. St. Paula was prejudiced in favour of corporal austerities and mortifications, that she might the more easily enjoy spiritual comfort; but she was under a greater obligation to obey her superiors, and therefore St. Jerome blamed her for using immoderate abstinences against her bishop's advice. The apostles, on the other hand, being commissioned to preach the Gospel and distribute the bread of heaven, judged that it would be wrong for them to interrupt these evangelical exercises to relieve the poor, though otherwise an excellent virtue. Every condition of life has its own peculiar virtues. The virtues of a prelate are different from those of a prince; those of a soldier from those of a married woman or a widow, and so on through every class of society. Though all ought to possess all the virtues, yet all are not equally bound to exercise them, but each ought to practise, in a more particular manner those virtues which are most requisite for the state of life to which he is called.

Among the virtues unconnected with our particular duty, we must prefer the most excellent to the most glittering and showy. Comets appear larger than stars, and occupy a greater space to our eyes, whereas, in reality, they cannot, either in magnitude or quality, be compared to the stars ; for, as they only seem large because they are nearer, and appear in a grosser manner than the stars, so there are certain virtues which, on account of their proximity, become more sensible, or, as I may say, more material, and therefore are highly esteemed, and always preferred by the vulgar. Hence it is that so many prefer corporal alms before spiritual ; the hair shirt, fasting, going barefoot, using the discipline, and other such corporal mortifications in preference to meekness, modesty, and other mortifications of the heart, which are, nevertheless, more excellent. Choose, then, Philothea, the best virtues, not the most esteemed ; the most excellent, not the most apparent ; those that are actually the best, not those that are most ostensible or shining.

It is profitable for everyone to exercise some particular virtue, yet not so as to abandon the rest, but to keep his spirit in a more settled condition. A fair virgin, in royal attire, more bright than the sun, whose head was decorated with a crown of olives, appeared to St. John, Bishop of Alexandria, and said to him : "I am the eldest daughter of the king ; if thou canst have me for thy friend I shall conduct thee to his presence." The holy prelate understood that she was mercy towards the poor, which God recommended to him ; and therefore, ever after, he gave himself up so absolutely to the practice of that virtue, that he obtained the title of St. John the Almoner. Eulogius the Alexandrian, desiring to do some particular service to God, and not having strength enough to embrace a solitary life, nor to subject himself to the obedience of another, took a poor wretch quite eaten up with the leprosy into his house, that he might exercise, in his regard, the virtues of charity and mortification ; and to perform them the more worthily, he made a vow to honour and serve him as his lord and master; now, on a temptation happening, as well to the leper as to Eulogius, to depart the one from the other, they addressed themselves to the great St. Anthony, who said: "Take care, my children, not to depart from one another, for being both of you near your end, if the angel shall not find you together, you run a great risk of losing your crown."

St. Louis, King of France, visited hospitals and the sick as diligently as if he served for wages. St. Francis had so extraordinary a love for poverty as to call her his lady; and St. Dominick for preaching, that his Order takes its name from it. St. Gregory the Great, following the example of the great Abraham, took pleasure in entertaining pilgrims, and like him received the King of Glory in the form of a pilgrim. Tobias exercised his charity in burying the dead. St. Elizabeth, though a great princess, delighted in nothing so much as in humbling herself. St. Catherine of Genoa, in her widowhood, dedicated herself to serve an hospital. Cassian relates that a devout lady, desirous to exercise the virtue of patience, came to St. Athanasius, who, at her request, placed her with a poor widow, so exceedingly peevish, choleric, and troublesome, as, by her insupportable temper, to give the good lady ample occasion to exercise the virtues of meekness and charity.

Thus, among the servants of God, some apply themselves to serve the sick; others to relieve the poor; others to propagate the knowledge of the Christian doctrine amongst children; others to reclaim souls that have gone astray; others to adorn churches and deck altars; others to restore peace and concord among such as have been at variance. As embroiderers lay gold, silver, and silk on the several articles which they are engaged in ornamenting, with such an admirable variety of colours as to resemb' all kinds of flowers, so those pious souls make choice of some particular devotion to serve as a ground for the spiritual embroidery of all other virtues, holding, by means thereof, all their actions and affections better united and ordered, by referring them to that principal end; and thus they show forth their spirit in its gilded clothing, surrounded with a variety of virtues.

When assaulted by any vice, we must embrace the practice of the contrary virtue, and refer all the others to it, by which means we shall overcome our enemy, and at the same time advance in all the virtues. Thus, if assaulted by pride or anger, we must in all our actions turn ourselves to humility and meekness, and make all our exercises of prayer, the sacraments, and the virtues of prudence, constancy and sobriety, subservient to this end. For as the wild boar, to sharpen his tusks, whets and polishes them with his other teeth, and by this means sharpens all at the same time, so a virtuous man, having undertaken to perfect himself in the virtue of which he stands most in need for his defence, files and polishes it by the exercise of the other virtues, which whilst they help to sharpen that one, make all of them become more excellent and better polished. It was thus that it happened to Job, who, exercising himself particularly in patience, against the many temptations wherewith he was assaulted, became confirmed in all kinds of virtues. Nay, St. Gregory Nazianzen says that, by the perfect exercise of one virtue a person may attain to the height of all the rest; for this he quotes the example of Rahab, who, having practised the virtue of hospitality, arrived at a great degree of glory. But this is only to be understood, when such a virtue is practised with great fervour and charity.

CHAPTER II.

Continuation of the former discourse on the choice of virtues.

Young beginners in devotion, says St. Augustine, commit certain faults, which, according to the rigour of the laws of perfection, are blameable and yet commendable, on account of the foreshadowing they give of the future excellence in piety, to which they serve as a disposition. That low and servile fear which begets excessive scruples in the souls of new converts from a course of sin, is commendable in beginners, and a certain foreboding of a future purity of conscience; but the same fear would be blamable in those who are far advanced and in whose heart love ought to reign, which, by imperceptible degrees, chases away this servile fear.

St. Bernard, in the beginning, was full of rigour towards those who put themselves under his direction; he told them that they must leave the body behind, and come to him only with the spirit. When he heard their confessions, he severely rebuked their most trivial faults, and urged them on to perfection with such vehemence, that, instead of making them advance forward, he drove them back; for they lost heart when they saw themselves so earnestly pressed up so steep and high an ascent. Observe, Philothea, it was an ardent zeal for perfect purity that induced this great saint to adopt that manner of proceeding. This zeal of the saint was a great virtue, but a virtue nevertheless reprehensible; of which, God Himself in a holy vision made him sensible, pouring at the same time into his soul so meek, amiable, and tender a spirit, that, being totally changed, he repented of his former rigour and severity, and became so gracious and condescending to everyone as to make himself all to all, that he might gain all. St. Je·

naving related how his dear daughter, St. Paula, was not only excessive, but obstinate, in the exercise of bodily mortification, to such a degree, that she would not yield to the contrary advice of Epiphanius, her bishop; and moreover, that she suffered herself to be carried away with such excessive grief for the death of her husband and children, as to be herself frequently in danger of death, concludes at length with these words: "Some will say, that instead of writing the praises of this holy woman, I blame her imperfections and faults; but I call Jesus to witness whom she served, and whom I desire to serve, that, I do not depart from the truth, either on the one side or the other, but set down sincerely what related to her, as one Christian should do of another; that is to say, I write her history, not her panegyric; and that her vices would have been virtues in many others:" meaning that the failings and defects of St. Paula would have been esteemed virtues in a soul less perfect; and that there are actions esteemed imperfections in the perfect, which would be held great perfections in those who are imperfect.

It is said to be a good sign, when, during convalescence, the legs of the sick person swell, for it shows that nature, now acquiring strength, casts out her superfluous humours; but this would be a bad symptom in one that was not sick, as it would show that nature had not sufficient strength to dissipate the noxious humours. We must, Philothea, have a good opinion of those who practise virtues, though they may have imperfections, since we see that the saints themselves have often had imperfections also. But as to ourselves, we must be careful to try to make ourselves as perfect as possible, faithfully but discreetly; and to this end we must strictly observe the advice of the wise man, "not to rely on our own ¬idence," but on the judgment of such as God has ¬ us for directors.

There are certain things which many esteem as virtues, though in reality they are not : I mean ecstasies or raptures, insensibilities, impassibilities, deifical unions, elevations, transformations, and such like perfections, treated of in certain books, which promise to elevate the soul to a contemplation purely intellectual, to the essential application of the spirit to a supernatural life. But observe well, Philothea, these perfections are not virtues, but rather the recompense of virtue, or small foreshadowings of the happiness of the life to come, which God sometimes grants to men, to make them desire the full possession of it in heaven.

But we must not aspire to such favours, since they are by no means necessary to the serving and loving of God, which ought to be our only pretension; neither are they such as can be obtained by labour and industry, since they are rather passions than actions which we may indeed receive, but cannot produce in ourselves. We have only undertaken to render ourselves good, devout, and godly; and we must strenuously endeavour to be so; but if it should please God to elevate us to these angelic perfections, we shall then be also good angels in this world. In the meantime, let us endeavour, humbly and devoutly, to acquire those simple virtues for which our Saviour exhorted us to labour; such as patience, meekness, mortification of the heart, humility, obedience, poverty, chastity, love for our neighbours, bearing with their imperfections, diligence, and holy fervour. Let us leave those super-eminent favours to elevated souls; we do not merit so high a rank in the service of God: we should be too happy to serve Him in his kitchen or pantry, or to be his domestics in much lower stations. If He should hereafter think proper to admit us into his cabinet, or privy council, it will be through the excess of his bountiful goodness. Yes, Philothea, the King of Glory does not recompense his servants according to the dignity of the offices they hold, but according to the measure of the love and humility with which they exercise them. Saul, seeking the asses of his father, found the kingdom of Israel. Rebecca, watering the camels of Abraham, became the spouse of his son. Ruth, gleaning after the reapers of Boaz, and lying down at his feet, was chosen as his wife. High and elevated pretensions to extraordinary favours are subject to illusion and deceit; and it sometimes happens that those who imagine themselves angels, are not even good men, and that there is more affectation and grandiloquence in their words and expressions than solidity in their manner of thinking and acting. We must neither despise nor censure anyone, but, blessing God for the super-eminence of others, keep ourselves in our lower but safer way, which may be less eminent, but better suited to our insufficiency and littleness: persuaded that, if we conduct ourselves with humility and fidelity in it, God will infallibly elevate us to a position that will be very great indeed.

CHAPTER III.

On Patience.

"Patience is necessary for you, that in doing the will of God, you may receive the promise" (Heb. x. 36). If our Saviour Himself has declared: "In your patience you shall possess your souls" (Luke, xxi. 19), should it not b ea man's great happiness, Philothea, to possess his soul? and the more perfect our patience, the more absolutely do we possess it. Let us frequently call to mind that as our Lord has saved us by patient suffering, so we also ought to

reputation, nor the love you owe to peace and meekness of heart.

Complain as little as possible of the wrongs done you; for, commonly speaking, he that complains, sins, because self-love magnifies the injuries done us, and makes us believe them greater than they really are. Make no complaints to passionate or censorious persons: but, if complaints are necessary, either to remedy the offence, or restore quiet to your mind, let them be made to the meek and charitable, who truly love God; otherwise, instead of easing your heart, they will provoke it to greater pain; for, instead of pulling out the thorn, they will force it in the deeper.

Many, on being sick, afflicted, or injured by others, refrain from complaining or showing a sensibility of what they suffer, lest it should appear that they wanted Christian fortitude and resignation to the will of God; but still they contrive divers artifices, that others should not only pity and compassionate their sufferings and afflictions, but also admire their patience and fortitude. Now this is not true patience, but rather a refined ambition and subtle vanity. "They have glory," says the apostle, "but not with God." The truly patient man neither complains himself, nor desires to be pitied by others; he speaks of his sufferings with truth and sincerity, without murmuring, complaining, or aggravating the matter; he patiently permits himself to be condoled by others, unless they pity him for an evil which he has not; for then he will modestly declare that he does not suffer on that account: and thus he preserves the tranquillity of his soul between truth and patience, acknowledging but not complaining of the evil.

Amidst the contradictions which shall infallibly befall you in the exercise of devotion, remember the words of our Lord (John, xvi. 21), "A woman when she is in labour hath sorrow because her hour is come, but when she hath brought forth her child, she remembereth no more the anguish, for joy that a man is born into the world." Now you desire absolutely to labour to have Jesus Christ in your heart and in your works and you cannot but suffer in your labour; but be of good courage, these sorrows once past, everlasting joy shall remain with you. Jesus, who will live in you, will fill your soul with ineffable happiness.

In sickness offer up all your griefs and pains as a sacrifice to our Lord, and beseech Him to unite them with the torments He suffered for you. Obey your physicians; take your medicines, food, and other remedies, for the love of God, remembering the gall He took for your sake; desire to be cured, that you may serve Him, but do not refuse to continue sick that you may obey Him; dispose yourself to die, if it be his pleasure, that you may praise and enjoy Him for ever.

Remember that as bees, whilst making their honey, live upon a bitter provision, so we can never perform acts of greater sweetness, nor better compose the honey of excellent virtues, than whilst we eat the bread of bitterness, and live in the midst of afflictions. And, as the honey that is gathered from the flowers of thyme, a small bitter herb, is the best, so the virtue which is exercised in the bitterness of the meanest and most abject tribulations is the most excellent.

Look frequently on Christ Jesus crucified, naked, blasphemed, slandered, forsaken, and overwhelmed with all sorts of troubles, sorrows, and labours, and consider that all your sufferings, neither in quality nor quantity, are comparable to his, and that you can never suffer anything for Him equal to what He has endured for you.

Consider the torments the martyrs have suffered, and those which many at present endure, more grievous beyond comparison than yours, and then say : Alas ! are not my sufferings consolations, and my pains pleasures, in comparison with those who, without any relief, assistance, or mitigation. live in a continual death, overwhelmed with afflictions infinitely greater than mine.

CHAPTER IV.

Exterior Humility.

"Borrow empty vessels not a few," said Eliseus to the poor widow (4 Kings, iv. 3), "and pour oil into them." To receive the grace of God into our hearts they must be emptied of vain-glory. As the castrel, a bird of the hawk kind, by crying and looking on the birds of prey, affrights them by a secret property peculiar to herself, which makes the dove love her above all other birds, and live in security with her, so humility repels Satan, and preserves the graces and gifts of the Holy Ghost within us ; and therefore all the saints, but particularly the King of Saints and his Mother, have always honoured and cherished this blessed virtue more than any other moral virtue. We call that glory vain which we assume to ourselves, either for what is not in us, or for what is in us, but does not deserve that we should glory in it. The nobility of our ancestors, the favour of great men, and popular honour, are things not in us, but either in our progenitors, or in the esteem of other men. Some become proud or insolent on account of riding a good horse, wearing a feather in their hat, or being dressed in a fine suit of clothes. But who does not see the folly of this? for if there be any glory in such things, the glory belongs to the horse, the bird, and the tailor ·

and what meanness of heart it must be to borrow
esteem from a horse, from a feather, or some ridiculous new fashion? Others value themselves on
account of a well-trimmed beard, curled locks, soft
hands; or because they can dance, sing, or play;
but are not these effeminate men, who seek to raise
their reputation by such frivolous and foolish
things? Others, on account of a little learning,
would be honoured and respected by the whole
world, as if everyone ought to become their pupils,
and account them their masters. Such persons are,
therefore, called pedants. Others strut like pea-
cocks, contemplating their beauty, and think themselves admired by everyone. All this is extremely
superficial, foolish, and impertinent; and the glory
which is raised on such weak foundations is justly
esteemed vain and frivolous.

True goodness is proved like true balm: for as
balm, when dropped into water, if it sinks and rests
at the bottom, is accounted the most excellent and
precious; so if you would know whether a man is
truly wise, learned, or generous, observe if his qua-
lifications tend to humility, modesty, and submission, for then they shall be good indeed; but if
they swim on the surface, and strive to appear above
water, they shall be so much the less true, in proportion as they are high. As pearls that are formed
during storms and thunder have nothing of the substance, but only the outside appearance of pearl, so
the virtues and good qualities of men that are bred
and nourished by pride, ostentation, and vanity,
have nothing but the appearance of good, without
any solidity.

Honours, rank, and dignities are like saffron,
which thrives best and grows most plentifully when
trodden under foot. It is no honour to be beautiful
when a man prizes himself for it: beauty, to be

pleasing, should be neglected ; and learning is a disgrace to us, when it puffs us up and degenerates into pedantry.

If we are exceedingly anxious for places, precedence, and titles, in addition to exposing our qualities to be examined, tried, and contradicted, we render them vile and contemptible ; for, as honour is beautiful when freely given, so it becomes base when exacted or sought after. When the peacock spreads his tail to admire himself, in raising up his beautiful feathers, he ruffles all the rest and discovers his deformities. Flowers that are fair whilst they grow in the earth wither and fade when handled ; and as they who smell the mandrake at a distance, or only in passing by, perceive a most agreeable odour, whilst they who smell it very near, and for a long time, become sick and stupefied, so honours give a pleasant satisfaction to those that smell them slightly and afar off, without stopping to amuse themselves with them, or being earnest about them ; but such as seek after them, or feed on them are exceedingly blamable, and worthy of reprehension.

The pursuit and love of virtue tend to make us virtuous ; but the pursuit and love of honour make us contemptible and worthy of blame. Generous minds do not amuse themselves with the petty toys of rank, honour, and salutation : they have other things to do ; such baubles only belong to degenerate spirits.

He that can have pearls never loads himself with shells ; and such as aspire to virtue do not trouble themselves about honours. Everyone, indeed, may take and keep his own place without prejudice to humility, so that it be done carelessly, and without ostentation. For as they that come from Peru, besides gold and silver, bring also from thence apes

and parrots, because they neither cost much nor
are burdensome, so such as aspire to virtue refuse
not the rank and honours due to them, provided
it does not cost them too much care and attention,
nor involve them in trouble, anxiety, or contentions.
Nevertheless, I do not here allude to those whose
dignity concerns the public, nor to certain particular
occasions of importance; for in these everyone ought
to keep what belongs to him with prudence and
discretion, accompanied by charity and suavity of
manners.

CHAPTER V.
Internal Humility.

But you desire, Philothea, to penetrate still deeper
into humility; for what I have hitherto said, rather
concerns wisdom than humility. Let us, then, pass
on farther. Many will not dare to consider the particular favours God has done them, lest it excite vain-
glory and self-complacency; but in so doing they
deceive themselves; for, since the best means to attain the love of God, says the great angelical doctor,
is the consideration of his benefits, the more we
know them, the more we shall love Him; and, as the
particular benefits He has conferred on us more
powerfully move us than those that are common to
others, so ought they to be more attentively considered. Certainly nothing can so effectually humble
us before God's mercy as the multitude of his benefits; nor so humble us before his justice as the enor-
mity of our innumerable offences. Let us, then,
consider what He has done for us, and what we have
done against Him; and, as we reflect on our sins
one by one, so let us consider his favours in the same
order. We must not fear that the knowledge of his
gifts may puff us up as long as we are attentive to
the truth, " that whatsoever there is of good in us,

is not from ourselves." Alas! do mules cease to be stupid and dirty animals even when laden with the precious and perfumed goods of a prince? "What hast thou which thou hast not received?" says the Apostle (1 Cor. iv. 7). "And if thou hast received, why dost thou glory?" Nay, on the contrary, the lively consideration of favours received makes us humble, because a knowledge of them begets gratitude. But if, in considering the favours that God has conferred on us, any thoughts of vanity should attack us, it will be an infallible remedy to recur to the consideration of our ingratitudes, imperfections, and miseries. If we consider how we acted when God was not with us, we shall easily be convinced that what we do while He is with us is not of our own doing or growth; we shall, indeed, rejoice in it, because we enjoy it; but we shall glorify God, because He alone is the Author of it. Thus the Blessed Virgin confesses that God did great things for her, but it is only to take occasion to humble herself and to glorify Him. "My soul," she says, "doth magnify the Lord, because He has done great things for me" (Luke, i. 46-49).

We often acknowledge ourselves to be nothing, nay, misery itself, and the refuse of the world; but we would be very sorry that anyone should take us at our word, or tell others that we are really such miserable wretches. On the contrary, we pretend to run away and hide ourselves, to the end that the world should run after us and seek us out. We pretend to consider ourselves the last in the company, and sit down at the lowest end of the table, but it is with a view that we may be told to pass to the upper end. True humility never makes a show of itself, nor does it use many humble words; for it desires not only to conceal all other virtues, but principally itself; and were it lawful to dissemble or scandalise its neighbour it would perform actions of arrogance and haughtiness, that 'it might conceal itself beneath them, and remain altogether unknown.

My advice, therefore, Philothea, is, that we should either not accustom ourselves to words of humility, or else use them with a sincere interior sentiment conformable to what we pronounce outwardly. Let us never cast down our eyes except when we humble our hearts; let us not seem to desire to be the lowest unless we sincerely desire it. Now I think this rule so general as to admit of no exception; I only add, that civility requires that we should sometimes offer precedence to those who will doubtless refuse it; and yet this is neither double-dealing nor false humility; for in this case, as the offer of precedence is only the beginning of honour, and since we cannot give it to them entirely, we do well to give them the beginning. I say, though some expressions of honour or respect may not seem strictly conformable to the truth, yet they are sufficiently so, provided the heart of him who pronounces them has a sincere intention to honour and respect him to whom they are addressed; for, although the words signify, with some excess, that which we would say, yet it is not wrong to make use of them, when common custom requires it; however, I wish our words were always as near as possible suited to our affections, that so we might follow in all, and through all, a cordial sincerity and candour. A man that is truly humble would rather another should say of him that he is miserable, that he is nothing, and that he is good for nothing, than that he should say it himself: at least, if he knows that any man says so, he does not contradict it, but heartily agrees to it; for, believing it himself firmly, he is glad to have others of the same opinion.

Many say that they leave mental prayer to those that are perfect; that, for their part, they are unworthy to use it. Others protest they dare not communicate often, because they do not find themselves sufficiently pure. Others fear they should bring disgrace upon devotion if they meddled with it by reason of their great misery and frailty. Others refuse to employ their talents in the service of God and their neighbour, saying, they know their own weakness, and fear they should become proud if they proved instruments of any good; and that, in giving light to others, they would consume themselves in the flames of vanity. All this is nothing but an artificial spirit of humility, false and malicious, whereby they tacitly and subtlely seek to find fault with the things of God; or, at the best, to conceal love of their own opinion, humour, and sloth, under the veil of humility. "Ask thou a sign of the Lord thy God, either unto the depth of hell, or to the height above," said the prophet Isaias to unhappy Achaz; and he answered: "I will not ask, neither will I tempt the Lord." Oh, the wicked man! He would seem to bear an extreme reverence to God, and he excuses himself under the colour of humility, from aspiring to that grace which Divine Goodness offers him; but does he see that when God desires to give us his graces, it is pride to refuse them? that the gifts of God oblige us to receive them; and that it is humility to obey and to comply as far as we can with his desires? Now, the desire of God is that we should be perfect, uniting ourselves to Him, and imitating Him as nearly as we possibly can. The proud man, who trusts in himself, has just reason not to attempt anything: but he that is humble is so much the more courageous, according as he acknowledges his own inability; and the more wretched he esteems himself, the more confident he becomes, because he places his whole trust in God, who delights to display his omnipotence in our weakness, and to elevate his

mercy upon our misery. We may, then, humbly
and devoutly presume to undertake all that may be
judged proper for our advancement by those who
guide our souls.

To imagine we know what we know not is very
great folly; to desire to be supposed to know that
of which we are ignorant is intolerable vanity. For
my part, as I would not make a parade of the knowledge, even of that which I know, so, on the other
hand, I would not pretend to be ignorant of it. When
charity requires it, we must freely and unobtru-
sively communicate to our neighbour, not only what
is necessary for his instruction, but also what is profitable for his consolation; since humility, which con-
ceals virtues, in order to preserve them, discovers
them nevertheless, when charity requires it, in order that we may enlarge, increase, and perfect them.
In this she imitates a certain tree in the isles of
Tylos, which at night closes up her beautiful carna-
tion flowers, and only opens them to the rising sun;
and, as the inhabitants of the country say that these
flowers sleep by night, so humility covers all our virtues and human perfections, and never lets them
appear but for the sake of charity, which, being not
a human and moral, but a divine and heavenly virtue, is the true sun of all other virtues, over which
she ought always to have dominion. So that the
humility which is prejudicial to charity is assuredly
false.

I would neither pretend to be a fool nor a wise
man; for if humility forbids me to conceal my wisdom, candour and sincerity also forbid me to counterfeit the fool; and, as vanity is the opposite of humility, so artifice, affectation, and dissimulation, are
contrary to plain dealing and sincerity. But if some
great servants of God pretended to be fools, in order
to render themselves more abject in the eyes of the

virtues which worldlings consider as mean and abject; whilst, on the contrary, they hold prudence, fortitude, and liberality in the highest estimation. There are also actions of *one and the same virtue,* some of which are despised, and others are honoured; to give alms and forgive injuries are both of them acts of charity; yet the first is honoured whilst the latter is despised, in the eyes of the world. A young lady or gentleman who refuses to join in the disorders of a frivolous company, or to talk, play, dance, drink, or dress as the rest do, incurs their scorn and censure, and their modesty is termed bigotry and affectation: to love this is to love our own abjection.

Behold an abjection of another kind. We go to visit the sick. If I am sent to the most miserable, it will be to me an abjection according to the world, for which reason I will love it. If I am sent to a person of quality, it is an abjection, according to the spirit; for there is not so much virtue nor merit in it, and therefore I will love this abjection. One falls in the midst of the street, and, besides his fall, receives shame: we must love this abjection. There are even faults which have no other ill in them but the abjection; and humility does not require that we should deliberately commit them, but that we should not vex ourselves when we have committed them. Such are certain follies, incivilities, and inadvertences, which, as we ought to avoid them before they are committed, for the sake of civility and discretion, so, when they are committed, we ought to be content with the abjection we meet with, and accept it willingly, for the sake of practising humility.

I say yet more: should I through passion or anger have spoken any unbecoming words, by which God and my neighbour may have been offended, I

will repent and be sorry for the offence, and endeavour to make the best reparation I can, but yet will
admit the abjection and the contempt which it has
brought upon me; and, could the one be separated
from the other, I would most cheerfully cast away
the sin, and humbly retain the abjection.

But though we love the abjection that follows the
evil, yet we must not neglect, by fit and lawful
means, to redress the evil that caused it, especially
when it is of importance. For example, should I
have some disagreeable disease in my face, I will
endeavour to have it cured, but not with the intention that I should forget the abjection I received by
it. If I have been guilty of some folly which has
given no one offence, I will make no apology for it;
because, although it were an offence, yet it is not
permanent! I could not, therefore, excuse it, but
only with the view to rid myself of the abjection,
which would not be agreeable to humility. But if,
through inadvertence, or otherwise, I should have
offended or scandalised anyone, I will repair the
offence by some true excuse, because the evil is permanent, and charity obliges me to remove it. Besides, it happens sometimes that charity requires
that we should remove the abjection for the good of
our neighbour, to whom our reputation is necessary;
but in such a case, though we remove the abjection
from before our neighbour's eyes, to prevent scandal,
yet we must carefully shut it up in our heart for its
edification.

But would you know, Philothea, which are the
best abjections, I tell you plainly, that those are the
most profitable to our souls, and most acceptable to
God, which befall us by accident, or by our condition
of life, because we have not chosen them ourselves,
but receive them as sent from God, whose choice is
always better than our own. But were we to choose

any, we should prefer the greatest; and those that are esteemed such as are most contrary to our inclinations, provided that they are conformable to our vocation; for, as I have already said, our own choice and election spoil or lessen almost all our virtues. Oh! who will enable us to say, "I have chosen to be abject in the house of God, rather than to dwell in the palaces of sinners" (Ps. lxxxi. 11). No one, certainly, Philothea, but He who exalts us, lived and died in such a manner as to become the reproach of men and the abjection of the people. I have said many things to you, which may seem hard in theory, but believe me, they will be sweeter than sugar or honey when you put them in practice.

CHAPTER VII.

How we are to preserve our good name in the practice of humility.

Praise, honour, and glory are not given to men for every degree of virtue, but for an excellence of virtue; for by praise we endeavour to persuade others to esteem the excellency of those whom we praise; by honour we testify that we ourselves esteem them; and glory, in my opinion, is nothing else but a certain lustre of reputation that arises from the concurrence of praise and honour; so that honour and praise are like precious stones, from a collection of which glory proceeds, like a certain enamelling. Now, humility, forbidding us to have any esteem for our own excellence, or think ourselves worthy to be preferred before others, consequently cannot permit that we should hunt after praise, honour, or glory, which are only due to excellence; yet it consents to the counsel of the wise man, who admonishes us to be careful of our good name (Ecclus. xli. 15), because a good name is an esteem, not of excellence, but of ordinary honesty and integrity of life, which humility does not forbid us to acknowledge in ourselves, nor, by consequence, to desire the reputation of it. It is true, humility would despise a good name if charity stood not in need of it; but because it is one of the foundations of human society, and because without it we are not only unprofitable but prejudicial to the public, on account of the scandal it would receive—charity requires and humility consents that we should desire it, and carefully preserve it.

Moreover, as the leaves, which in themselves are of little value, are, nevertheless, necessary, not only to beautify the tree, but also to preserve its young and tender fruits, so a good reputation, which of itself is a thing not much to be desired, is, notwithstanding, very profitable, not only for the ornament of life, but also for the preservation of virtue, especially of such virtues as are as yet but weak and tender.

The obligation of preserving our reputation, and of being actually such as we are thought to be, urges a generous spirit forward with a strong and agreeable impulse. Let us, then, preserve our virtues, Philothea, because they are acceptable to God, the sovereign object of all our actions. But as they who desire to preserve fruits are not content to candy them with sugar, but also enclose them in proper vessels, so, although the love of God may be the principal preserver of our virtue, we may, in addition, employ our good name as very convenient and profitable for that purpose.

Yet we must not be over-nice with respect to the preservation of our good name; for such as are too tender and sensitive on this point are like those who, for every slight indisposition, take physic, and, thinking to preserve their health, quite destroy it; so do those who endeavour so delicately to maintain their reputation, entirely lose it; for, by this tenderness, they become whimsical, quarrelsome, and insupportable, and thus provoke the malice of detractors.

The overlooking and despising of an injury or calumny is, generally speaking, by far a more effectual remedy than resentment, contention, and revenge; for a contempt for them causes them to vanish; whereas if we are angry on account of them, we seem to acknowledge them.

An excessive fear of losing our good name betrays a great distrust of its merit, or of the virtue which is its foundation. As the inhabitants of towns which have wooden bridges over great rivers fear their being carried away by every little flood, but they that have bridges of stone apprehend only extraordinary inundations, so they that have a soul solidly grounded in Christian virtue despise the overflowing of injurious tongues; but those that find themselves weak are disturbed by every discourse. In a word, Philothea, he that is over-anxious to preserve his reputation loses it; and that person deserves to lose his honour who seeks to obtain it from those whose vices render them truly infamous and dishonourable.

Reputation is but a sign to point out where virtue resides; it is virtue, then, that must be preferred in all, and through all. Therefore, should anyone call you a hypocrite, because you addict yourself to devotion, or a coward because you have pardoned an injury, laugh at him; for, in addition to the fact that such judgments are passed on us by the weak and foolish, we must not forsake or turn aside from the path of virtue, although we should thereby lose our reputation, because we must prefer the fruit to the leaves, viz., interior and spiritual graces to all external goods. It is lawful to be jealous, but not a worshipper of our reputation; and as we should not offend the eyes of the good, so we must strive to satisfy those of the wicked. The beard is an ornament to the face of a man, and the hair to the head of a woman : if one pluck out by the root the beard from the chin, and the hair from the head, it will seldom grow again ; but if it be only cut, nay, though it be shaved close, it will soon bud forth anew, and grow stronger and thicker than before ; so, although our reputation may be cut, or even shaved close, by the tongues of detractors, which David compares to sharp razors, we must not let ourselves be uneasy, for it will soon shoot forth again, not only as fair as before, but much more firm and durable. But if our vices and wicked course of life take away our reputation it will seldom return, because it is pulled up by the root ; for the root of a good name is virtue and probity, which, as long as they remain in us, can always recover the honour due to them.

If any vain conversation, idle habit, fond love, or custom of frequenting improper company, blast our reputation, we must forsake these gratifications, because our good name is of more value than such vain contentments. But if, for the exercise of piety, the advancement of devotion, or making our way towards heaven, men grumble, murmur, and speak evil of us, let us leave them, like curs, to bark at the moon; for should they, at any time, be able to cast an aspersion on our good name, and by that means cut and shave the beard of our reputation, it will quickly spring up again, and the razor of detraction will be as advantageous to our honour as the pruning-knife to the vine, which makes it spread and multiply in fruit.

Let us incessantly fix our eyes on Jesus Christ crucified, and march on in his service with confidence and sincerity, but yet with wisdom and discretion : He will be the protector of our reputation ; and should He suffer it to be taken from us, it will be either to restore it with advantage, or to make us profit in

the enraged elephant as the sight of a little lamb, and nothing so easily breaks the force of cannonshot as wool. We value not the correction which proceeds from passion, though it be accompanied with reason, as much as that which proceeds from reason alone; for the reasonable soul, being naturally subject to reason, is never subject to passion, but through tyranny; and therefore when reason is accompanied by passion it makes itself odious, its just government being debased by the fellowship of tyranny. Princes do honour to their people, and make them rejoice exceedingly when they visit them with a peaceable train; but when they come at the head of armies, though it be for the common good, their visits are always disagreeable; for, although they cause military discipline to be rigorously observed among their soldiers, yet they can never do it so effectually but that some disorders always happen, by which the countrymen will be sufferers. In like manner, as long as reason rules, and peaceably exercises chastisements, corrections, and reproaches, although severely and rigorously, everyone loves and approves it; but when it brings anger, passion, and rage, which St. Augustine calls its soldiers, along with it, it makes itself more feared than loved, and even its own disordered heart is always the sufferer. It is better, says the same St. Augustine, writing to Profuturus, to deny entrance to just and reasonable anger than to admit it, be it ever so little; because, being once admitted, it is with difficulty driven out again; for it enters as a little twig, and in a moment becomes a beam; and if the sun sets upon it, which the apostle forbids, it turns into hatred, from which we have scarcely any means to rid ourselves; for it nourishes itself under a thousand false pretexts, since there was never an angry man that thought his anger unjust.

It is better, then, to attempt to find the way to live without anger than to pretend to make a moderate and discreet use of it; and when, through our imperfections and frailty, we find ourselves surprised, it is better to drive it away speedily than to enter into a parley; for, if we give it ever so little leisure, it will become mistress of the place, like the serpent, which easily draws in its whole body where it can once get in its head.

But how shall I drive it away? you will say. You must, Philothea, at the first alarm, speedily muster your forces, not violently and tumultuously, but mildly and seriously; for, as we hear the ushers in public halls and courts of justice, crying "silence," make more noise than the whole assembly, so it frequently happens that by endeavouring with violence to restrain our anger, we stir up more trouble in our heart than the wrath had excited before, and the heart being thus agitated, can be no longer master of itself. After this meek effort, practise the advice which St. Augustine, when old, gave the new Bishop Auxilius: Do, says he, that which a man should do, if that befall you which a man of God speaks of in the Psalms: "My eye is troubled with wrath" (Ps. xxx.) Have recourse to God, crying out: "Have mercy on me, O Lord;" that He may stretch forth his right hand to repress your anger: I mean that we must invoke the assistance of God when we find ourselves excited to wrath, in imitation of the Apostles, when they were tossed by the wind and the storm upon the waters; for He will command our passions to cease, and a great calm shall ensue. But the prayer which is offered up against present and pressing danger must always be performed calmly, and not violently—and this must be observed in all the remedies against this evil. Moreover, as soon as ever you perceive yourself guilty of an act of wrath, repair the fault immediately, by an act of meekness towards the person with whom you were angry. For as it is a sovereign remedy against a lie to contradict it upon the spot, as soon as we perceive we have told it; so we must repair anger instantly by a contrary act of meekness, for recent wounds, it is said, are most easily cured.

Again, when your mind is in a state of tranquillity, lay in a plentiful store of meekness, speaking all your words and doing all your actions, small and great, in the mildest manner possible, calling to mind, as the spouse in the Canticles has not only honey on her lips, her tongue, and in her breast, but milk also, so we must not only have our words sweet towards our neighbour, but also our whole breast, that is to say, the whole interior of our soul; neither must we have the aromatic and fragrant sweetness of honey, viz., the sweetness of civil conversation with strangers, but also the sweetness of milk amongst our family, and neighbours—those greatly fail in this who in the street seem to be angels, and in their houses demons.

CHAPTER IX.

Of Meekness towards Ourselves.

One of the best exercises of meekness we can perform is that of which the subject is within ourselves, in never fretting at our imperfections; for, though reason requires that we should be sorry when we commit a fault, yet we must refrain from that bitter, gloomy, spiteful, and passionate displeasure for which many are greatly to blame, who being overcome by anger, are angry for having been angry, and vexed to see themselves vexed, for by this means they keep their hearts perpetually steeped in passion; and though it seems as if the second anger destroyed the first, it serves nevertheless to open a passage for fresh anger on the first occasion that may present itself. Besides, this anger and vexation against ourselves tends to pride, and flows from no other source than self-love, which is troubled and disquieted when we see ourselves imperfect. We must then be displeased with our faults, but in a tranquil, settled, and firm manner; for, as a judge punishes malefactors much better, when he is guided in his sentences by reason and proceeds with a tranquil spirit, than when he acts with violence and passion (because, judging in passion, he does not punish the faults according as they are, but according as he is himself), so we correct ourselves much better by a calm and steady repentance than by that which is harsh, hasty, and passionate; for repentance exercised with violence proceeds not according to the quality of our faults, but according to our inclinations. For example, he that effects chastity will vex himself beyond all bounds at the least fault he commits against that virtue, and will, on the other hand, think nothing of a gross detraction which he has been guilty of; whilst he who hates detraction torments himself for a slight murmur of it, and makes no account of a gross fault committed against chastity; and so of others. Now, all this springs from no other fountain but that in the judgment of their consciences, these men are not guided by reason, but by passion.

Believe me, Philothea, as the mild and affectionate reproofs of a father have far greater power to reclaim his child than rage and passion, so, when we have committed any fault, if we reproach our hearts with mild and calm remonstrances, having more compassion for it than passion against it, sweetly encouraging it to amendment, the repentance it shall ~~eive~~ by this means, will sink much deeper, and penetrate it more effectually than a fretful, hasty, and stormy repentance.

For if I myself, for example, had formed a strong resolution not to yield to the sin of vanity, and yet had fallen into it, I would not reprove my heart after this manner : " Art thou not wretched and abominable, that, after so many resolutions, thou hast suffered thyself to be thus carried away by vanity. Die with shame, lift up no more thine eyes to heaven, blind, impudent, traitor as thou art, a rebel to thy God !" but I would correct it thus rationally, saying compassionately: " Alas ! my poor heart, behold we have fallen into the pit which we had so firmly resolved to avoid. Well, let us get out again, and quit it for ever; let us call upon the mercy of God, and hope that He will assist us to be more constant for the time to come; and let us put ourselves again into the way of humility. Courage ! let us from this day forward be more upon our guard ; God will help us; we shall do better in future ;" and on this reprehension I would build a firm and constant resolution never more to relapse into that fault, using the proper means to avoid it, by the advice of my director.

However, if anyone should find his heart not sufficiently moved with this mild manner of reprehension, he may use one more sharp and severe, to excite it to deeper confusion, provided that he afterwards closes up all his grief and anger with a sweet and consoling confidence in God, in imitation of that illustrious penitent, who, seeing his soul afflicted, raised it up in this manner : " Why art thou so sad, O my soul, and why dost thou disquiet me ? Hope in God, for I will still give praise to Him, who is the salvation of my countenance, and my God " (Ps. xlii. 5).

Raise up your heart, then, again whenever it falls, but tranquilly and softly ; humbling yourself before

God', through the knowledge of your own misery, but without being surprised at your fall ; for it is no wonder that weakness should be weak, or misery wretched ; detest, nevertheless, with all your power, the offence God has received from you, and return to the way of virtue which you had forsaken, with a great courage and confidence in his mercy.

CHAPTER X.

We must treat of our affairs with diligence, but without eagerness or solicitude.

That care and diligence wherewith we ought to attend to our affairs must never be confounded with anxiety and solicitude. The angels are careful of our salvation, and procure it with diligence, yet they are never agitated either by anxiety or solicitude ; for care and diligence naturally result from their charity, whereas solicitude and anxiety are utterly incompatible with their felicity ; because the former may be accompanied by a calm and tranquil state of mind, whereas the latter never can.

Be careful and attentive then, Philothea, to all those affairs which God has committed to your care, for such a disposition in you is agreeable to the will of his Divine Majesty, without suffering your care and attention to degenerate into inquietude and anxiety ; do not worry your spirits about them, for an over-solicitude disturbs the reason and judgment, and prevents us from doing that properly, for the execution of which we are so eager and anxious.

When our Lord reproached Martha, He said : "Martha, Martha, thou art solicitous and art troubled about many things !" You must here observe that he would not have been troubled had she been but merely diligent ; but being over-concerned and disquieted, she hurried and troubled herself, and therefore received this reprehension from our Lord.

As rivers that flow slowly through the plains bear large boats and rich merchandise, and the rain which falls gently in the open fields makes them fruitful in grass and corn; or. as torrents and rivers, which run rapidly, and overflow the grounds, ruin the bordering country, and render it unprofitable for traffic, so in like manner violent and tempestuous rains injure the fields and meadows. That work is never well executed which is done with too much eagerness and hurry. We must hasten leisurely, says the old proverb: "He that is in haste," says Solomon, "is in danger of stumbling" (Prov. xix. 2). We do our business soon enough when we do it well. As drones, although they make more noise, and seem more eager to work than bees, make only wax and no honey, so they that hurry themselves with a tormenting anxiety and eager solicitude never do much, nor is what they do profitable.

As flies trouble us, not by their strength but by their multitude, so affairs of importance give us not so much trouble as trifling ones when they are great in number. Undertake, then, all your affairs with a calm and peaceable mind, and endeavour to despatch them in order, one after another; for if you make an effort to do them all at once, or without order, your spirit will be so overcharged and depressed that it will probably lie down under the burden without effecting anything.

In all your affairs rely wholly on Divine Providence, through which alone you must look for success; labour, nevertheless, quietly on your part to co-operate with its designs, and then you may be assured if you trust, as you ought, in God, that the success which shall come to you, will be always that which is the most profitable for you, whether it appeared good or bad, according to your private judgment. Imitate little children, who, as they with one hand cling to their father, and with the other gather berries along the hedges, so you, gathering and holding the goods of this world with one hand, must with the other always cling, to the hand of your heavenly Father, turning towards Him from time to time to see if your actions or occupations are pleasing to Him; but, above all things, take heed that you never let go his protecting hand, through a desire to gather too much worldly goods; for should He forsake you you will not be able to go a step further without falling to the ground. My meaning is, Philothea, that amidst those ordinary affairs and occupations which do not require so earnest an attention, you should look more to God than on them; and when they are of such importance as to require your whole attention, that then also you should look from time to time towards God, like mariners, who, in order to arrive at the port to which they are bound, look more up towards heaven than down on the sea, in order to guide their ship; thus will God work with you, in you, and for you, and your labour shall be followed by consolation.

CHAPTER XI.

Obedience.

Charity alone can place us in perfection, but obedience, chastity, and poverty, are the three principal means by which to attain to it. Obedience consecrates our heart, chastity our body, and poverty our means to the love and service of God. These three branches of the spiritual cross are grounded on a fourth, viz., humility. I shall say nothing of these three virtues, when they are solemnly vowed, because this subject concerns religious orders only; nor even when they are simply vowed; for though a vow may add many graces and merits to virtues, yet, to make us perfect, it is not necessary that vows should be made, provided they be observed. For though being vowed, and especially solemnly, they place a man in the state of perfection; yet, to arrive at perfection itself, they must be observed, there being a very great difference between the state of perfection and perfection itself; since all bishops and religious are in a state of perfection; and yet, alas, all have not arrived at perfection itself, as is too plainly to be seen. Let us endeavour then, Philothea, to practise well these virtues, each one according to his vocation; for though they do not place us in the state of perfection, yet they will make us perfect: and, indeed, everyone is obliged to practise them, though not all after the same manner.

There are two sorts of obedience, the one necessary, the other voluntary. By that which is necessary, you must obey your ecclesiastical superiors, as the Pope, the bishop, the parish priest, and such as represent them: also your civil superiors, such as your prince, and the magistrates he has established for administering justice; and, finally, your domestic superiors, viz., your father and mother, master and mistress. Now this obedience is called necessary, because no man can exempt himself from the duty of obeying his superiors, God having placed them in authority to command and govern, each in the department that is assigned to him. You must, then, of necessity obey their commands; but to be perfect follow their counsels also, nay, even their desires and inclinations, so far as charity and discretion will permit. Obey them when they order that which is agreeable, such as to eat or to take your

10

recreation: for though there seems to be no great virtue to obey on such occasions, yet it would be a great vice to disobey. Obey them in things indifferent, such as to wear this or that dress, to go one way or another, to be silent, and this will be a very commendable obedience; obey them in things hard, troublesome, and disagreeable, and this will be a perfect obedience. Obey, in fine, meekly, without reply; readily, without delay; cheerfully, without repining; and, above all, obey lovingly, for the love of Him, who through his love for us, made Himself obedient unto death, even to the death of the cross, and who, as St. Bernard says, rather chose to part with his life than his obedience.

That you may learn effectually to obey your superiors, yield easily to the will of your equals, when you see no evil in doing so, without being contentious or obstinate. Accommodate yourself cheerfully to the reasonable desires of your inferiors; never exercise an imperious authority over them, so long as they act well. It is an illusion to believe that we should obey with ease, if we were in a religious order, when we feel ourselves so backward and stubborn in what regards obedience to such as God has placed over us.

We call that obedience voluntary which we practise of our own choice, and which is not imposed upon us by another. We do not commonly choose our king, our bishop, our father or mother, nor even do wives always choose their husbands; but we choose our confessor and director: if then in choosing we make a vow to obey, as the holy mother Teresa did, who as has been already observed, besides her obedience solemnly vowed to the superior of her Order, bound herself by a simple vow to obey Father Gratian; or if, without a vow, we resolve to obey anyone, this obedience is called voluntary, on account of its being grounded on our own free will and choice.

We must obey each one of our superiors, according to the charge he has over us. In political matters we must obey the laws; in ecclesiastical, our prelates; in domestic, our parents, master, or husband; and, in what regards the private conduct of soul, our spiritual father or director.

Request your spiritual father to impose upon you all the actions of piety you are to perform, in order that they may acquire a double value; the one of themselves, because they are works of piety; the other of obedience to his commands, and in virtue of which they are performed. Happy are the obedient, for God will never suffer them to go astray.

CHAPTER XII.
The Necessity of Chastity.

For the first degree of that virtue never voluntarily permit anything which is forbidden with regard to chastity.

For the second degree, limit as far as you can all superfluous and useless pleasures, although they may be harmless and permitted to you.

For the third degree, do not attach your affections to those which may be necessary and even imposed on you.

St. Augustin admired in his dear Alipius the admirable purity which had entirely freed him from the sentiments, and even from the remembrance of former disorders. Indeed everyone knows that it is easy to preserve for a long time fruits which are still whole; but however little they may be tainted or broken they can only be preserved in sirups. I say that we have several means for preserving safely our chastity whilst it remains in its full integrity; but when it has once lost it, nothing can preserve it but a solid devotion, the sweetness of which I have often compared with that of honey.

In the state of virginity, chastity demands great simplicity of soul, and great delicacy of conscience, in order to keep at a distance all kinds of curious thoughts, and to raise itself above all sensual pleasures by means of an absolute and entire contempt of everything which man has in common with the beasts, and which they have even more than he. Let these pure souls never doubt in any way that chastity is not incomparably better than anything which is incompatible with perfection. "For," as St. Jerome says, "the demon not being able to endure that salutary ignorance of pleasure, desires at least to excite the desire of it in those souls, and gives them, therefore, ideas of it, so seductive, although false, that they remain very much troubled, because," adds that holy Father, "by degrees they go on to esteem more and more that which they have been ignorant of." It is thus that so many young persons, surprised by a false and foolish esteem for the pleasures of the senses, and by a sensual and restless curiosity, give themselves up to them, and compromise their temporal and eternal interests, like unto butterflies, which believing the flame to be as pleasant as it appears beautiful, foolishly burn themselves in it.

You know how necessary chastity is: "Seek peace with all and holiness," says the Apostle, "without which no one shall see God." Now remark that by holiness he means chastity, according to the interpretation of Ss. Jerome and Chrysostom. No; no person shall see God without chastity; no person shall inhabit his holy tabernacles if he has not a pure heart; as our Saviour says, "Dogs and the impure shall be banished from it." Also, " Blessed are the clean of heart, for they shall see God."

CHAPTER XIII.

How to preserve Chastity.

Keep always a great guard over yourself in order to drive away promptly everything which might tempt to impurity ; for it is an evil which develops itself by insensible degrees, weak in the beginning, but their progress very rapid. In a word, it is more easy to fly from it than to cure it.

Chastity is a treasure which, according to St. Paul, " we keep in fragile vessels ; and in truth it has much of the fragility of those vases which break by knocking against each other." The freshest water, when we try to preserve it in a vessel, quickly loses its freshness if any animal touches it. Never permit yourself, Philothea, to practise, and preserve yourself from, those external liberties, equally contrary to Christian modesty and to the respect you owe yourself ; for, although one may preserve an absolutely chaste heart in spite of actions which arise rather from want of thought than from malice, and which are not usually practised, nevertheless, chastity always receives from them some lamentable injury. You sufficiently understand that I do not speak here of what virtually ruins chastity.

Chastity takes its origin in the heart, and its exterior practice consists in regulating and purifying the senses ; this is why it is lost by means of all the external senses, as well as by the thoughts of the mind, and the desires of the heart. Thus, every sensation which we allow ourselves regarding an immodest object, or with a spirit of immodesty, is

really an unchaste act, and the Apostle recommended the first Christians not even to mention
the vice amongst them.   Bees not only do not
touch a body in a state of putrefaction, but they
fly from the bad smell which it exhales.   Remark,
I beseech you, what holy Scripture tells us of the
Spouse of the Canticles.   Everything is mysterious in them.   Myrrh distils from her hands, and
you know that this liquor preserves from corruption ; her lips are bordered by a red riband, and
that teaches us that modesty blushes at words, even
when they are ever so little indecent ; her eyes are
compared to the eyes of the dove, on account of their
purity ; she wears earrings of gold, and that metal
is also a symbol of purity ; her nose is compared to
a cedar of Lebanon, the odour of which is exquisite,
and its wood incorruptible.   What does all that
mean ?   That the soul should be, in all its senses,
devout, chaste, open, pure, and honourable.

Chastity can be lost in so many ways that there
are kinds of indecencies, which, according as they
are great or small, weaken it or dangerously wound
it, or even destroy it entirely.   There are certain indiscreet and vulgar liberties which, properly speaking,
do not violate chastity ; but which weaken and dim
its brightness.   There are other liberties not only indiscreet, but vicious ; not only vulgar, but immodest
and sensual, which wound it mortally.   There are
others again which destroy it entirely.

Never be intimate with persons whose manners
you know to be corrupt, especially when impudence
is joined with impurity, which is almost always
the case.

It is said that he-goats, touching the sweet almond
tree with their tongues, make them become bitter,
so these corrupted souls and infected hearts, scarcely
speak to any person, either of the same or a different
but they cause them to fall in some degree

from purity : they have poison in their eyes and in their breath like basilisks. On the contrary, keep company with the chaste and virtuous ; often meditate upon and read about holy things ; for the Word of God is chaste, and makes those also chaste that delight in it ; this made David compare it to the topaz, a precious stone, which is said to have the property of cooling the heat of concupiscence.

Keep yourself always near to Jesus Christ crucified, both spiritually by meditation and really by the Holy Communion. For as they who lie on the herb called *agnus castus* become chaste and modest, so you, laying down your heart to rest upon our Lord, who is the true, chaste, and immaculate Lamb, shall find that your soul and your heart shall soon be cleansed from all the defilements of impurity.

CHAPTER XIV.

Poverty of Spirit to be observed by the Rich.

"Blessed are the poor in spirit, for theirs is the kingdom of heaven" (Matt. v. 3). Accursed, on the other hand, are the rich in spirit, for hell is their portion. He is rich in spirit who has his riches in his spirit, or his spirit in his riches : he is poor in spirit who has no riches in his spirit, nor his spirit in riches. The halcyons form their nest like an apple, and leave only a little opening at the top ; they build them on the seashore, and make them so firm and impenetrable that when the waves sweep over the strand the water can never get into them, but keeping always uppermost and following its motion, they remain in the midst of the sea, upon the sea, and masters of the sea. Your heart, Philothea, ought to be in this manner, open only to heaven, and impenetrable to riches and all transitory things.   Whatever portion of them you may possess, keep your heart free from the least affection towards them ; keep it always above them, and in the midst of riches let it hold them in contempt and be their master.   Do not suffer this heavenly spirit to be the captive of earthly goods, let it be always their master, but never their slave.

There is a material difference between having poison and being poisoned. As apothecaries keep almost all kinds of poison for use on various occasions, but yet are not poisoned, because they have not poison in their bodies, but in their shops : so you possess riches without being poisoned by them, if you keep them in your house or purse, and not in your heart.   To be rich in effect, and poor in affection, is the great happiness of the Christian ; for by this means he has all the advantages of riches for this world, and the merit of poverty for the world to come.

Alas ! Philothea, no one ever acknowledges that he is covetous ; everyone disavows that base and mean passion ; persons excuse themselves on account of the charge of children which oppresses them and of that wisdom which requires that men should establish themselves in the world : they never have too much : some pretence is always discovered to get more : nay, the most covetous not only deny that they are avaricious, but even think in their conscience that they are not so.   Covetousness is a malignant fever which is less and less felt according as it becomes more violent and ardent. Moses saw the sacred fire which burned the bush, and yet consumed it not ; but this profane fire of avarice, on the contrary, consumes and devours the covetous person, and yet burns him not ; for in the midst of the most excessive heats of his avarice, he boasts of the most agreeable coolness in the world, and esteems his insatiable drought to be a natural and pleasing thirst.

If you have a longing desire to possess goods which you have not, though you may say you would not unjustly possess them, yet you are nevertheless truly covetous. He that has a longing, ardent, and restless desire to drink, although he may drink nothing but water, shows nevertheless that he is feverish.

O Philothea, I know not if it is a justifiable desire to wish to justly obtain that which another justly possesses: for it seems that by this desire we would serve our own convenience to the prejudice of another. If a man possesses anything justly, has he not more reason to keep it justly than we have to desire it justly? Why then do we extend our desires to his possessions, to deprive him of them? At the best, if this desire is just, yet certainly it is not charitable, for we would not in any case, that another man should desire, although justly, that which we have a desire to keep justly. This was the sin of Achab, who desired to have Naboth's vineyard justly, which Naboth much more justly desired to keep: Achab desired it with an ardent and impatient desire, and therefore offended God.

It is time enough, Philothea, to desire your neighbour's goods when he is desirous to part with them; for then his desire will make yours not only just, but charitable also; yes, for I am willing that you should take care to increase your substance, provided it may be done not only justly, but with peace and charity.

If you have a strong attachment to the goods which you possess, if you are over-solicitous about them, set your heart on them, have them always in your thoughts, and fear the loss of them with a sensible apprehension, believe me you are feverish;

for they that have a fever drink the water that is given them with a certain eagerness and satisfaction which the healthy are not accustomed to feel. It is impossible to take such pleasure in laughing without having an extraordinary affection for it.

If when you suffer loss of goods, you find your heart quite disconsolate, believe me you have too great an affection for them : for nothing can be a stronger proof thereof than your affliction for their loss.

Desire not, then, with a full and express desire, the wealth which you have not, nor fix your heart much on what you have ; grieve not for the losses which may befall you, and then you shall have some reason to believe, that though rich in effect, you are not so in affection, but rather poor in spirit, and consequently blessed, and that the kingdom of heaven belongs to you.

CHAPTER XV.

How to practise true and real Poverty, being notwithstanding really rich.

The painter, Parrhasius, painted the people of Athens in a very ingenious manner, representing, by means of numerous figures in one picture, their several variable dispositions—choleric, unjust, inconstant, courteous, gentle, merciful, haughty, proud, humble, resolute, and timorous. But I, Philothea, would put together into your heart riches and poverty, a great care for and a great contempt of temporal things.

Be more careful to make your goods profitable and fruitful than worldly men are. Are not the gardeners of great princes more careful and diligent in cultivating and embellishing the gardens committed to their charge, than if they were their own? And why? Simply because they consider them as the gardens of kings and princes, to whom they desire to make themselves acceptable by their services. Philothea, our possessions are not our own, but were lent to us by God to cultivate them, and it is his will that we should render them fruitful and profitable, and therefore we perform services agreeable to Him in being careful of them; but then it must be a greater and more solid care than that which worldlings have of their goods, for they labour only for love of themselves, but we must labour for the love of God. Now as self-love is violent, and turbulent, and impetuous, so the care which proceeds therefrom is full of trouble, uneasiness, and disquiet; and as the love of God is sweet, peaceable, and calm, so the care which proceeds from it, although it is for worldly goods, is yet amiable, sweet, and agreeable. Let us, then, exercise this peaceable care of preserving, nay, even of increasing our temporal goods whenever just occasions present themselves, and as far as our condition requires, for God wishes us to do so for the love of Him.

But beware lest self-love deceives you; for sometimes it counterfeits the love of God so closely that one would imagine it to be the same. Now, that it may not deceive you, and that the care of your temporal goods may not degenerate into covetousness, in addition to what I said in the last chapter, we must practise a real poverty in the midst of all the riches which God has given us.

Deprive yourself, then, frequently of some part of your property, by bestowing it on the poor with a willing heart; for to give away what we have is to impoverish ourselves by so much as we give; and the more we give the poorer we make ourselves. It is true God will repay it back to us, not only in the next world, but even in this; for nothing mak͏ us prosper so much in this world as alms; but till such time as God shall restore it to us we must remain so much the poorer by what we have given. Oh, how holy and rich is that poverty which is occasioned by giving alms!

Love the poor and poverty, and you shall become truly poor, since, as the Scripture says, "we are made like the things which we love." Love makes lovers equal. "Who is weak," says St. Paul, "with whom I am not weak?" He might have likewise said, Who is poor with whom I am not poor? For love made him resemble those whom he loved. If, then, you love the poor, you shall be truly a partaker of their poverty, and poor like them. Now if you love the poor, be often in their company, be glad to see them in your house, and to visit them in theirs; converse willingly with them, be pleased to have them near you in the church, in the streets, and elsewhere. Be poor in tongue with them, speaking to them as their companion; but be rich in hand, by bestowing your goods on them, as having more abundance.

Nay, more, Philothea, do not rest content with being as poor, but be poorer than the poor themselves. But how may that be? The servant is lower than his master; make yourself, then, a servant of the poor; go and serve them in their beds when they are sick, serve them, I say, with your own hands; be their cook yourself, and at your own expense; be their seamstress and laundress. O Philothea, such service is more glorious than a kingdom.

I cannot sufficiently admire the ardour with which this counsel was put in practice by St. Louis, one of the greatest kings the sun ever shone on. I say a great king in every kind of greatness. He frequently served at table the poor whom he maintained, and caused three poor men almost every day to dine with him, and many times eat the remainder of their pottage with an incomparable love. When he visited the hospitals, which he frequently did, he commonly served those suffering from leprosy and ulcers, and such as had the most loathsome diseases, kneeling on the ground, respecting, in their persons, the Saviour of the world, and cherishing them as tenderly as any fond mother cherishes her own child. St. Elizabeth, daughter of the King of Hungary, often went amongst the poor, and for her recreation sometimes clothed herself like a poor woman amongst her ladies, saying to them: "If I were a poor woman I would dress in this manner." Good God, Philothea, how poor were this prince and princess in the midst of their riches, and how rich in their poverty? Blessed are they who are poor in this manner, for to them belongs the kingdom of heaven. "I was hungry, and you gave me to eat; I was naked, and you clothed me; come, possess the kingdom prepared for you from the foundation of the world:" these words the King of the poor, as well as of kings, will say when He addresses Himself to the elect at the Day of General Judgment.

There is no one but, upon some occasion or other, feels a want of some convenience. Sometimes we receive a visit from a guest whom we would wish to entertain very well, but for the present have not the means; at other times our best clothes are in one place, whilst we want them in another place where we must be seen. Again, sometimes all the wines in our cellar ferment and turn sour, so that there remain only such as are bad; at another time we happen to stop at some poor village where all things are wanting, where we have neither bed, chamber, table, nor attendance; in fine, it is very often easy to suffer for the want of something, b we ever so rich.   Now this is to be poor in effect with regard to the things we want.   Philothea, rejoice on these occasions, accept them with a good heart, and bear them cheerfully.

But should you meet with losses which impoverish you more or less, as in the case of tempests, fires, inundations, bad harvests, robberies, or lawsuits, oh, then is the proper season to practise poverty, receiving those losses with meekness, and submitting to your losses with patience and constancy.   Esau presented himself to his father with his hands covered with hair, and Jacob did the same ; but as the hair on Jacob's hands stuck not to his skin, but to his gloves, one might take away the hair without hurting the skin ; on the contrary, because the hair on the hands of Esau stuck to his skin, which was hairy by nature, he that would attempt to pluck off his hair would have put him to such excessive pain as to force him to cry aloud, and be very warm in his own defence.   Thus, when our worldly goods cleave to our heart, if tempest, a thief, or a cheat, should pluck any part of them from us, what complaints, trouble, and impatience do we not show ? But when our goods do not cleave to our hearts, and are only considered according to the care God would have us take of them, should they be taken from us, we lose neither our peace nor our senses.   Hence the difference between beasts and men as to their garments ; for the garments of the former, viz., their skins stick fast to their flesh, and those of the latter are only put upon them, so that they may be put on or taken off at pleasure.

CHAPTER XVI.

How to practise Richness of Spirit in real Poverty.

But if you are really poor, Philothea, be likewise, for God's sake, actually poor in spirit ; make a virtue of necessity, and value this precious jewel of poverty at the high rate it deserves ; its lustre is not discovered in this world, and, nevertheless, it is exceedingly rich and beautiful.

Be patient ; you are in good company ; our Lord Himself, his Blessed Mother, the Apostles, and innumerable saints, both men and women, have been poor, and even when they might have been rich they have scorned to be so. How many great personages have there been who, in spite of contradictions from the world, have gone to search after holy poverty in cloisters and hospitals, and who took indefatigable pains to find it ! Witness St. Alexius, St. Paula, St. Paulinus, St. Angela, and so many others ; and behold, Philothea, this holy poverty more gracious in your own lodging ; you have met her without being at the trouble of seeking her ; embrace her, then, as the dear friend of Jesus Christ, who was born, who lived, and who died in poverty : poverty was his nurse during the whole course of his life.

Your poverty, Philothea, enjoys two great privileges, by means of which you may considerably enhance its merits. The first is that it did not come to you by your choice, but by the will of God, who has made you poor without any concurrence of your own will. Now that which we receive entirely from the will of God is always very agreeable to Him, provided that we receive it with a good heart, and through love of his holy will : where there is least of our own, there is most of God's ; the simple and pure acceptance of God's will makes our offerings extremely pure.

The second privilege of this kind of poverty is that it is truly poverty. That poverty which is praised, caressed, esteemed, succoured, and assisted, bears some resemblance to riches—at least, it is not altogether poverty; but that which is despised, rejected, reproached, and abandoned, is poverty indeed. Now such is ordinary poverty; for as the poor are not poor by their own choice, but from necessity, their poverty is not much esteemed, for which reason their poverty exceeds that of numbers of religious orders; although, otherwise, their poverty has a very great excellence, and is much more commendable, by reason of the vow and intention for which it is chosen.

Complain not, then, Philothea, of your poverty; for we never complain but of that which displeases us, and if poverty displeases you, you are no longer poor in spirit, but rich in affection.

Be not disconsolate for not being as well assisted as may appear necessary, for in this consists the excellence of poverty. To be willing to be poor and not to feel the hardships of poverty, is to desire the honour of poverty with the convenience of riches.

Be not ashamed to be poor, nor to ask alms in charity. Receive with humility what may be given to you, and bear refusals with meekness. Frequently remember the journey Our Blessed Lady undertook into Egypt to preserve the life of her dear Son, and how much contempt, poverty, and misery she was obliged to suffer: provided you live thus, you shall be very rich in your poverty.

CHAPTER XVII.

Friendship : and, first, concerning that which is evil and frivolous.

Love holds the first place among the several passions of the soul; it is the sovereign of all the emotions of the heart, and directs all the rest towards it, and makes us such as are the objects of its love. Be careful then, Philothea, to entertain no evil love, for if you do you will presently become evil. Now friendship is the most dangerous love of all; because other loves may be without communication, but friendship, being wholly grounded upon it, we can hardly *have* close friendship for any person without partaking of his qualities.

All love is not friendship; for when one loves without being again beloved, then there is love but not friendship; because friendship is intercommunication of love, therefore where love is not mutual there can be no friendship. Nor is it enough that it be mutual, the parties that love each other must besides know of their mutual affection; for if they know it not they have love but not friendship. There must be also some kind of communication between them, so as to form the ground of friendship. Now, according to the diversity of the communications, the friendship also differs, and the communications are different according to the variety of the good things they communicate to each other; if they are false and vain, the friendship is also false and vain; if they are true the friendship is likewise true; and the more excellent the goods may be, the more excellent also is the friendship. For as that honey is best which is gathered from the most exquisite flowers, so also that friendship is best which is founded upon the most exquisite communication. And as there is honey in Heraclea which is poisonous, and makes those mad that eat it, because it is gathered from poisonous plants which abound in that country; even so, friendship grounded upon false and vicious communications is also false and vicious.

Communications founded on sensual pleasures is so gross that it does not merit the name of friendship among men; and if there were no other communication in marriage, there would be no friendship in it; but because, besides that, there is a communication in marriage, of life, of industry, of goods, of affections, and of an indissoluble fidelity, therefore the friendship of matrimony is a true and holy friendship. Such is also friendship that is grounded on accomplishments which are frivolous and vain, because these also depend on the senses. I call those pleasures sensual which are immediately and principally annexed to the exterior senses: such as the pleasures to behold a beautiful person, to hear a sweet voice, and the like. I call certain vain endowments and qualities frivolous accomplishments which weak minds call virtues and perfections. Observe how the greater part of silly girls, women, and young people talk: they hesitate not to say, Such a gentleman has many virtues and perfections, for he dances gracefully, he plays well at all sorts of games, he dresses fashionably, he sings delightfully, speaks eloquently, and looks well; it is thus that mountebanks esteem those in their way the most virtuous who are the greatest buffoons.

But as all these things regard the senses, so the friendships which proceed from them are termed sensual, vain, and frivolous, and deserve rather the name of foolish fondness than of friendship: such are the ordinary friendships of young people, which are grounded on curled locks, a fine head of hair, smiling glances, fine clothes, affected countenances, and idle talk—a friendship suited to the age of those lovers whose virtue is, as yet, only in the blossom, and whose judgment is only in the bud; and, indeed, such friendships, being but transitory, melt away like snow in the sun.

CHAPTER XVIII.
Sensual Friendship.

When these foolish friendships are kept up between persons of different sex, without intention of marriage, being but phantoms of friendship, they deserve not the name either of true friendship or true love by reason of their excessive vanity and imperfection. Now, by means of these fondnesses the hearts of men and of women are caught and entangled with each other in vain and foolish affections, founded upon these frivolous communications, and wretched complacencies, of which I have been just speaking.

And although these dangerous loves, commonly speaking, terminate at last in downright immorality, yet that is not the first design or intention of the persons between whom they are carried on, otherwise they would not be merely sensual friendships, but absolute impurity. Sometimes even many years pass before anything directly contrary to chastity happens between them, whilst they content themselves by giving to their hearts the pleasures of wishes, sighs, and such like foolish vanities.

Some have no other design than to satisfy a natural desire of affection; and these regard nothing in the choice of the objects of their love but their own taste and instinct; so that, at the first meeting with an agreeable person, without examining his interior or comportment, they begin this fond communication, and entangle themselves in these wretched nets, out of which afterwards they find great difficulty in disengaging themselves. Others suffer themselves to be carried on by the vanity of esteeming it no small glory to conquer hearts by love. Now these, aiming at glory in the choice they make, set their net and lay their snares in high, rare, and illustrious places. Others are led away at the same time, both by their amorous inclination and by vanity; for though their hearts are altogether inclined to love, nevertheless they will not engage themselves in it without some advantage of glory. Such affections are all criminal, foolish, and vain: criminal, because they usually terminate in great sin, and because they rob God, the wife, or the husband of that love, and consequently of that heart which belonged to them; foolish, because they have neither foundation nor reason; vain, because they yield neither profit, honour, nor content; on the contrary, they are attended by loss of time, are prejudicial to honour, and bring no other pleasure than that of an eagerness in pretending and hoping, without knowing what they would have, or what they would pretend to. For these wretched and weak minds still imagine they have something, they know not what to hope for, from the testimonies given them of reciprocal love, and yet they cannot tell what this is; the desire of which can never end, but goes on continually, oppressing their hearts with perpetual distrusts, jealousies, and inquietudes.

St. Gregory Nazianzen, in his discourse addressed, indeed, to vain women, yet also suitable for men, says: " Thy natural beauty is sufficient for thy husband; but if it be for many men, like a net spread out for a flock of birds, what will be the consequence? He shall be pleasing to thee who shall please himself with thy beauty; thou wilt return him glance for glance, look for look; presently will follow smiles and little amorous words, dropping by stealth at the beginning, but soon after becoming more familiar, and passing on to open courtship. Take heed, oh, my talking tongue, of telling what will follow; yet, will I say this one truth : nothing of all those things which young men and women say and do together in these foolish complacencies is exempted from grievous stings. All the links of wanton loves hold one to another, as one piece of iron touched by the loadstone draws divers others after it."

Oh, how wisely has this great bishop spoken? What is it you think to do? To give love? No; for no one gives love voluntarily that does not receive it necessarily. He that catches in this chase is likewise caught himself. Our hearts, as soon as they see a soul inflamed with love for them, are presently set on fire with love for it. But someone will say, I am willing to entertain some of this love, but not too much. Alas! you deceive yourself, the fire of love is more active and penetrating than you imagine; you think to receive but a spark, and will wonder to see it in a moment take possession of your whole heart, reduce all your resolutions to ashes, and your reputation to smoke. " Who will have pity on a charmer struck by a serpent?" (Eccles. xii. 13). And I also, like unto the wise man, cry out, Oh foolish and senseless people, think you to charm love in such a manner as to be able to manage it at your pleasure? You would play with it, but it will sting and torment you cruelly; and do you not know that everyone will laugh at and deride you for attempting to charm or tie down love, and on a false pretence put into your bosom a dangerous serpent which has undermined and destroyed both your soul and your honour.

Good God! what blindness is this, to play away

thus at hazard against such frivolous stakes, the principal power of our soul? Yes, Philothea, for God regards man only for his soul; his soul only for his will; his will only for his love. Alas! we have not nearly as much love as we stand in need of—I mean to say that we fall infinitely short of having sufficient wherewith to love God; and yet, wretches as we are, we lavish it foolishly on vain and frivolous things, as if we had some to spare. Ah! this great God, who hath reserved to Himself the whole love of our souls in acknowledgment of our creation, preservation, and redemption, will exact a most strict account of all these criminal deductions we make from it; for, if He will examine so rigorously into our idle words, how strictly will He not examine into our impertinent, foolish, and pernicious loves?

The walnut-tree is very prejudicial to the vines and fields wherein it is planted; because, being so large, it attracts all the moisture of the surrounding earth, and renders it incapable of nourishing the other plants; the leaves are also so thick that they make a large and close shade; and, lastly, it allures passers-by to it who, to beat down the fruit, spoil and trample upon all about it. These sensual friendships cause the same injury to the soul, for they possess her in such a manner, and so strongly draw her emotions to themselves, that she has no strength left to produce good works; the leaves, that is, idle talk, amusements, and dalliance, are so frequent, that all leisure time is squandered away on them; and, finally, they beget so many temptations, distractions, suspicions, and other evil consequences, that the whole heart is trampled down and destroyed by them. In a word, these sensual friendships not only banish heavenly love, but also the fear of God from the soul; they waste the spirit, and ruin the reputation; they are the sport of the world and the plague of hearts.

CHAPTER XIX.

True Friendship.

Love everyone, Philothea, with a great love of charity, but have no friendship except for those that communicate unto you the things of virtue ; and the more exquisite the virtues are, which shall be the matter of your communications, the more perfect shall your friendship also be. If this communication be in the sciences, the friendship is certainly very commendable, but still more so if it be in the moral virtues—in prudence, discretion, fortitude, and justice. But should your reciprocal communication relate to charity, devotion, and Christian perfection, how precious will friendship be ! It will be excellent, because it comes from God, excellent because it shall last eternally in God. Oh, how good it is to love on earth as they love in heaven, to learn to cherish each other in this world as we shall do eternally in the next.

I speak not here of that simple love of charity which we must have for all men, but of that spiritual friendship by which two, three, or more souls communicate one to another their devotion and spiritual affections, and make themselves all but one spirit. Such happy souls may justly sing : "Behold how good and pleasant it is for brethren to dwell together in unity" (Ps. cxxxi. 1) ; for the delicious balm of devotion distils out of one heart into another by so continual a participation, that it may be said that God has poured out upon this friendship his blessing and life everlasting. I consider all other friendships as but so many shadows in comparison with this, and that their bonds are but chains of glass or of jet in comparison with that bond of holy devotion which is more precious than gold.

Form no other kind of friendship than this. I speak of such friends as you choose yourself; but you must not, therefore, forsake or neglect the friendships which nature or former duties oblige you to cultivate with your parents, kindred, benefactors, neighbours, and others.

Many perhaps may say: "We should have no kind of particular affection and friendship, because it occupies the heart, distracts the mind, and begets envy;" but they are mistaken, because having seen, in the writings of many devout authors, that particular friendships and extraordinary affections are of infinite prejudice to religious persons, they therefore imagine that it is the same with regard to the rest of the world; there is, however, a material difference; for as in a well-ordered monastery, the common design of all tends to true devotion, it is not requisite to make these particular communications of friendship, lest by seeking among individuals for that which is common to the whole, they should fall from particularities to partialities; but for such as dwell among worldlings and desire to embrace true virtue, it is necessary for them to unite themselves together by a holy and sacred friendship, since by this means they encourage, assist, and conduct each other to good; for as they that walk on level ground need not lend each other a hand, whilst they that are on a rugged and slippery road hold one by the other to walk more securely, so they that are in religious orders stand in no want of particular friendships, but they that are in the world have need of them to secure and assist each other amidst the many dangerous passages through which they are to pass. In the world all are not directed by the same views, nor actuated by the same spirit; we must therefore separate ourselves, and contract friendships according to our several pretensions. This particularity begets, indeed, a partiality; but it is a holy partiality, which creates no other division but that which, of necessity, should always exist between good and evil.

No one surely can deny but that our Lord loved St. John, Lazarus, Martha, and Magdalen, with a sweet and special friendship. We know that St. Peter tenderly cherished St. Mark and St. Petronilla, as St. Paul did Timothy and St. Thecla. St. Gregory Nazianzen boasts, a hundred times, of the incomparable friendship he had with the great St. Basil, and describes it in this manner: "It seemed that in the one and the other of us there was but one soul dwelling in two bodies; and if those are not to be believed, who say that all things are in all things, yet of us two you may believe that we were both in each of us, and one in the other: we had each of us only one pretension to cultivate virtue, and to accommodate all the designs of our life to future hopes; going in this manner out of this mortal earth, before we died in it." St. Augustine testifies that St. Ambrose loved St. Monica entirely, for the real virtues he saw in her, and that she reciprocally loved him as an angel of God. But I am to blame in detaining you so long on this very clear subject. St. Jerome, St. Augustine, St. Gregory, St. Bernard, and all the greatest servants of God have had very particular friendships, without prejudice to their perfection. St. Paul, reproaching the disorders of the Gentiles, accuses them of being people without affection, that is to say, that they had no true friendship. And St. Thomas, with all the wisest philosophers, acknowledges that friendship is a virtue; and he speaks of particular friendship, since, as he says, "Perfect friendship cannot be extended to a great many persons." Perfection therefore consists. not in having no friendship, but in having none but with such as are good, saint-like, and holy.

CHAPTER XX.

The difference between true and vain Friendships.

Observe, Philothea, this important admonition. As the poisonous honey of Heraclea is so like the other that is wholesome, that there is great danger of mistaking the one for the other, or of taking them mixed together (for the goodness of the one cannot destroy the poison of the other), so he must stand upon his guard, who would not be deceived in friendships, particularly when contracted between persons of different sexes, under any pretext whatsoever. The devil often effects a change in those that love : they begin with virtuous love, which if not attended by the utmost discretion, sensual love will begin to mingle, and afterwards carnal love ; yes, there is even danger in spiritual love, if we are not extremely upon our guard : though in this it is more difficult to be imposed upon, because its purity and whiteness make the spots and stains which Satan seeks to mingle with it more apparent, and, therefore, when he takes this in hand he does it more craftily, and endeavours to slip in impurities by almost insensible degrees.

You may distinguish worldly friendship from that which is holy and virtuous as the poisonous honey of Heraclea is known from the other ; for, as the honey of Heraclea is sweeter to the tongue than the ordinary honey, because of the juice of the deadly nightshade which gives it additional sweetness, so worldly friendship ordinarily produces a great profusion of sweet words, passionate expressions, together with admiration of beauty, behaviour, and other sensual qualities, whereas, holy friendship speaks a plain and sincere language, and commends nothing but virtue and the grace of God, the only foundations on

possible to stop a torrent that descends a mountain, so it is hard to prevent the love which has entered in at the ear from falling suddenly into the heart.

Alcmæon pretended that goats breathe by the ears and not by the nostrils, which Aristotle of course denied; but this I know, that our heart breathes by the ear, and as it sends forth its own thoughts by the tongue, so it draws in the thoughts of others by the ear. Let us then keep a diligent guard upon our ears, that we may not draw in the corrupt air of filthy words, for otherwise our hearts will soon be infected. Hearken to no conversation of this kind under what pretext soever.

Remember that you have dedicated your heart to God, and, that being so, it would be a sacrilege to alienate the least part of it from Him. Rather dedicate it to Him anew, by a thousand resolutions and protestations: and keeping yourself close within them, as a deer within its thicket, call upon God, and He will help you, and his love will take yours under its protection. that it may live for Him alone.

But if you are already caught in the meshes of such evil friendships, how difficult will it be to extricate yourself from them! Place yourself before the Divine Majesty, acknowledging, in his presence, the excess of your misery, frailty, and vanity. Then, with the greatest effort of which your heart is capable, detest them; renounce all the promises received, and, with the greatest and most absolute resolution, determine in your heart never to permit them to occupy your thoughts in the slightest degree for the remainder of your life.

If you could withdraw yourself to a distance from the object, I know of no better remedy, for change of place contributes very much to calm the excess and pain either of grief or of love. The youth of whom St. Ambrose speaks, in his Second Book of Penance, having made a long journey, returned home altogether freed from the vain love he had formerly entertained, and so much changed that his foolish mistress meeting him, and saying: Dost thou not know me? am I not the same that I was? Yes, answered he; but I am not the same that I was. Absence had wrought in him this happy change. Thus St. Augustine relates, that to mitigate the grief he suffered for the death of his friend he quitted Tagasta, the place where his friend died, and went to Carthage.

But what must he do who cannot withdraw himself? Let him absolutely give up all private familiarity and conversation, amorous looks, smiles, and in general all kinds of intercourse which may nourish the impure fire; or, if he must speak to the other party, let it be only to declare with a bold, short, and serious protestation, the eternal divorce which he has sworn. I cry aloud to everyone who has fallen into these wretched snares: Cut them, break them, tear them; you must not amuse yourself in unravelling these criminal friendships: you must tear and rend them asunder; wait not to untie the knots, but break them or cut them, so that the cords and strings may be worth nothing; we must not stand on ceremony with love which is contrary to the love of God.

But after I have thus broken the chains of this infamous bondage, there will still remain some feelings: the marks and prints of the iron will still be imprinted in my feet, that is to say, in my affections. No, Philothea, they will not, provided you have conceived as great a detestation of the evil as it deserves: you shall now be excited with no other feeling but that of an extreme horror of this infamous love and of all that relates to it; and you shall remain free from all other affection towards the forsaken object, except that of a most pure charity, for God's sake.

But if, through the imperfection of your repentance, there should yet remain in you any evil inclinations, seek a mental solitude for your soul, according to what I have taught you before, and retire into it as often as you can, and, by a thousand reiterated ejaculations of the spirit, renounce all your criminal inclinations, and reject them with your whole strength. Read pious and holy books with a more than ordinary application; go to confession, and communicate more frequently; humbly and sincerely consult your director, or some prudent, faithful friend, concerning all the suggestions and temptations of this kind which may come upon you, and doubt not but that God will deliver you from those criminal passions, provided you continue faithfully in such good exercises. And, you will ask, will it not be ingratitude to break off a friendship so unmercifully? Oh, how happy is that ingratitude which makes us pleasing to God! But no, Philothea, I tell you, in the name of God, that this will be no ingratitude, but a great benefit which you shall do to your lover; for in breaking your own bonds asunder, you shall also break his, since they were common to you both; and though, for the present, he may not be sensible of his happiness, yet he will acknowledge it soon after, and jointly sing with you in thanksgiving: "O Lord, thou hast broken my bonds; I will sacrifice to thee a sacrifice of praise, and call upon thy holy name." (Ps. cxv.)

CHAPTER XXII.

More Advice on Friendship.

I have another important piece of advice to give you on this subject. Friendship requires great communication between friends, otherwise it can neither grow nor subsist. Therefore it often happens that, with this communication of friendship, divers other communications insensibly glide from one heart to another, by a mutual infusion and reciprocal intercourse of affections, inclinations, and impressions. But this happens especially when we have a high esteem for him whom we love; for then we open our heart in such a manner to his friendship that, together with it, his inclinations and impressions enter rapidly in their full stream, be they good or bad. Certainly the bees that gather the honey of Heraclea seek nothing but honey; but yet, with the honey they insensibly suck the poisonous qualities of the aconite, from which they gather it. On these occasions, Philothea, we must carefully put in practice what the Saviour of our souls was accustomed to say: "Be ye good bankers, or changers of money:" that is to say, "Receive not bad money with the good, nor base gold with the fine;" separate that which is precious from that which is vile; for there is scarcely any person that has not some imperfection. For why should we receive promiscuously the faults and imperfections of a friend, together with his friendship? We must love him indeed, notwithstanding his imperfections, but we must neither love nor receive his imperfections; for friendship requires a communication of good, not of evil. Therefore, as they that draw gravel out of the river Tagus separate the gold which they find to carry it away and leave the sand on the banks. so they who have the intercommunication of some good friendship ought to separate from it the sand of imperfections, and not suffer it to enter into their souls. St. Gregory Nazianzen testifies, that many, loving and admiring St. Basil, were brought insensibly to imitate him, even in his outward imperfections, as in his slow speech, his abstracted and pensive spirit, the fashion of his beard, and in his gait. And we often

see husbands, wives, children, and friends, who,
having a great esteem for their friends, parents, husbands, and wives, get, either by condescension or imitation, a thousand little bad habits, which they have
one with another. Now, this ought by no means to
be so, for everyone has evil inclinations enough of his
own, without charging himself with those of others;
and friendship is so far from requiring it that, on the
contrary, it obliges us mutually to aid and assist
one another, with a view to our being freed from all
kinds of imperfections. We must indeed meekly bear
with our friend in his imperfections, but we must
not lead him into imperfections, much less imitate
his imperfections ourselves. But I speak only of imperfections; for as to sins, we must neither occasion
them, nor tolerate them in our friends. It is either
a weak or a wicked friendship to behold our friend
perish and not to help him; to see him die of an
abscess, and not to dare to open it with a lancet of
correction, to save his life. True and living friendship cannot subsist in the midst of sin. It is said
that the salamander extinguishes the fire in which
he lies, so sin destroys the friendship in which it
lodges. If it be but a transient sin, friendship will
presently put it to flight by correction; but if it be
habitual, and take up a permanent abode, friendship
immediately perishes, for it cannot exist but upon
the solid foundation of virtue. We must never, then,
commit sin for friendship's sake. A friend becomes
an enemy when he would lead us to sin; and he deserves to lose his friend when he would destroy his
soul. It is an infallible mark of false friendship to
see it exercised towards a vicious person, whatsoever kind his sins may be; for if he whom we love
is vicious, without doubt our friendship is also vicious; since, seeing that it cannot respect true virtue,
it must needs be grounded on some frivolous virtue,

12

or sensual quality. Society formed for trade purposes among merchants is but a shadow of true
friendship, since it is not made for the love of the
persons, but for the love of gain.

Finally, the two following divine sentences are the
two main pillars to secure a Christian life; the one
is that of the wise man : "He that fearh God shall
likewise have a good friendship; " thether is that
of the Apostle St. James : "The friendship of this
world is the enemy of God."

CHAPTER XXIII.

The exercise of Exterior Mortification.

Old writers on agriculture and country affairs tell
us that if any word be written upon a sound almond,
and it is again enclosed in the shell and planted, all
the fruit upon the tree growing from it will have the
same word engraven upon it. For my part, Philothea, I could never approve of the method of those
who, to reform a man begin with his exterior, such
as his gestures, his dress, or his hair. On the contrary, I think we ought to begin with his interior :
" Be converted to me, with your whole heart " (Joel,
ii.) " Son, give me thine heart." (Prov. xxiii.) For
the heart being the genuine source of our actions,
our works will be always such as our heart is. The
Divine Spouse inviting the soul : " Put me as a seal
upon thy heart, as a seal upon thy arm." (Cantic. v.)
Yes, truly ; for whosoever has Jesus Christ in his heart
will quickly show Him in all his exterior actions.
I desire, therefore, dear Philothea, above all things to
engrave upon your heart this sacred motto, " Live
Jesus ; " being assured that your life, which proceeds
from the heart, as an almond-tree from an almond,
will afterwards bring forth the same words of salva-

tion written upon all your actions; for, as this sweet Jesus lives within your heart, so will He also live in your exterior, in your eyes. your mouth, your hands, and even the hair on your head; so that you will be able to say with St. Paul: " I live, no, not I, but Christ liveth in me." In a word, he that has gained the heart has gained the whole man; but even this heart. by which we would begin, requires to be instructed how it ought to frame its outward behaviour, to the end that men may not only behold holy devotion therein, but also wisdom and discretion; for this reason I crave your serious attention to the following short admonitions:

If you are able to endure fasting, you would do well to fast some days besides those which are commanded by the Church; for, besides the usual effects of fasting, viz., to elevate the spirit, to keep the flesh in subjection, to exercise virtue, and to acquire a greater reward in heaven, it is a great means to restrain gluttony, and keep the sensual appetites and the body subject to the law of the spirit: and although we may not fast much, yet the enemy fears us when he knows we know how to fast. Wednesdays, Fridays, and Saturdays are the days on which the ancient Christians exercised themselves most in abstinence; choose, then, some one of those days to fast on, as far as your devotion and the discretion of your director shall advise you.

I would willingly say to you, as St. Jerome said to the good Lady Læta: " Long and immoderate fastings displease me much, especially in those that are yet in their tender age." I have learned by experience that the young ass, being weary in his journey, seeks to go off from the straight road: that is to say, that young people, being brought into infirmities through excess of fasting, easily turn to a delicate and luxurious way of living. Deer cannot run well under two circumstances—when they are either too fat or too lean. We are greatly exposed to temptations, both when our body is too much pampered, and when it is too much weakened ; for the one makes it insolent with ease, and the other desperate with affliction ; and as we cannot bear it when it is too fat, so it cannot bear us when it is too lean. The want of this moderation in the use of fasting, discipline, hair-shirts, and other austerities, renders the best years of many unprofitable in the service of charity, as it did even in the case of St. Bernard, who repented that he had used overmuch austerity ; and the more they exceeded in the ill-treatment of their bodies in the beginning, the more they were constrained to favour them in the end. Would they not have done better to have mortified their bodies moderately, and in proportion to the offices and labours to which their condition obliged them ?

Labour, as well as fasting, serves to mortify and subdue the flesh. Now, provided the labour you undertake contributes to the glory of God and your own welfare, I had rather you would suffer the pain of the labour than that of fasting. This is the sense of the Church, since, on account of such labours as contribute to the service of God and our neighbour dispenses persons engaged in them, even from the fasts commanded. Some find it painful to fast ; others to serve the sick or visit prisoners ; others to hear confessions, to preach, pray, and perform such like exercises. These latter kind of pains are of more value than the former ; for, besides subduing the body, they produce fruits much more desirable, and therefore, generally speaking, it is better to preserve our bodily strength more than may be necessary than to weaken it too much ; for we can always decrease it when we will, but we cannot always repair it when e would desire to do so.

We should attend with great reverence to the admonition given by our Blessed Saviour to his disciples : "Eat the things that are set before you" (Luke, x. 9). It is, in my opinion, a greater virtue to eat without choice that which is laid before you, and in the same order as it is presented, whether it be more or less agreeable to your taste, than to always choose the worst ; for although this latter way of living seems more austere, yet the former has, notwithstanding, more resignation, since by it we renounce not only our own taste, but even our own choice ; and it is no small mortification to accommodate one's taste to every kind of meat, and keep it in subjection to all occurrences. Besides, this kind of mortification makes no parade, gives no trouble to anyone, and is happily adapted to civil life. To set one kind of meat aside to take another, to pick and scrape off every dish, to think nothing well dressed or sufficiently nice, and make a mystery of every morsel, bespeaks a heart over-nice, and too much attached to eating and drinking. I esteem more St. Bernard's drinking oil instead of water or wine than if he had drank wormwood water purposely ; for it was a plain sign that he thought not of what he drank ; and in this indifference respecting our food consists the perfection of the practice of the sacred rule : " Eat that which is set before you." I except, however, such meats as may prejudice the health, or incommode the spirit, such as hot or high-seasoned meats : as also certain occasions in which nature requires recreation and assistance, in order to be able to support some labour for the glory of God. A continual and moderate sobriety is preferable to violent abstinence, practised by fits and followed by intemperance.

A moderate use of discipline awakens the fervour of devotion. The hair-shirt mortifies the flesh exceedingly, but the use of it, generally speaking, is not proper either for married persons or tender complexions, or for such as have other great pains to support. However, on some remarkable days of penance, it may be used with advice of a discreet confessor.

We must dedicate the night to sleep, everyone as much as his constitution requires, in order to enable him to watch and spend the day profitably; and also because the Holy Scripture, the examples of the saints, and natural reason, strenuously recommend the morning to us as the most useful portion of the day, and that our Lord Himself is named the Rising Sun, and our Blessed Lady the dawning of the day. I think it a point of virtue to take care to go to rest early in the evening, that we may be enabled to awake and arise early in the morning, which is certainly of all other times the most favourable to piety and to the health, the most agreeable, and that which least disposes to disturbance and distractions; when the very birds invite us to awake and praise God; so that early rising is equally serviceable to health and holiness.

Balaam, mounted on his ass, was going to King Balak, but because he had not a right intention, the angel waited for him on the way, with a sword in his hand to kill him. The ass, on seeing the angel, stood still three several times, and became restive; Balaam, in the meantime, beat it cruelly with his staff to make it advance, until the beast, at the third time, falling down under Balaam, by an extraordinary miracle, spoke to him: "What have I done to thee? why strikest thou me, lo! now this third time?" (Numb. xxii. 28). But soon after Balaam's eyes were opened and he saw the angel, who said to him: "Why beatest thou thy ass? If she had not turned out of the way, giving place to me, I had

slain thee, and she should have lived." Then Balaam
said to the angel: "I have sinned, not knowing
that thou didst stand against me." Behold, Philothea, although Balaam is the cause of the evil, yet he
strikes and beats his poor ass that could not prevent
it. It is often the same case with us; for example,
a woman sees her husband or child sick, and presently betakes herself to fasting, haircloth, and
such discipline, as David did on the like occasion.
Alas! my dear friend, you beat the poor ass, you
afflict your body, but it cannot remedy the evil, nor
is it on that account that God's sword is drawn
against you: correct your heart, which is an idola-
tor of your husband, and which has permitted a
thousand vices in your child; has encouraged it on
to pride, vanity, and ambition. Again, a man perceives that he frequently relapses in a shameful
manner into the sin of impurity; an inward remorse
comes, sword in hand, against his conscience, to
pierce it through with a holy fear; and presently,
his heart returning to itself, he says: "Ah, wicked
flesh! ah, treacherous body! thou hast betrayed
me;" and immediately he lays great blows on
his flesh, with immoderate fasting, excessive dis-
ciplining, and unsupportable hair-shirts. Oh, poor
soul, if thy flesh could speak, as Balaam's ass did, it
would say to thee: "Why, O wretch, dost thou
strike me?" It is against thee, O soul, that God
arms his vengeance; it is thou that art the criminal:
why dost thou lead me into bad company? why
dost thou employ mine eyes, my hands and my lips
in wantonness? why dost thou trouble me with impure imaginations? Cherish thou good thoughts, and
I shall have no evil impulses; keep company with
such as are modest and chaste, and I shall not be
provoked to impurity. It is thou, alas! that throwest
me into the fire, and yet thou would not ha·

me burn; thou castest smoke into my eyes, and yet wouldst not have them inflamed. And God, without doubt, says to you in these cases: Beat, break, bend, and crush your hearts to pieces, for it is against them principally that my anger is excited. As to cure diseases of the skin it is not so necessary to wash or bathe the body as it is to purify the blood and strengthen the liver; so to cure our vices, although it may be good to mortify the flesh, yet it is, above all, necessary to purify our affections, and to refresh our hearts effectually. But in and through all, let us be sure never to undertake corporal austerities, but with the advice of our spiritual guide.

CHAPTER XXIV.

Conversation and Solitude.

To seek and to avoid conversation are two blameable extremes in the devotion of those that live in the world, which is that of which we are now treating. To shun all conversation savours of disdain and contempt of our neighbours; and to be fond of it is a mark of sloth and idleness. We must love our neighbours as ourselves, and to show that we love them we must not fly their company: and to testify that we love ourselves, we must stay with ourselves, when we are only by ourselves. "Think first of thyself," says St. Bernard, "and then of others." If, then, nothing presses you to go abroad into company, or to receive company at home, stay in yourself, and entertain yourself with your own heart; but if company visit you, or any just cause invite you into company, go, in God's name, Philothea, and see your neighbour with a benevolent heart and a kindly eye.

We call those conversations evil which are carried

on with some evil intention, or when the company is vicious, indiscreet, and dissolute : such as these we must avoid, as much as bees shun the company of wasps and hornets. For, as when persons are bitten by mad dogs, their perspiration, their breath, and their spittle become infectious, so vicious and dissolute persons cannot be visited without the utmost risk and danger, more especially by those whose devotion is as yet but young and tender.

There are some unprofitable conversations held merely to recreate and divert us from our serious occupations to which we must not be too much addicted, although we allow them to occupy the leisure destined for recreation. Other conversations have politeness for their object, as in the case of mutual visits and certain assemblies brought together to do honour to our neighbour. With respect to these, as we ought to be most cautious in the practice of them, so neither must we be uncivil in condemning them, but modestly comply with our duty in their regard, to the end that we may equally avoid both ill-breeding and levity.

It remains that we should speak of the profitable conversation of devout and virtuous persons. To converse frequently, Philothea, with such as these, will be to you of the utmost benefit. As the vine that is planted among the olive-trees bears oily grapes, which have the taste of olives, so the soul which is often in the company of virtuous people cannot but partake of their qualities. As drones alone cannot make honey, but make it with the help of the other bees, so it is of great advantage to us in the exercise of devotion to converse with those that are devout.

In all conversations, sincerity, simplicity, meekness, and modesty, are to be ever preserved. There are a sort of people who make gestures and motions

with so much affectation that they cause trouble to
the company ; and as he who could never walk but
by counting his steps, nor speak but by singing,
would be troublesome to the rest of mankind, so they
who affect an artificial carriage, and do nothing but
with airs, are very disagreeable in conversation, for
in such there is always some kind of presumption.
Let a moderate cheerfulness be ordinarily predominant in our conversation. St. Romuald and St.
Anthony are highly commended for having always,
notwithstanding their austerities, both their countenance and their discourse adorned with joy, gaiety,
and courtesy; "Rejoice with them that rejoice"
(Rom. xii. 15). And again I say to you with the
Apostle. "Rejoice always but in the Lord. Let
your modesty be known to all men" (Phil. iv. 4).
To rejoice in our Lord, the subject of your joy must
not only be lawful, but also decent; and this I say,
because there are some things lawful which yet are
not decent : and to the end that your modesty may
be known to all, keep yourself free from insolence,
which is always reprehensible. To cause one of the
company to fall down, to blacken another's face, to
prick or pinch a third, to hurt a fool, are foolish
and insolent merriments.

But still, besides that mental solitude to which
you may retreat, even amidst the greatest conversations, as I have hitherto observed (Ps. ii. 12), you
ought also to love local and real solitude : not that I
expect you should go into the desert, as St. Mary of
Egypt, St. Paul, St. Antony, St. Arsenius, and the
other ancient solitaries did, but to be for some time
alone by yourself in your chamber or garden, or in
some other place where you may at leisure withdraw
your spirit into your heart and recreate your soul
with pious meditations, holy thoughts, or spiritual
reading. St. Gregory Nazianzen, speaking of him-

self, says : "I walked, myself with myself, about sunset, and passed the time on the seashore; for I am accustomed to use this recreation to refresh myself, and to shake off a little my ordinary troubles :" and afterwards he relates the pious reflections he made, which I have already mentioned elsewhere. St. Augustine relates that often going into the chamber of St. Ambrose, who never denied entrance to anyone, he always found him reading, and that after staying awhile, for fear of interrupting him, he departed again without speaking a word, thinking that the little time that remained to that great pastor for recreating his spirit, after the hurry of so many affairs as he had upon his hands, ought not to be taken from him.   And when the Apostles one day had told our Lord how they had preached, and how much they had done, he said to them : "Come ye apart into a desert place and rest a little " (Mark, vi. 13).

CHAPTER XXV.

Decency in Attire.

St. Paul desires that devout women, and the same may be said of men, should be attired " in decent apparel, adorning themselves with modesty and sobriety" (1 Tim. ii. 9). Now, the decency and the ornaments of apparel, depend on the matter, the form, and the cleanliness of them. As to their cleanliness, it should be always very great, and we should not suffer any kind of dirt on them.   Exterior neatness represents in some measure the cleanliness of the interior ; and God Himself requires corporal cleanliness in those that approach his altars, and have the principal charge of devotion.

As to the matter, form, and decency of our dress,

it should be considered according to the several circumstances of the time, the age, the quality, the company, and the occasions. People are ordinarily better dressed on holidays, in proportion to the solemnity of the feast which is celebrated. In times of penance, as in Lent, ornaments are laid aside. At marriages wedding garments are worn; at funerals, mourning.

The married woman may and ought to adorn herself when she is with her husband, and he desires it; but if she should do so when she is at a distance from him, it will be asked whose eyes she desires to favour with that particular care? A greater liberty in point of ornaments is allowed to maidens, because they may lawfully desire to appear agreeable to many, although with no other intention but that of gaining a husband. Neither is it considered amiss that widows who purpose to marry should adorn themselves in some measure, provided they betray no levity; for, having already been mistresses of families and passed through the griefs of widowhood, they should be considered as being of a more mature and settled mind. But as for those that are widows indeed, not only in body but in heart, no other ornament becomes them but humility, modesty, and devotion; for if they have an inclination to make men fall in love with them, they are not widows indeed, and if they have no such desire, why do they carry about them the instruments of love? The host that ceases to receive guests must pull down the sign from his inn. Old people are always ridiculous when they try to make themselves look youthful.

Be neat, Philothea; let nothing hang loose about you, or be put on in a slovenly manner. It is a kind of contempt of those with whom we converse to come into their company in unseemly apparel; but, then, avoid all affectation, vanity, strangeness, or levity in your dress. Keep yourself always, as much as possible, on the side of plainness and modesty, which, without doubt, is the greatest ornament of beauty, and the best way to make up for the want of it.

St. Peter (1 Epist. iii. 3), admonishes women, in particular, not to wear their hair much curled and frizzled in rings and wreaths; but men who are so weak as to amuse themselves about such foppery are justly ridiculed for their effeminacy. They say they think no evil in these things; but I repeat, as I have said elsewhere, that the devil thinks quite other-wise. For my part, I desire that devout people, whether men or women, should be the best clad in any company, but the least pompous and affected: I would have them adorned with gracefulness decency, and dignity. St. Louis says that each one should dress according to his condition; so that the wise and the good may have no reason to complain that you dress too much, nor young people say you do too little. But in case young people will not content themselves with what is decent, we must conform to the judgment of the wise.

CHAPTER XXVI.

Conversation; and, first, how we must speak of God.

As physicians discover the health or sickness of a man by looking on his tongue, so our words are true indications of the quality of our souls. Our Saviour says: "By thy words thou shalt be justified, and by thy words thou shalt be condemned" (Matt. xii. 37). We readily move our hand to the pain that we feel, and the tongue to the love that we entertain.

If, then, Philothea, you love God, you will often speak of Him in your familiar conversation, wit' the members of your household, your friends, and your neighbours: "For the mouth of the just will meditate on wisdom, and his tongue will speak judgment." (Ps. xxxvi. 30). As bees with their little mouths sip nothing but honey, so should your tongue be always sweetened with God, and find no greater pleasure than in the sweet praises and blessings of his name flowing between your lips, like St. Francis, who used to suck and lick his lips after pronouncing the holy name of the Lord, to draw as it were from thence the greatest sweetness in the world.

But speak always of God, as of God; that is, reverently and devoutly; not with ostentation or affectation, but with a spirit of meekness, charity, and humility, distilling, as much as you can, as is said of the Spouse in the Canticle (Cant. iv. 11), of the delicious honey of devotion, and of the things of God, drop by drop, into the ears sometimes of one and sometimes of another, praying to God in secret, that it may please Him to make this holy dew sink deep into the hearts of those that hear you.

Above all things, this angelic office must be done meekly and swiftly; not by way of correction, but inspiration: for it is surprising how powerfully a sweet and amiable manner of proposing good things attracts the hearts of hearers.

Never, therefore, speak of God or of devotion in a light and thoughtless manner, or for talk-sake, but rather with the utmost attention and reverence. I give you this advice, that you may avoid that remarkable vanity which is found in many false devotees, who upon every occasion speak words of piety and godliness, by way of entertainment, without ever thinking of what they say, and afterwards falsely imagine themselves to be such as their words imply.

CHAPTER XXVII.

Modesty in our words, and the respect we owe to persons.

" If any offend not in words he is a perfect man " (James, iii. 2). Be careful, then, never to let slip an indecent word : for although you do not speak it with an ill intention, yet it may be hurtful to those that hear it. An evil word falling into a weak heart spreads itself like a drop of oil falling on linen : nay, it sometimes seizes on the heart in such a manner as to fill it with a thousand impure thoughts and temptations to sin, for as the poison of the body enters by the mouth, so the poison of the soul enters by the ear, and the tongue that utters it is a murderer. For although perhaps the poison which it has poured in has not worked its effect, because it found the souls of the hearers guarded with some preservative, nevertheless the malice was in the tongue to occasion their death. Let no man therefore tell me that he has no such thought; for our Lord, the searcher of hearts, has said : " That out of the abundance of the heart the mouth speaketh." But if we think no evil on such occasions, yet the enemy, who is of a contrary opinion, always secretly makes use of immodest words to pierce the soul of some one. As they that have eaten the herb *angelica* have always sweet and agreeable breaths, so they that have honesty and chastity, which is an angelic virtue, in their hearts, have their words always pure, modest, and chaste. As for indecent and obscene things, the Apostle will not have them even named amongst us, assuring us, " That nothing so much corrupts good manners as wicked discourse."

When immodest words are uttered under a disguise, cleverly and craftily, they become infinitel-

more poisonous; for, as the sharper the dart is
the more easily it enters our bodies, so the more
pointed an obscene word is the deeper it penetrates
into the soul; and they who esteem themselves men
of gallantry for speaking such words should know
that, in conversation, they should be like a swarm
of bees, brought together to collect honey for a
sweet and virtuous entertainment, and not like a
nest of wasps, assembled to suck corruption. If
some fool should address himself to you in a lascivious manner, convince him that your ears are offended, either by turning immediately away, or by
such other mark of resentment as your discretion
may direct.

To become a scoffer is one of the first qualities of
a wit: God, who detests this vice, has heretofore
inflicted terrible punishments on its perpetrators.
Nothing is so opposite to charity or devotion as despising and speaking scandal of your neighbour;
now, as derision or mockery is never without
scoffing, divines consider it as one of the worst
kind of offences, by words, a man can be guilty of
against his neighbour, for other offences may be
committed, still having some esteem for the party,
offended, but by this he is treated with scorn and
contempt.

As for certain good-humoured, jesting words,
spoken by one to another, by way of modest and
innocent mirth, they belong to the virtue called
eutrapela by the Greeks, which we may call the art
of agreeable conversation; and by those we take an
honest and friendly recreation from such frivolous
occasions as human imperfections furnish us with:
only we must be careful not to pass from honest
mirth to scoffing; for scoffing provokes to laughter
in the way of scorn and contempt of our neighbour;
whereas innocent mirth and drollery excite laugh-

ter by innocent liberty, confidence, and familiar freedom, joined to the sprightly wit of some ingenious conceit. St. Louis, when ecclesiastics offered to speak to him after dinner, of high and sublime matters, told them : " It is not now time to quote texts, but to divert ourselves with some cheerful conceits ; let every man say what he desires, but innocently." This he said when any of the nobility were present to receive marks of kindness from him. But let us remember, Philothea, so to pass our time of recreation that we may never lose sight of the greatest of all concerns—et rnity.

CHAPTER XXVIII.
Rash judgments.

" Judge not, and you shall not be judged," says the Saviour of our souls; "condemn not, and you shall not be condemned" (Luke, vi. 37). "No," says the holy apostle, " judge not before the time, until the Lord come, who both will bring to light the hidden things of darkness, and will make manifest the counsels of the heart " (2 Cor. iv. 5). Oh, how displeasing are rash judgments to God! The judgments of the children of men are rash, because they are not the judges of one another, and therefore usurp to themselves the office of our Lord. They are rash, because the principal malice of sin depends on the intention of the heart, which is an impenetrable secret to us. They are not only rash, but also impertinent, because everyone has enough to do to judge himself, without taking upon him to judge his neighbour. In order that we may not be hereafter judged, it is equally necessary to refrain from judging others; and to be careful to judge ourselves. For, as our Lord forbids the one, so the apostle enjoins the other, saying, that "if we judge ourselves, we should not be judged." But, O good God! we do quite the contrary; for by judging our neighbour on every occasion we do that which is forbidden; and by not judging ourselves, we neglect to put into practice that which we are strictly commanded to do.

We must apply remedies against rash judgments, according to their different causes. There are some hearts naturally so sour, bitter, and harsh, as to make everything bitter and sour that comes into them: "turning judgment," as the prophet Amos says, into wormwood, by never judging their neighbour but with rigour and harshness. Such have great need to fall into the hands of a good spiritual physician; for this bitterness of heart being natural to them, it is hard to overcome it, and though it be not in itself a sin, but an imperfection, yet it is dangerous, because it introduces and causes rash judgment and detraction to remain in the soul. Some judge rashly, not through harshness, but through pride, imagining that in the same proportion as they lower the honour of other men they raise their own. Arrogant and presumptuous spirits, who admire themselves so much and place themselves so high in their own esteem, look on all the rest of mankind as mean and abject. "I am not like the rest of men," saith the foolish Pharisee (Luke, xviii. 11). Others, who have not altogether this manifest pride, feel a certain satisfaction in thinking over the evil qualities of other men, in contradistinction to the good qualities wherewith they think themselves endowed. Now, this self-complacency is so imperceptible as not to be discovered even by those who are tainted with it. Others, to excuse themselves to themselves and to assuage the remorse of their own conscience, very willingly judge others to be guilty of the same 'nd of vice to which they themselves are addicted, or some other as great; thinking that the multitude of offenders make the sin the less blamable. Many take the liberty to judge others rashly, merely for the pleasure of delivering their opinion and conjectures on their manners and humours, by way of exercising their wit; and if, unhappily, they sometimes happen not to err in their judgment, their rashness increases to so violent an excess as to render it, in a manner, impossible ever to effect their cure. Others judge through passion and prejudice, always thinking well of what they love, and ill of what they hate; excepting in one case only, not less wonderful than true, in which the excess of love incites them to pass an ill judgment on that which they love; and this is jealousy, through which, as everyone knows, one simple look, or the least smile may convict the beloved person of disloyalty or infidelity. In fine, fear, ambition, and other such weaknesses of the mind frequently contribute towards the forming of suspicions and rash judgments.

But what is the remedy? As they who drink the juice of the herb of Ethiopia, called *ophiusa*, imagine that they everywhere behold serpents and other frightful objects; so they who have swallowed pride, envy, ambition, and hatred, think everything they see evil and blamable. The former, to be healed, must drink palm wine; and I say to the latter, drink as much as you can of the sacred wine of charity, and it will deliver you from those noxious humours that beget rash judgment. As charity fears to meet evil, so she never goes to seek after it; but whenever it falls in her way, she turns her face aside and takes no notice. At the first alarm of evil she shuts her eyes, and afterwards believes, with an honest simplicity, that it was not evil, but only its shadow or apparition; and if she cannot help sometimes acknowledging it to be really evil, she presently turns from it, and endeavours to forget even its shadow. Charity is the sovereign remedy against all evils, but especially this. All things appear yellow to the eyes of those who are afflicted with the jaundice; and it is said that to cure them of this evil they must wear celandine under the soles of their feet. The sin of rash judgment is, indeed, a spiritual jaundice, and makes all things appear evil to the eyes of such as are infected with it. He that desires to be cured of it must apply the remedies, not to his eyes, nor to his understanding, but to his affections, which are the feet of the soul. If your affections are mild, your judgment will be mild also; if your affections are charitable, your judgment will also be charitable. I shall here present you with three admirable examples: Isaac had said that Rebecca was his sister; Abimelech saw him playing with her, that is to say, caressing her in a tender manner (Gen. xxvi. 8); and presently he judged she was his wife; a malicious eye would rather have judged her to have been his mistress. But Abimelech followed the most charitable opinion he could gather from such an action. We must always do the like, Philothea, ever judging, as much as possible, in favour of our neighbour; and if one action could bear a hundred faces, we should always look on that which is the fairest.

Our Blessed Lady was with child (Matt. i. 9), and St. Joseph plainly perceived it; but, on the other hand, as he saw her quite holy, pure, and angelical, he could not believe she became pregnant in any unlawful way; he resolved, therefore, to leave her privately, and commit the judgment of her case to God; and though the argument was very strong to make him conceive an ill opinion of his Virgin Spouse, yet he would never judge her by it, and why? Because, says the spirit of God, he was a just man. A just

man, when he can nò longer excuse either the action
or the intentiou of him that he sees otherwise to be
virtuous, nevertheless will not judge him, but puts
the remembrance of it out of his mind, and leaves
the judgment to God. Thus, our Blessed Saviour
on the cross (Luke, xxxi. 24), not being able altogether to excuse the sin of those that crucified Him,
yet at least extenuated the malice of it by alleging
their ignorance. When we cannot excuse the sin,
let us at least render it deserving of compassion,
attributing it to the most favourable cause, such as
ignorance or weakness.

But may we never then judge our neighbour? No,
verily, never. It is God, O Philothea, that judges
criminals in public justice. It is true He uses the
voice of the magistrate to make himself intelligible
to our ears; they are his interpreters, and ought to
pronounce nothing but what they have learned of
Him, as being his oracles; if they do otherwise, by
following their own passions, then it is they indeed who judge, and who consequently shall be
judged; for it is forbidden to men, as of men, to
judge others.

To see or know a thing is not to judge it; for
judgment, at least according to the phrase of the
Scriptures, presupposes some difficulty, great or
small, true or apparent, which is to be decided;
wherefore they say: "That he who believeth not,
is already judged" (John, iii. 1), because there is no
doubt of his damnation. Is it not then evil to doubt
of our neighbour? No, for we are not forbidden to
doubt but to judge; however, it is not allowable
either to doubt or suspect any farther than pre-
cisely so far as reason and argument may force us,
otherwise our doubts and suspicions will be rash.

If some evil eye had seen Jacob when he kissed
Rachel by the well, or had seen Rebecca rece·

bracelets and ear-rings from Eliezer, a man unknown
in that country, he would no doubt have thought
ill of these two patterns of chastity, but without reason or ground; for, when an action is of itself indifferent, it is a rash suspicion to draw an evil conclusion from it, unless many circumstances give strength
to the argument. It is also a rash judgment to draw
an inference from an action, in order to blame the
person, but this I shall explain more clearly hereafter.

In fine, those who have tender consciences are not
very subject to rash judgments; for, as the bees in
misty or cloudy weather keep themselves close in
their hives in order to arrange their honey, so the
thoughts of good souls go not in search of objects
that lie concealed amidst the cloudy actions of their
neighbours; but, rather to avoid meeting them, they
withdraw themselves into their own hearts, there to
arrange and set in order good resolutions for their
own amendment.

It is the part of a useless soul to amuse herself
with examining into the lives of other men; I except
spiritual directors, fathers of families, magistrates,
&c., for a large portion of their duty consists in
looking to or watching over the conduct of others;
let them discharge that duty with love, and having
done so, let them then keep themselves within themselves.

CHAPTER XXIX.
Of Detraction.

Rash judgment begets inquietude, contempt of our
neighbour, pride, self-complacency, and several other
most pernicious effects; amongst which detraction,
the true plague of conversation, holds the first place.
Oh, that I had one of the burning coals of the holy
altar, to touch the lips of men, to the end that their

iniquities might be taken away, and their sins cleansed, in imitation of the seraphim that purified the mouth of the prophet Isaias! He that could deliver the world from detraction would free it from a great part of the sins of iniquity.

Whosoever robs his neighbour of his good name, besides repenting of the sin he commits, is also bound to make reparation; for no man can enter into heaven with the goods of another; and amongst all exterior goods, a good name is the best. Detraction is a kind of murder, for we have three lives, viz.: the spiritual, which consists in the grace of God; the corporal, which depends on the soul; and the civil, which consists in our good name; sin deprives us of the first, death takes away the second, and detraction robs us of the third. But the detractor, by one blow of his tongue, commits three murders: he kills not only his own soul, and the soul of him that hears him, but also, by a spiritual murder, takes away the civil life of the person detracted. "For," as St. Bernard says, "both he that detracts, and he that hearkens to the detractor, have each the devil about them—the one in his tongue, and the other in his ear." David, speaking of detractors, says: "They have whet their tongues like serpents" (Ps. cxxxix). Now, as the serpent's tongue is forked, and has two points, so is that of the detractor, who at one stroke stings and poisons the ear of the hearer and the reputation of him against whom he is speaking.

I earnestly conjure you then, Philothea, never to detract either directly or indirectly; take heed of imputing false crimes and sins, or of aggravating those that are manifest; or of putting an evil interpretation on his good works; or of denying the good which you know to be in him, or of maliciously concealing it, or diminishing it by words; for in all these ways you will highly offend God; but most of all by false accusations, and denying the truth to the prejudice of a third person ; for it is a double sin to belie and hurt your neighbour at one and the same time.

They who preface detraction by protestations of friendship and regard for the person detracted, or who make apologies in his favour, are the most subtle and venomous of all detractors. "I protest," say they, "that I love him ; in every other respect he is a worthy man ; but yet the truth must be told, he did ill to commit such a treacherous action ; she was very virtuous, but, alas ! she was surprised," &c. Do you not perceive the artifice? As the dexterous archer draws the arrow as near to himself as he can, that he may shoot it away with greater force, so, when these detractors seem to draw the detraction towards themselves, it is only with a view to shoot the dart away with more violence, that it may enter the deeper into the hearts of their hearers. But the detraction which is uttered by way of a jest is more cruel than the rest. For, as the hemlock is not of itself a very quick, but rather a slow poison, which may be easily remedied, yet being taken with wine is incurable, so detraction, which of itself might pass lightly in at one ear and out at another, sticks fast in the minds of the hearers, when it is couched under some subtle and merry jest : "They have," says David, "the venom of asps under their lips." The bite of the asp is almost imperceptible, and its venom at first causes a delightful itching, by means of which the heart and the bowels expand and receive the poison, against which there is afterwards no remedy.

Say not such a one is a drunkard, because you have seen him drunk, for one single act does not constitute a habit. The sun stood still once in favour of the victory of Josue, and was darkened another time in favour of our Saviour, yet none will say that the sun is either motionless or dark. Noah and Lot were once drunk, yet neither the one nor the other was a drunkard; nor was St. Peter bloody-minded, for having once shed blood, nor a blasphemer, though he once blasphemed. To bear the name of a vice or a virtue it must be habitual—one must have made some progress in it. It is, therefore, very wrong to say, such a man is passionate, or a thief, because we have seen him once in a passion or guilty of stealing. Although a man has been a long time vicious, yet we are in danger of belieing him if we call him vicious. Simon the Pharisee called Magdalen a sinner, because she had been one long before, yet he belied her, for she was then no longer a sinner, but a most holy penitent, and therefore our Saviour defended her against him. The vain Pharisee held the humble publican to be a great sinner (Luke, xviii.), or even perhaps an unjust man, an adulterer, an extortioner, but was greatly deceived, for at that very time he was justified. Alas! since the goodness of God is so immense that one moment suffices to obtain and receive his grace, what assurance can we have, that he who was yesterday a sinner is not a saint to-day? The day that is past ought not to judge the present day, nor the present day judge that which is past: it is only the last day that judges all. We can then never say that a man is wicked, without the danger of lying; all that we can say, if we must speak, is, that he did bad actions, or lived ill at such a time, that he does ill at present; but we must never draw consequences from yesterday to to-day, nor from to-day to yesterday, much less to-morrow.

Now, though we must be extremely cautious of speaking ill of our neighbour, yet we must avoid the contrary extreme into which some fall, who, to avoid the sin of detraction, commend and speak well of vice. If a person is indeed a detractor, say not in his excuse that he is a frank and free speaker; if a person be notoriously vain, say not that he is genteel and elegant; never call dangerous familiarities by the name of simple and innocent acts; nor disobedience by the name of zeal; nor arrogance by the name of freedom; nor lasciviousness by the name of friendship. No, Philothea, we must not think to avoid the vice of detraction by favouring, flattering, or cherishing vice; but we must boldly and freely call evil evil, and blame that which is blamable : for in doing this we glorify God, provided we observe the following conditions :

To speak against the vices of another it is necessary we should have the profit, either of him of whom we speak, or of them to whom we speak in view. For instance, when the indiscreet or dangerous familiarities of such or such persons are related in the company of young maids, or the liberties taken by this or that person, in their words or gestures, are plainly immodest; if I do not freely blame the evil, but rather excuse it, those tender souls who hear of it may take occasion to imitate those of whom we speak. Their profit, then, requires that I should freely reprehend these liberties upon the spot, except I could reserve this good office to be done better, and with less prejudice to the persons spoken of on some other occasion.

It is moreover requisite, nay, it is my indispensable duty to speak on the spot, when I am one of the chief of the company, for if I should keep silence, it would look as though I approved of the vice; but if I am one of the least, I must not take upon me to pass censure. But, above all, it is necessary that I should be so exactly just in my words as not to say a single word too much. For example : if I blame the familiarity of this young man, and that young maid, because it is apparently indiscreet and dangerous, I must hold the balance so even as not to make the fault a single grain heavier. Should there be but only a slight appearance, I will call it no more; if but a mere indiscretion, I will give it no worse name; should there be neither indiscretion nor real appearance of evil, but only that from which some malicious spirit may take a pretext to speak ill, I must either say nothing whatever, or say that and no more. My tongue, whilst I am speaking of my neighbour, shall be in my mouth like a knife in the hand of a surgeon, that would cut between the sinews and the tendons. The blow I shall give shall be neither more nor less than the truth. In fine, it must be our principal care in blaming any vice, to spare, as much as possible, the person in whom it is found.

It is true we may speak freely of infamous, public, and notorious sinners, provided it be in the spirit of charity and compassion, and not with arrogance and presumption, nor with the complacency in the evils of others, which is always the part of a mean and abject heart. Amongst all these, the declared enemies of God and his Church, such as the ringleaders amongst heretics and schismatics, must be excepted, since it is charity to cry out against the wolf wherever he is, more especially when he is among the sheep.

Everyone takes the liberty to censure princes, and to speak ill of whole nations, according to the different opinions they hold concerning them. Philothea, avoid this fault; for besides the offence to God, it may bring you into a thousand quarrels.

When you hear anyone spoken ill of, make the accusation doubtful, if you can do it justly; if you cannot, excuse the intention of the party accused; if that cannot be done, express a compassion for him, divert the discourse, remembering yourself, and reminding the company that they who do not fall should return thanks to God ; recall the detractor to himself with meekness, and mention some good action of the party in question, if you know of any.

CHAPTER XXX.

Other counsels touching Discourse.

Let your speech be meek, frank, open, and sincere, without the least mixture of equivocation, artifice, or dissimulation ; for, although it may not be advisable to tell all that is true, yet it is never allowable to speak against the truth. Accustom yourself, therefore, never to tell a deliberate lie, either by way of excuse or otherwise ; remembering always that God is the God of truth. Should you tell a lie unawares, fail not to correct it on the spot by some explanation or reparation : an honest excuse has always more grace and force to bear one harmless than a lie.

Though one may sometimes prudently disguise the truth by some artifice of words, yet it must never be done but when the glory and service of God manifestly require it ; in any other case such artifices are dangerous. "Thy Holy Spirit will have nothing to do with the deceitful." (Wisd. i.) No artifice is so good and desirable as plain dealing : worldly prudence or artifice belongs to the children of the world, but the children of God walk uprightly and their hearts are without guile. "He that walketh sincerely," says the wise man, "walketh confidently" (Prov. x. 9). Lying, double-dealing, and dissimulation are always signs of a weak and mean spirit. St. Augustine has said, in the Fourth Book of his Confessions : "That his soul and that of his friend were but one soul; and that he had a horror of his life after the death of his friend, because he was not willing to live by halves; and yet that, for the same cause he was unwilling to die, lest his friend should die wholly." These words seemed to him afterwards so artificial and affected, that he recalled them, and censured them in his Book of Retractations. Observe, Philothea, the tenderness of that holy soul with respect to the least artifice in his words. Fidelity, plainness, and sincerity of speech are the greatest ornaments of a Christian life. "I will take heed," says David, "of my ways, that I offend not with my tongue" (Ps. xxxviii.); and again: "Set, O Lord, a watch before my mouth, and a door round about my lips." (Ps. cxi.) It was the advice of St. Louis, in order to avoid contention, not to contradict anyone in discourse, unless it were either sinful, or some great prejudice to acquiesce with him; but should it be necessary to contradict, or oppose our own opinion to that of another, we must do it with such mildness and dexterity as not to exasperate his spirit, for nothing is ever gained by harshness and violence.

To speak little (a practice so much recommended by all wise men), is not to be understood that we should utter but few words, but that we should not speak unprofitable words; for in speaking the quantity should not be considered so much as the quality of the words; but, in my opinion, we ought to fly both extremes. For to be too reserved, and to refuse to join in conversation, looks like disdain or a want of confidence; and, on the other hand, constant talking, so that others are not afforded either leisure or opportunity to speak when they desire to do so, is a mark of shallowness and levity.

St. Louis condemned whispering in company, and particularly at table, lest it should give others occasion to suspect that some evil was spoken of them. He said : "He that is at table, in good company, and has something to say that is merry and pleasant, should speak it so that all the company may hear him, but if it be a thing of importance let him keep silent."

CHAPTER XXXI.

Pastimes and Recreations : and first, of such as are lawful and commendable.

It is necessary sometimes to relax our minds as well as our bodies by some kind of recreation. St. John the Evangelist, as Cassian relates, amusing himself one day with a partridge on his hand, was asked by a huntsman : How such a man as he could spend his time in so unprofitable a manner? St. John said to him : Why do you not carry your bow always bent? Because, answered the huntsman, if it were always bent I fear it would lose its spring and become useless. Be not surprised, then, replied the apostle, that I should sometimes remit somewhat of my close application and attention of spirit in order to enjoy a little recreation, that I may afterwards employ myself more fervently in divine contemplation. It is doubtless a vice to be so rigorous and austere, as neither to be willing to take any recreation ourselves, nor allow it to others.

To take the air, to walk, to entertain ourselves with cheerful and friendly conversations, to play on musical instruments, to sing, or to hunt, are recreations so innocent, that in a proper use of them there needs but that common prudence, which gives to everything its due order, time, place, and measures.

Those games in which the gain serves as a recompense for the dexterity and industry of the body or of the mind, such as tennis, ball-playing, chess, backgammon, &c., are recreations in themselves good and lawful: provided that excess, either in the time employed in them, or in stakes played for, is avoided, because if too much time is spent in them, they are no longer an amusement, but an occupation, in which neither the mind nor the body is refreshed, but, on the contrary, stupefied and oppressed. After playing five or six hours at chess the mind is quite fatigued and exhausted. To play long at tennis is not to recreate but to fatigue the body; and if the sum played for is too great the passion for gambling is excited; besides, it is unjust to hazard so much upon abilities of so little importance as those which are exercised at play. But above all, Philothea, take especial care not to set your affections upon these amusements; for how innocent soever any amusements may be, when we set our hearts upon them they become vicious. I do not say that you must take no pleasure whilst at play, for then it would not be recreation; but I say, you must not fix your affection on it, nor amuse yourself too long with it, nor be too eager after it.

CHAPTER XXXII.

Prohibited Games.

Games of dice, cards, and the like, which depend principally upon chance, are not only dangerous recreations, like dances, but evidently bad and reprehensible; hence they have been forbidden by the laws, both ecclesiastical and civil. You will ask, perhaps, what great harm can there be in them? There is: for the gain is not acquired at these games according to reason, but chance, which often falls upon him whose ability and industry deserves nothing; and reason is offended at such a proceeding. But you will say it is according to an agreement entered into by the persons concerned. That serves, indeed, to show that the winner does no wrong to the loser, but it justifies neither the agreement nor the game : for the gain which ought to be the recompense of industry is made the reward of chance, which deserves none whatever, since it in no way depends upon us. Besides, although these games bear the name of recreations, yet they are by no means recreations, but tiresome occupations; for is it not tiresome to keep the mind incessantly occupied, intent to a high degree, and annoyed by perpetual apprehensions and solicitudes? Can there be any attention more painful, gloomy, and melancholy than that of gamesters? You must neither speak, laugh, nor cough, whilst they are at play, for fear of giving them offence. In fact, they feel no joy at play but when they win: and is not that joy iniquitous, which can only be caused by the loss and displeasure of a friend or companion. Surely such satisfaction is infamous. For these three reasons this species of gaming is prohibited.

St. Louis, on hearing that the Count of Anjou, his brother, and Monsier Gautier de Nemours, were gaming, arose from his sick-bed, went staggering to their chamber, and cast the tables, the dice, and part of the money out at the window into the sea, and was very angry with them. The holy and chaste damsel Sara, addressing God in prayer, brings forward this argument of her innocence: "Thou knowest, O Lord, that I have never joined myself with them that play." (Tob. iii.)

CHAPTER XXXIII.

Balls and Pastimes which are lawful, but dangerous.

Although balls and dancing are recreations in their nature indifferent, yet according to the ordinary manner in which they are conducted they preponderate very much on the side of evil, and are consequently extremely dangerous. Being generally carried on at night, it is by no means surprising that several vicious circumstances should obtain easy admittance, since the subject is of itself so susceptible of evil. The lovers of these diversions, by sitting up late at night, disable themselves from discharging their duty to God on the morning of the day following. Is it not, then, a kind of madness to turn day into night, light into darkness, and good works into criminal fooleries? Everyone strives who shall carry most vanity to the ball; and vanity is so congenial, as well to evil affections as to dangerous familiarities, that both are easily engendered by dancing.

I have the same opinion of dancing, Philothea, as physicians have of mushrooms, that the best of them, in their opinion, are good for nothing; so I tell you the best ordered balls are good for nothing. If, nevertheless, you must eat mushrooms, be sure they are well cooked. If, upon some occasions which you cannot well avoid, you must go to a ball, see that your dancing is properly guarded. But you will ask me how must it be guarded? I answer, by modesty, dignity, and a good intention. Eat but sparingly and seldom of mushrooms, physicians say, for, be they ever so well cooked, the quantity makes them poisonous : dance but little, and very seldom, I say, lest otherwise you put yourself in danger of contracting an affection for it.

14

Mushrooms, according to Pliny, being spongy and porus, easily attract infection to themselves from the things that are about them; so that being near serpents and toads they imbibe their venom. Balls, dancing, and other nocturnal meetings, ordinarily attract together the reigning vices and sins, namely, quarrels, envy, scoffing, and impurity; and, as these exercises open the pores of the bodies of those that practise them, so they also open the pores of their souls, and expose them to the danger of some serpent, taking advantage therefrom to breathe some loose words or immodest suggestions into the ear, or of some basilisk casting an impure look or glance into the heart, which being thus opened, is easily seized upon and poisoned. O Philothea, these idle recreations are ordinarily very dangerous; they chase away the spirit of devotion, and leave the soul in a languishing condition; they cool the fervour of charity; and excite a thousand evil affections in the soul, and therefore they ought not to be used but with the greatest caution.

But physicians say that after mushrooms we must drink good wine; and I say that after dancing it is necessary to refresh our souls with some good and holy considerations, to prevent the baneful effects of these dangerous impressions which the vain pleasure taken in it may have left in our minds.

1. Consider that during the time you were at the ball innumerable souls were burning in the flames of hell for the sins they had committed at dancing, or which were occasioned by it. 2. That many religious and devout persons of both sexes were at that very time in the presence of God, singing his praises, and contemplating his divine goodness. Ah! how much more profitable was their time employed than yours! 3. That whilst you were dancing many souls departed out of this world in great

anguish, and that thousands and thousands of men and women then suffered great pain in their beds, in hospitals, in the streets, from burning fevers, and other diseases. Alas! they have no rest, and will you have no compassion for them? and do you not think that you may some day groan as they did, whilst others dance as you did? 4. That our Blessed Saviour, his Virgin Mother, the angels and saints, beheld you at the ball. Ah, how greatly did they pity you, seeing your heart pleased with so vain an amusement, and taken up with such childish toys! 5. Alas! whilst you were there, time was passing away, and death was approaching nearer: behold how he mocks you, and invites you to his dance, in which the groans of your friends shall serve for the music, and where you shall make but one step from this life to the next. The dance of death is, alas! the true pastime of mortals, since by it we instantly pass from the vain amusements of this world to the eternal pleasures or pains of the next.

I have set down these little considerations for you; God will suggest to you many more to the like effect, provided you fear Him.

CHAPTER XXXIV.

At what time we may play or dance.

In order that playing and dancing may be lawful, we must use them by way of recreation, without having any affection for them; we may use them for a short time, but not till we are wearied or stupefied by them; and we must use them but seldom, lest we should otherwise turn a recreation into an occupation. But on what occasions may we lawfully play and dance? Lawful occasions for ir

nocent games are frequent, whilst those for games
of chance are rare, on account of their being more
blamable and dangerous; therefore, in one word,
dance and play as your own prudence and discretion may direct you to comply with the requests of
the company in which you are; for condescension, as
a branch of charity, makes indifferent things good,
and even dangerous things allowable; it even takes
away the harm from those things that are, in some
measure, evil; and therefore games of hazard, which
otherwise would be reprehensible, are not so, if we
use them sometimes by a just condescension.

I was very much pleased to read, in the Life of St.
Charles Borromeo, how he yielded to the Swiss in
certain things, in which otherwise he was very strict;
and that St. Ignatius of Loyola, being invited to play,
did not refuse. As to St. Elizabeth of Hungary,
she played and danced sometimes, when she was
present at assemblies of recreation, without any prejudice to her devotion; for devotion was so deep in
her soul, that her devotion increased amongst the
pomps and vanities to which her condition exposed
her. Great fires increase by the wind, but little
ones are soon blown out, if they are not well pro-
tected.

CHAPTER XXXV.

*We must be faithful both on great and small
occasions.*

The sacred Spouse in the Canticles, says: "That
his spouse has wounded his heart with one of her
eyes, and one of the hairs of her neck" (chap. iv. 9).
Now, among all the exterior parts of the human
body none is more noble, either for its construction
or activity, than the eye, and none more mean than

the hair. Wherefore the Divine Spouse would give us to understand that He is pleased to accept not only the great works of devout persons, but also the least and most trivial; and that to serve Him according to his liking, we must take care to serve Him well, not only in great and high things, but in those that are small and low, as we can both by the one and the other wound his heart with love.

Prepare yourself, then, Philothea, to suffer many great afflictions, even martyrdom itself, for our Lord; resolve to surrender to Him whatever is most dear to you, when it shall please Him to take it: father, mother, husband, wife, children, brother, sister, nay, even your eyes, or your life; for all these sacrifices you ought to prepare your heart. But as long as God does not send you afflictions so sensible or so great, since He requires not your eyes, give Him at least your hair. I mean, suffer meekly these small injuries, little inconveniences, and inconsiderable losses which daily befall you; for, by means of such little occasions as these, managed with love and affection, you shall engage his heart entirely, and make it all your own. Little daily charities, a headache, a toothache, or a cold; the bad humour of a husband or a wife; the breaking of a glass, contempt or scorn; the loss of a pair of gloves, of a ring, or of a handkerchief; little inconveniences to which we put ourselves by going too soon to bed, and rising early to pray or communicate; that little bashfulness we feel in doing certain acts of devotion in public; in short, all these trivial sufferings being accepted and embraced with love, are highly pleasing to the Divine Goodness, who for a cup of cold water only has promised a throne of felicity to his faithful servants. Therefore, as these occasions present themselves every moment, the good management of them will be a great means to heap u· score of spiritual riches.

When I saw in the Life of St. Catherine of Sienna her many raptures and elevations of spirit, her many words of wisdom, nay, even sermons uttered by her, I doubted not but that, with the eye of contemplation, she had ravished the heart of her Heavenly Spouse. But I was no less comforted when I found her in her father's kitchen, humbly turning the spit, blowing the fire, dressing the meat, kneading the bread, and doing the meanest offices of the house with a courage full of love and affection for her God; for I esteem no less the little and humble meditation she made amongst these mean and abject employments, than the ecstasies and raptures she so often had, which, perhaps, were given her only in recompense of her humility and abjection. Her manner of meditating was as follows: Whilst she was dressing meat for her father she imagined that she was preparing it for our Saviour, like another St. Martha, and that her mother held the place of Our Blessed Lady, and her brothers that of the apostles: exciting herself in this manner to serve the whole court of heaven in spirit, whilst she employed herself with great delight in these low services, because she knew such was the will of God. I have produced this example, Philothea, in order that you may know of what importance it is to direct all your actions, be they ever so mean, with a pure intent to the service of God's Divine Majesty.

Therefore, I earnestly advise you to imitate the valiant woman, whom the great Solomon so highly commends: "She put out her hand," as he says, "to strong things," that is, to high, generous, and important things, and yet disdained not to take hold of the spindle (xxxi.) Put out your hand to strong things, exercise yourself in prayer and meditation, in frequenting the sacraments, in exciting souls to the love of God, and in infusing good inspirations into their hearts, and, in a word, in the performance of great and important works, according to your vocation; but never forget your distaff or spindle, or, in other words, take care to practise those low and humble virtues, which grow like flowers at the foot of the cross, such as serving the poor, visiting the sick, taking care of your family, and attending to all your domestic concerns with that profitable diligence which will not suffer you to be idle : and amidst all these occupations mingle considerations similar to those which I have related above of St Catherine.

Great occasions of serving God present themselves but seldom, but little ones frequently. " Now he that shall be faithful in small matters," says our Saviour, " shall be set over great things." Perform all things, then, in the name of God, and you will do all things well : whether you eat, drink, sleep, recreate yourself, or turn the spit, provided you know how to refer all your actions to God, you will profit much in the sight of his Divine Majesty,

CHAPTER XXXVI.

How to keep your mind just and reasonable.

It is reason that makes us men, and yet it is a rare thing to find men truly reasonable, because self-love turns us away from the paths of reason, leading us insensibly to a thousand small, yet dangerous injustices and partialities, which, like the little foxes spoken of in the Canticles, destroy the vines ; for, because they are little we take no notice of them ; but, because they are great in number, they fail not to hurt us very much.

Are not those things of which I am about to speak unjust and unreasonable ? We cond-

every little thing in our neighbours, and excuse ourselves in things that are great—we want to sell very dear and to buy very cheap; we desire that justice should be executed in another man's house, but that there should be mercy and connivance in our own; we would have everything we say taken in good part, but we are delicate and touchy with regard to what others say of us; we would have our neighbour to sell us his goods, but is it not more reasonable that he should keep his goods if he prefers to do so? We take it ill that he will not yield to our requirements; but has he not more reason to be offended that we should expect him to do so?

If we love one particular exercise we despise all others, and set ourselves against everything that is not according to our own taste. If there is any one of our inferiors who has not a good grace, or to whom we have once taken a dislike, do what he will we take it in ill part, we cease not on every occasion to mortify him, and find fault with all he does. On the contrary, if anyone is agreeable to us, by a behaviour pleasing to our mind, he can do nothing that we are not willing to excuse. There are some virtuous children whom their parents can scarcely bear to see, on account of some bodily imperfections, and there are vicious children who are favourites for some beauty or gracefulness. On all occasions we prefer the rich to the poor. Although one person is neither of better condition, nor more virtuous than another, we prefer him because he is the best clad. We desire to have debts due to us paid punctually, but would have others to be gentle in demanding theirs: we keep our own rank with precision, but would have others humble and condescending: we complain easily of our neighbour, but none must complain of us: what we do for others seems always very considerable, but what others do for us seems as nothing. In a word, we are like the partridges in Paphlagonia, which are said to have two hearts; for we have one heart mild, favourable, and courteous towards ourselves, and another hard, severe, and rigorous towards our neighbour. We have two balances, one to weigh out to our own advantage, and the other to weigh in to the detriment of our neighbour. " Deceitful hearts," says the Scriptures (Ps. xi. 3.), "have spoken with a double heart," namely, two hearts; and to have two weights, the one greater by which we receive, and the other less, by which we deliver out, is an abominable thing in the sight of God (Deut. xxv. 13).

Philothea, in order to perform all your actions with equity and justice, you must exchange situations with your neighbour: imagine yourself the seller whilst you are buying, and the buyer whilst you are selling, and thus you will sell and buy according to equity and justice; for although small injustices that exceed not the limits of rigour, in selling to our advantage may not oblige to restitution; yet, being defects, contrary to reason and charity, we are certainly obliged to correct and amend them; at the best, they are nothing but mere illusions; for, believe me, a man of a generous, just, and courteous disposition is never on the losing side. Neglect not then, Philothea, frequently to examine whether your heart is such with respect to your neighbour as you would have his to be in respect to you, were you in his situation; for this is the touchstone of true reason. Trajan, being blamed by his confidants for making the imperial majesty, as they thought, too accessible, asked: "Ought I not then be such an emperor towards my subjects as I would desire an emperor to be towards me, were I myself a private individual?

CHAPTER XXXVII.

Desires.

Everyone knows that we are obliged to refrain from the desires of vicious things, since even the desire of evil is of itself criminal : but I tell you, moreover, Philothea, you must not be anxious about balls, plays, or such like diversions, nor covet honours and offices, nor yet visions and ecstasies, for there is a great deal of danger and deceit in such vanities. Desire not that which is at a great distance, nor that which cannot happen for a long time, as many do, who by this means weary and distract their hearts unprofitably. If a young man earnestly desires to be settled in some office before the proper time, what does all his anxiety avail him? If a married woman desires to be a nun, to what purpose? If I desire to buy my neighbour's goods before he is willing to sell them, is it not loss of time to entertain such a desire? If, while sick, I desire to preach, to celebrate Mass, to visit others that are sick, and perform the exercises of those who are in health ; are not all these desires vain, since it is out of my power to put them in execution? Yet, in the meantime, these unprofitable desires occupy the place of the virtues of patience, resignation, mortification, obedience, and meekness under sufferings, which are what God would have me practise at that time.

I can by no means approve of persons desiring to amuse themselves in any other kind of life than that in which they are already engaged ; nor in any exercises that are incompatible with their present conditions ; for this distracts the heart, and makes it unfit for its necessary occupations. If I desire to practise the solitude of a Carthusian, I lose my time ;

and this desire occupies the place of that, which I ought to have, of employing myself well in my present office; no, I would not that anyone should even desire to have a better wit or judgment than what he is already possessed of, for these desires answer no purpose, and only occupy the place of that which everyone ought to have, of cultivating the talents which he inherits from nature; nor would I have anyone desire those means to serve God which he has not, but rather diligently employ those which he has. Now, this is to be understood only of desires which totally occupy the heart; for, as to simple wishes, if they be not too frequent, they do no harm whatsoever.

Do not desire crosses, except in proportion to the patience wherewith you have supported those which have been already sent you; for it is presumptuous to desire martyrdom, and not to have the courage to bear an injury. The enemy often suggests a great desire of things that are absent, and which never shall come to pass, that so he may divert our mind from present objects, from which, however trivial they may be, we might obtain considerable profit to ourselves. We fight with the monsters in Africa in imagination, and in the meantime, for want of attention, we suffer ourselves to be killed by some insignificant reptile that lies in our way. Desire not temptations, for that would be rashness; but accustom your heart to expect them courageously, and to defend yourself against them when they come.

A variety of food, taken in any considerable quantity, overloads the stomach, and if it is weak destroys it: overcharge not then your soul, neither with a multitude of worldly desires, which may end in your ruin, nor even with such as are spiritual, as they are apt to beget distractions. When the purified soul finds herself freed from bad inclinations she feels a craving after spiritual things, and as one famished she longs for a variety of exercises of piety, mortification, penance, humility, charity, and prayer. Philothea, it is a good sign of health to have a keen appetite; but you must consider whether you can digest all that you would eat. Amongst so many desires, choose, then, by the advice of your spiritual director, such as you may execute at present, and turn them to the best advantage afterwards; God will send you others, which you must also practise in their proper season, and thus you will never lose your time in unprofitable desires, but bring them all forth in good order; but as to those that cannot be immediately executed, they should be locked up in some corner of the heart till their time comes. This advice I not only give to spiritual persons, but also to those in the world; for without attending to it, there would be no living without anxiety and confusion.

CHAPTER XXXVIII.

Instructions for Married People.

"Matrimony is a great sacrament, but I speak in Christ, and in the Church." (Eph. v. 32). It is honourable to all, in all, and through all: that is, in all its parts to all; because even virgins ought to honour it with humility; in all, because it is equally holy in the rich and poor; through all, because its origin, its end, its advantages, its form, and its matter, are all holy. It is the nursery of Christianity, that supplies the earth with fruitful souls, to complete the number of the elect in heaven; in a word, the conservation of marriage is of the last importance to the commonwealth, for it is the origin and source of all its streams.

Above all things, I exhort married people to that mutual love which the Holy Ghost so much recommends in the Scriptures. Oh, you that are married, it is unnecessary to tell you to love each other with a mutual love, like turtle doves; nor to say, love one another with a human love like heathens; but I say to you, after the great Apostle: "Husbands, love your wives, as Christ has loved his Church. And you, wives, love your husbands, as the Church loveth her Saviour." (Eph. v.) It was God that brought Eve to our first father Adam, and gave her to him as his wife; it is also God, O my friends, who with his invisible hand, has tied the knot of the holy bond of your marriage, and given you to one another; why do y .u not then cherish each other with a holy, sacre l, and divine love?

The first effect of this love is an indissoluble union of your hearts. Two pieces of fir glued together, if the glue be good, cleave so fast one to the other, that you may sooner break the piece in any other place than that wherein they are joined. But God joins the husband to the wife with his own blood; for which cause this union is so strong that the soul must sooner separate from the body of the one or the other than the husband from the wife. Now this union is not understood principally of the body, but of the heart, and of the affections.

The second effect of this love ought to be the inviolable fidelity of the one to the other-party. Seals were anciently graven upon rings worn on the fingers, as the Holy Scripture itself testifies. Behold, then, the mystery of this ceremony in marriage. The Church, which by the hand of the priest, blesses a ring, and giving it first to the man, testifies that she puts a seal upon his heart by this sacrament, to the end that henceforward neither the name nor the love of any other woman may enter therein so long as she shall live, who has been given to him; afterwards the bridegroom puts the ring on the hand of the bride that she reciprocally may understand that her heart must never admit an affection for any other man, so long as he shall live upon earth, whom our Lord here gives to her as a husband.

The third fruit of marriage is the lawful production and education of children. It is a great honour to you that are married, that God, designing to multiply souls, which may bless and praise Him to all eternity, makes you co-operate with Him in so noble a work, by the production of the bodies into which He infuses immortal souls, like heavenly drops, as He creates them.

Preserve, then, O husbands, a tender, constant, and heartfelt love for your wives; for the woman was taken from that side of the first man which was nearest to his heart, to the end she might be loved tenderly by him. The weaknesses and infirmities of your wives, whether in body or mind, ought never to provoke you to any kind of disdain, but rather to a sweet and an affectionate compassion; since God has created them such, to the end that, depending upon you, you should receive from them more honour and respect, and that you should have them in such a manner for your companions, that nevertheless, you should be their heads and superiors. And you, O wives, love the husbands whom God has given you tenderly and cordially, but with a respectful love, and full of reverence, for therefore, indeed, did God create them of a sex more vigorous and predominant; and was pleased to ordain that the woman should depend upon the man, being a bone of is bone, and flesh of his flesh, and that she should made of a rib taken from under his arm, to show that she ought to be under the hand and guidance of her husband. The holy Scripture, which strictly recommends to you this subjection, renders it also pleasant, not only by prescribing that you should accommodate yourselves to it with love, but also by commanding your husbands to exercise it over you with charity, tenderness, and complacency: "Husbands," says St. Peter, "behave yourselves discreetly towards wives, as the weaker vessels, giving honour to them" (1 Epist. iii. 7).

But while I exhort you to advance more and more in this mutual love which you owe to one another, beware lest it degenerate into any kind of jealousy; for it often happens, that as the worm is bred in the apple which is most delicate and ripe, so jealousy grows in that love of married people, which is the most ardent and exacting, but of which, nevertheless, it spoils and corrupts the substance; breeding, by insensible degrees, strifes, dissensions, and separations. But jealousy never comes where the friendship on both sides is grounded on solid virtue, and therefore where it enters, it is an infallible mark that the love is in some degree sensual and gross, and has fallen upon a subject where it has met with but an imperfect and inconstant virtue, subject to distrust. It is then a stupid ostentation of friendship to try to exalt it by jealousy; for jealousy may be a sign of the greatness and grossness of the friendship, but never of its goodness, purity, and perfection; since the perfection of friendship presupposes an assurance of the virtue of those whom we love, and jealousy a doubt of it.

If you desire, O husbands, that your wives should be faithful to you, give them a lesson by your example. "With what face," says St. Gregory of Nazianzen, "can you exact purity from your wives when you yourselves live in impurity? How can you require of them that which you give them not ? If you would have them chaste, behave yourselves chastely towards them." And, as St. Paul says: "Let every man know how to possess his own vessel in holiness." But if, on the contrary, you yourselves teach them not to be virtuous, it is no wonder if you are disgraced by their fall. But you, O wives, whose honour is inseparably joined with purity and modesty, be zealous to preserve this your glory, and suffer no kind of loose behaviour to tarnish the whiteness of your reputation. Fear all kinds of assaults, be they ever so small ; never suffer any wanton address to come near you : whosoever praises your beauty, or your genteel behaviour, ought to be suspected, tor he who praises the ware which he cannot buy is strongly tempted to steal it ; but if to your praise he adds the dispraise of your husband, he offers you a heinous injury ; for it is evident that he not only has a mind to ruin you, but accounts you already half lost, since the bargain is half made with the second merchant, when one is disgusted with the first.

Ladies, formerly as well as now, were accustomed to wear a number of pearls on their ears, for the pleasure, says Pliny, of the jingling which they make in touching one another. But for my part, as I know that the great friend of God, Isaac, sent earrings as the first earnest of his love to the chaste Rebecca, I believe that this mysterious ornament signifies, that the first part of his wife which a husband should take possession of, and which his wife should faithfully keep for him, is her ears: to the end that no language or noise should enter there, but the sweet and amiable music of chaste and pure words, which are the Oriental pearls of the Gospel ; for we must always remember that souls are poisoned by the ear, as the body is by the nouth.

Love and fidelity joined together, beget always familiarity and confidence : and therefore the saints have used many reciprocal caresses in their marriage, but always pure, tender, and sincere. Thus Isaac and Rebecca, the most chaste married couple of ancient times, were seen through a window caressing one another (Gen. xxvi. 8), in such a manner that, although there was no immodesty, Abimelech was convinced that they could be no other than man and wife. The great St. Louis, equally rigorous to his own flesh, and tender in the love of his wife, was almost blamed for the abundance of caresses, though, indeed, he rather deserved praise for being able to bring his martial and courageous spirit to stoop to these little offices, requisite to the conservation of conjugal love; for, although these little demonstrations of pure and free affection bind not their hearts, yet they bring them near one another, and serve for an agreeable disposition of mutual conversation.

St. Monica, before the birth of the great St. Augustine, dedicated him by frequent oblations to the Christian religion, and to the service and glory of God, as he himself witnesses, saying: "That he hath already tasted the salt of God in his mother's womb." This is a great lesson for Christian women to offer up to his Divine Majesty the fruit of their wombs, even before they come into the world; for God, who accepts the offerings of an humble and willing heart, commonly at that time seconds the affections of mothers; witness Samuel, St. Thomas of Aquin, St. Andrew of Fiesola, and divers others. The mother of St. Bernard, a mother worthy of such a son, as soon as her children were born, took them in her arms, and offered them up to Jesus Christ, and from thenceforward loved them with respect, as things consecrated and entrusted to her by God;

which succeeded so happily to her, that in the end the
whole seven became very holy.   But when children
begin to have the use of reason both their fathers and
mothers ought to take great care to imprint the fear
of God in their hearts.   The good Queen Blanche
performed this office fervently with regard to the
king, St. Louis her son; she often said to him: I
had much rather, my dear child, see you die before
my eyes, than see you commit even one mortal sin;
which caution remained so deeply engraved on his
soul, that, as he himself related, not one day of his
life passed in which he did not remember it, and
take all possible care strictly to observe it.   Families
and generations in our language, are called houses;
and even the Hebrews called the generations of children the building up of a house; for it is in this sense
it is said that God built houses for the midwives of
Egypt.   Now, this is to show that the raising of a
house or family, consists not in storing up a quantity
of worldly goods, but in the good education of children in the fear of God, and in virtue, in which no
pains or labours ought to be spared, for children are
the crown of their parents.   Thus, St. Monica, with
so much fervour and constancy, fought against the
evil inclinations of her son, St. Augustine, that having followed him by sea and land, she made him more
happily the child of her tears, by the conversion of
soul, than he had been of her blood by the genera-
tion of his body.

St. Paul leaves to wives the care of the household,
as their portion; for which reason many think, with
truth, that their devotion is more profitable to the
family than that of the husband, who, not residing
so constantly amongst the domestics, cannot consequently so easily frame them to virtue.   On this
consideration Solomon (Prov. xxxi.), makes the happiness of the whole household to depend on the care

and industry of the valiant woman whom he describes.

It is said in Genesis (chap. xxv. 21), that Isaac seeing his wife Rebecca barren, prayed to the Lord for her, or, according to the Hebrew, prayed to the Lord over against her, because the one prayed on the one side of the oratory, and the other on the other; so the prayer of the husband, made in this manner, was heard. Such union as this of the husband and wife, in holy devotion, is the greatest and most fruitful of all; and to this they ought mutually to encourage and to draw each other. There are fruits like the quince, which on account of the harshness of their juice, are not agreeable except when they are preserved with sugar; there are others, which, because of their tenderness cannot be long kept, unless they are preserved in like manner, such as cherries and apricots; thus wives ought to wish that their husbands should be preserved with the sugar of devotion; for a man without devotion is a kind of animal, severe, harsh, and rough. And husbands ought to wish that their wives should be devout, because without devotion a woman is very frail, and subject to fall from, or to become weak in virtue. St. Paul says: "That the unbelieving husband is sanctified by the believing wife, and the unbeliving wife by the believing husband;" because, in this strict alliance of marriage, the one may draw the other to virtue; but what a blessing is it, when the man and wife being both believers, sanctify each other in the true fear of God.

As to the rest: the mutual bearing with one another ought to be so great, that they should never be both angry with each other at the same time, nor suddenly, to the end that there should never be a division or contention seen between them. Bees cannot stay in a place where there are echoes, loud sounds, or voices : nor can the Holy Ghost remain in a house where there are sounds of clamour, strife, and contradictions. St. Gregory Nazianzen relates that in his time married people made a feast on the anniversary day of their wedding. For my part, I should approve of introducing this custom, provided it were not attended with worldly and sensual recreations ; but that the husband and wife should confess and communicate on that day, and recommend to God with more than ordinary fervour the happy progress of their marriage ; renewing their good purposes to sanctify it still more and more by mutual love and fidelity, and recovering breath, as it were, in our Lord, for the better supporting the burdens of their calling.

CHAPTER XXXIX.

Instructions for Widows.

St. Paul instructs all prelates in the person of Timothy, saying: "Honour widows that are widows indeed " (1 Tim. v. 3). Now, to be a widow indeed, the following things are required :

1. That the widow be not only a widow in body, but in heart also ; that is, that she make an inviolable resolution to keep herself in a state of chaste widowhood ; for those that are only widows till an opportunity presents itself of being married again, are still joined to men, according to the will of the heart. But if she that is a widow indeed, in order to confirm herself in the state of widowhood, will offer her body and her chastity by vow to God, she adds a great ornament to her widowhood, and gives great security to her resolution ; for since, after her vow, she has it no longer in her power to quit her

chastity without giving up her title to heaven, she
will be so jealous of her design, that she will not
suffer even the least thought of marriage to occupy
her heart for a single moment; so that this sacred
vow will serve as a strong barrier between her soul
and all manner of projects contrary to her resolution. St. Augustine advises this vow very strenuously to the Christian widow; and the ancient and
learned Origen goes much farther, for he exhorts
married women to vow and dedicate themselves to a
chaste widowhood, in case their husbands die before
them; to the end that, amidst the sensual pleasures
of marriage, they may also, by means of this anti-
cipated promise, enjoy the merit of a chaste widowhood. A vow not only makes the good works done
in consequence thereof more acceptable to God, but
also encourages us to put them into execution; it
gives to God not only the good works which are the
fruits of our good will, but dedicates likewise to
Him the will itself, which is the tree of all our
actions. By simple chastity we lend, as it were,
our body to God, retaining, notwithstanding, a
liberty to subject it another day to sensual pleasures, but by the vow of chastity we make Him an
absolute and irrevocable gift of it, without reserving
to ourselves any power of recalling it, and thus happily render ourselves bond-slaves to Him, whose
bondage is better than any kingdoms. Now, as I
highly approve of the advice of those two great persons, so I should wish that those souls which are so
happy as to desire to follow it, should do it prudently, holily, and solidly, having first well examined
their resolutions, invoked the light and grace of
heaven, and taken the advice of some wise and devout director : by this means all will be done with
more fruit.

2. Moreover, this renunciation of second marriage

must be done with the simple intent of turning all the affections of the soul towards God, and of joining the heart on every side with that of his Divine Majesty; for if the desire to leave her children rich, or any other worldly consideration, should keep the widow in the state of widowhood, she may perhaps have praise for it, but certainly not before God; for in the eyes of God nothing can truly merit praise but that which is done for his sake.

3. Moreover, the widow that would be a widow indeed, must voluntarily separate and restrain herself from profane satisfactions: "For she that liveth in pleasures is dead while she is living" (1 Tim. v. 6). To desire to be a widow, and to be nevertheless pleased with being courted, flattered, and caressed; to be fond of balls, dancing, and feasting; to be perfumed, finely dressed, &c., is to be a widow, living as to the body, but dead as to the soul. The widow, then, who lives in these fond delights, is dead while she lives, and therefore, properly speaking, she is but a semblance of widowhood.

"The time for pruning is come, the voice of the turtle hath been heard in our land," says the Canticle. All who would live devoutly must prune and cut away all worldly superfluities. But this is more particularly necessary for the true widow, who like a chaste turtle-dove comes fresh from weeping, bewailing, and lamenting the loss of her husband. When Noemi returned from Moab to Bethlehem, the women of the town who had known her when she was first married, said one to another: "Is not that Noemi?" (Ruth, i. 20.) "But she answered, Call me not Noemi, I pray you, for Noemi signifies comely and beautiful; but call me Mara, for the Lord hath filled my soul with bitterness:" this she said on account of having lost her husband. Even so the devout widow never desires to be esteemed either beautiful or comely, contenting herself with being such as God will have her to be, that is to say, humble and abject in her own eyes.

As lamps that are fed with aromatic oil cast a more sweet smell when their flame is put out, so widows whose love has been pure in their marriage, send forth a more sweet perfume of virtue and chastity, when their light, namely, their husband, is extinguished by death. To love the husband as long as he lives is an ordinary thing among women; but to love him so well, that after his death she will hear of no other, is a degree of love which appertains only to those that are widows indeed. To hope in God, whilst the husband serves as a support, is a thing not so rare; but to hope in God, when one is destitute of this support, is a thing worthy of great praise. Therefore it is more easy to know, in widowhood, the perfection of the virtues which a woman had during her married life.

The widow that has children, who stand in need of her assistance and guidance, principally in what relates to their soul and their establishment in life, ought not on any account abandon them; for the Apostle Paul says clearly, that they are obliged to take care of their children, that they may make a like return to their parents (Tim. ii. 1), and those who have no solicitude for those that belong to them, and especially for their own family, are worse than infidels. But if the children are in such a state as to stand in no need of her guidance, then the widow should gather together all her affections and thoughts, to apply them more purely to her own advancement in the love of God.

If some absolute necessity does not oblige the conscience of the true widow to external troubles, such as lawsuits, I counsel her to avoid them altogether, and to follow that method in managing her affairs which appears the most peaceable and quiet, although it may not seem the most advantageous. For the advantages to be reaped from worldly troubles must be very great, if they are to bear any comparison with the happiness of a holy tranquillity. Moreover, disputes and lawsuits distract the heart, and often open a gate to the enemies of the soul, while to please those whose favour they stand in need of, they are forced to adopt such behaviour as is neither suitable to devotion, nor pleasing to God.

Let prayer be the widow's continual exercise; for seeing that she ought now to have no other love but for God, she should, by the same rule, have scarcely any words but for God. Her heart, which could not well give itself up entirely to God, nor follow the attraction of his divine love, during the life of her husband, ought immediately after his death to run ardently after the sweet odour of the heavenly perfumes, saying, in imitation of the heavenly Spouse: O Lord, now that I am all my own, receive me so that 1 may be all thine: "Draw me after Thee, we will run after the odour of thy ointment."

The virtues proper for the exercise of a holy widow, are perfect modesty, a renunciation of honours, ranks, assemblies, titles, and of all such vanities; serving the poor and sick, comforting the afflicted, instructing girls in a devout life, and making themselves perfect patterns of all virtues to young women. Cleanliness and plainness should be the ornaments of their dress; humility and charity the ornaments of their actions; courtesy and mildness the ornaments of their speech; modesty and purity the ornaments of their eyes; and Jesus Christ crucified the only love of their heart. In fine, the true widow should be in the Church like a little violet of March, and send forth an incomparable sweetness by the odour of her devotion, and almost always keep herself concealed under the broad leaves of her humility; since by her dress, rather dark than bright in colour, she testifies her mortification. She grows in cool and uncultivated places, not willing to be importuned with the conversation of worldlings, the better to preserve the coolness of her heart against all the heats which the desire of riches, of honours, or even of vain love might bring upon her. "She shall be blessed," says the holy apostle, "if she continue in this manner" (1 Cor. vii. 8).

I could say a great many other things upon this subject; but I shall have said enough in advising the widow who is solicitous for the honour of her condition to read attentively the excellent epistles which the great St. Jerome wrote to Furia, to Salvia, and to other ladies who were so happy as to be the spiritual children of so great a father; for nothing can be added to that which he says, except this one admonition—that the true widow ought never to blame or censure those who marry a second, or even a third or fourth time; for in some cases God so disposes with regard to them for his greater glory; and that she must always have before her eyes this doctrine of the ancients, that neither widowhood nor virginity have any place or rank in heaven but that which is assigned to them by humility.

CHAPTER XL.

A Word to Virgins.

O virgins, I have only three words to say to you, for the rest you will find elsewhere. If you pretend to a temporal marriage, be careful to keep your first love for your first husband. In my opinion, it is a great deceit to present, instead of an entire and sincere heart, a heart quite worn away, spoiled, and tired out in love. But if your happiness calls you to the pure and virginal espousals of Christ, and that you desire to preserve for ever your virginity, in the name of God, keep your love with all possible diligence for your Divine Spouse, who, being purity itself, loves nothing so much as purity, and to whom are due the first-fruits of all things, but principally those of our love. St. Jerome's epistles will furnish you with all advice necessary for you ; and as your condition obliges you to obedience, choose a guide, under whose direction you may, in a more holy manner, dedicate your heart and body to his Divine Majesty.

PART THE FOURTH.

CONTAINING

NECESSARY ADVICE AGAINST THE MOST ORDINARY TEMPTATIONS.

CHAPTER I.

We must not concern ourselves about what the children of the world may say.

As soon as worldlings perceive that you desire to follow a devout life, they will discharge arrows of mockery and detraction against you without number. The most malicious will attribute your change to hypocrisy, bigotry, or artifice. They will say that, being frowned upon and rejected by the world, you are now having recourse to God. Your friends will make a thousand remonstrances which they imagine to be very wise and charitable. They will say that you will fall into a state of melancholy, that you will lose your credit in the world, and make yourself insupportable; that you will grow old before your time; that your domestic affairs will suffer; that you must live in the world, like one in the world; that salvation may be gained without so many mysteries; and a thousand like impertinences.

Dear Philothea, what is all this but foolish and empty babbling? These people have no concern for your health or for your affairs. "If you were of the world," says our Saviour, "the world would

its own ; but because you are not of the world, there·
fore the world hateth you" (John, xv. 19). We have
seen gentlemen and ladies pass the whole night, nay,
many nights together, at chess or cards ; and can
there be any occupation more absurd, stupid, or
gloomy than that of gamesters ? and yet worldlings
say not a word, nor do friends ever trouble themselves about them ; but should they spend an hour
in meditation, or rise in the morning a little earlier
than usual, to prepare themselves for communion,
everyone would run to the physician to cure them
of their hypochondria.   You may pass thirty nights
in dancing and no person will complain of it, but for
watching during only one Christmas night everyone
coughs, and complains that he is sick the next morning.   Who sees not that the world is an unjust
judge, gracious and favourable to its own children,
but harsh and rigorous towards the children of God ?
   We can never be well with the world without
losing ourselves with the world : it is so fantastical
that it is impossible to content it.   "John the
Baptist came neither eating bread nor drinking
wine," says our Saviour, "and you say he hath a
devil: the Son of Man is come eating and drinking,
and you say, Behold a man that is a glutton, and a
drinker of wine" (Luke, vii. 33).   It is the truth,
Philothea, if through condescension to the world we
take the liberty to laugh, play, or dance, the world
will be scandalised at us ; and if we do not, it will
accuse us of hypocrisy and melancholy.   If we adorn
ourselves, the world will interpret it to be done for
some ill end ; if we neglect our dress, it will impute
it either to meanness or avarice.   Our mirth will be
termed dissoluteness ; and our mortification sullen-
ness : and as it thus looks upon us with an evil eye,
we can never be agreeable to it.   It aggravates our
imperfections, publishing them as sins, makes our

venial sins mortal, and our sins of frailty sins of malice. Charity is benevolent and kind, says St. Paul, but the world is malicious; charity thinks no evil, whereas the world, on the contrary, always thinks evil; and when it cannot condemn our actions it will accuse our intentions. So that whether the sheep have horns or not, be they white or black, the wolf will devour them if he can.

Do what we can, the world will still wage war against us. If we are long at confession it will wonder how we can have so much to say, if we stay but a short time it will say we have not confessed all. It will watch our entire conduct, and if we utter one word of anger it will protest that our temper is insupportable; the care of our affairs will be made to appear covetousness, and our meekness folly. But with regard to the children of the world, their anger is called generosity, their avarice proper economy, their familiarities honourable entertainments. The spiders always spoils the work of the bees.

Let us turn a deaf ear to this blind world, Philothea; let it screech as long as it pleases, like an owl, to disturb the birds of the day. Let us be constant in our designs, and invariable in our resolutions. Our perseverance will demonstrate whether we have, in good earnest, sacrificed ourselves to God, and dedicated ourselves to a devout life. Comets and planets appear to be almost equally bright; but as comets are only fiery exhalations which pass away and, after a short time, disappear, whereas planets remain in perpetual brightness; so hypocrisy and true virtue have a great resemblance in outward show, but the one is easily distinguished from the other, because hypocrisy cannot stand its ground long, but is quickly dissipated like smoke, whereas true virtue is always firm and constant.

It highly contributes towards the security of devotion, if, at the beginning, we bear reproaches and calumny on its account, since we thereby avoid the danger of pride and vanity, which may be compared to the midwives of Egypt, who killed the male children of the Israelites on the very day of their birth, by the order of the inhuman Pharaoh. As we are crucified to the world, the world ought to be crucified to us; since worldlings look upon us as fools, let us look upon them as madmen.

CHAPTER II.

We must always have courage.

Light, though it is beautiful and lovely to our eyes, nevertheless dazzles them after we have been long in the dark. Before we become familiar with the inhabitants of any country, be they ever so courteous and gracious. we find ourselves somewhat strange amongst them. It may probably happen, Philothea, that this general farewell which you have bid to the follies and vanities of the world may make some impressions of sadness and discouragement on your mind. If this should be the case, have a little patience, I beg of you, for it will come to nothing. It is but a little strangeness, occasioned by novelty; when it has passed away you will feel ten thousand consolations.

It may perhaps be painful to you at first to relinquish that praise which your vanities extorted from foolish worldlings; but would you for the sake of that forfeit the eternal glory with which God will suredly recompense you? The vain amusements pastimes in which you have hitherto employed time will again present themselves to allure your heart, and cause it to turn towards them; but will you resolve to renounce eternal happiness for such deceitful fooleries? Believe me, if you persevere, you will quickly receive consolations so delicious and agreeable as shall oblige you to confess that the world has nothing but gall in comparison with this honey, and that one day of devotion is preferable to a thousand years expended in all the pleasures it can afford.

But you see that the mountain of Christian perfection is exceeding high: O my God, you say, how shall I be able to ascend. Courage, Philothea. When the young bees begin to assume their form they are unable to fly to the flowers, the mountains, or the neighbouring hills, to gather honey; but, by continuing to feed on the honey which the old ones have prepared, their wings appear, and they acquire sufficient strength to fly and seek their food all over the country. It is true we are yet young bees in devotion, and consequently unable to rise so high as to reach the top of Christian perfection; but, according as our desires and resolutions take shape, and our wings grow, we may reasonably hope that we shall one day become spiritual bees, and be able to fly; in the meantime let us feed upon the honey of the many good instructions which other devout persons have left us, and pray to God to give us wings like a dove, that we may not only be enabled to fly up during this present life, but also rest on the mountain of eternity in the life to come.

CHAPTER III.

The nature of Temptations, and the difference between the feeling of temptation and the consenting to it.

Imagine to yourself, Philothea, a young princess extremely beloved by her spouse, and that some wicked man, in order to corrupt her fidelity, sends an infamous messenger to treat with her concerning his design : First, the messenger proposes the intention of his master ; secondly, the princess is pleased or displeased with the proposition ; thirdly, she either consents or refuses. It is in the same manner that Satan, the world, and the flesh, seeing a soul espoused to the Son of God, send her temptations and suggestions by which, 1, sin is proposed to her ; 2, she is either pleased or displeased with the proposal ; 3, she either consents or refuses. These are the three steps which lead to iniquity—temptation, delectation, and consent. But though these three things are not so manifestly discerned in all other kinds of sins, they are nevertheless palpably seen in great sins.

Though the temptation to any sin whatsoever should last during life, it could never render us displeasing to the Divine Majesty, provided we were not pleased with it, and did not yield our consent to it ; the reason is, because we do not act, but suffer in temptation, and as in this we take no pleasure, so we cannot incur any guilt. St. Paul suffered for a long time the temptations of the flesh, and yet so far from being displeasing to God on that account, that, on the contrary, God was glorified on account of them. The blessed Angela de Foligny felt such cruel temptations of the flesh, that she moves us compassion when she relates them. St. Francis and St. Benoit also suffered such violent temptations as obliged the one to cast himself naked into thorns and the other into snow, in order to combat them, and yet they lost nothing of God's favour, but increased very much in grace.

You must then be courageous, Philothea, amidst temptations, and never think yourself overcome as long as they displease you, observing well this difference between feeling and consenting, viz., we may feel temptations, though they displease us, but we can never consent to them, unless they please us, since being pleased with them ordinarily serves as a step towards our consent. Let then the enemies of our salvation lay as many baits and allurements in our way as they please; let them remain always at the door of our heart, in order to try to gain admittance; let them make us as many proposals as they can—still, as long as we remain steadfast in our resolution to take no pleasure in the temptation, it is utterly impossible for us to offend God, any more than that the prince whom I have mentioned could be displeased with his spouse, on account of the infamous message sent to her, if she took no kind of pleasure whatever in it. Yet, in this case, there is this difference between her and the soul, that the princess having heard the wicked proposition, may, if she please, drive away the messenger, and never again suffer him to appear in her presence; but it is not always in the power of the soul not to feel the temptation, though it is in her power not to consent to it; for which reason, although the temptation may last ever so long a time, yet it cannot hurt us as long as it is disagreeable to us.

But with respect to the pleasure which may follow the temptation, it may be observed that, as there are two parts in the soul, the inferior and the superior, and that the inferior does not always fol-

16

low the superior, but acts for itself apart, it frequently happens that the inferior part takes delight in the temptation without the consent, nay, against the will of the superior. This is that warfare which the Apostle describes, when he says: "That the flesh lusteth against the spirit, and the spirit against the flesh; for these are contrary one to another" (Gal. v. 17).

Have you never seen, Philothea, a great wood-fire covered with ashes? Should one come to that place ten or twelve hours after in search of fire, he finds but little in the midst of the hearth, and that scarcely to be noticed; yet there it is, and with it he may kindle again the remainder of the cinders which were dead. So it is with charity, which is our spiritual life, in the midst of violent temptations; for the temptation, casting the pleasure which accompanies it into the inferior part, covers the whole soul, as it were with ashes, and reduces the love of God into a narrow compass: for it appears nowhere but in the midst of the heart, in the centre of the spirit, and even there is scarcely perceptible, and it is only with much difficulty that we find it; yet there it is in reality, since, notwithstanding all the trouble and the disorder we feel in our soul and our body, we still retain a resolution never to consent to the temptation; and the pleasure which the outward man feels displeases the inward, so that although it surrounds the will, yet it is not within it; by which we see that such pleasure, being involuntary, can be no sin.

CHAPTER IV.

Two remarkable examples on this subject.

As it so nearly concerns you to understand this matter perfectly, I will explain it more fully. A young man, as St. Jerome relates, being fastened down with bands of silk, on a delicate soft bed, was provoked by the most violent temptations, employed by his persecutors, in order to stagger his constancy. Ah! must not his chaste soul have felt strange disorders? Nevertheless, amongst so many conflicts, in the midst of such a terrible storm of temptations, he testified that his heart was not vanquished, and that his will gave no consent. Having no part of his body at command but his tongue, he bit it off, and spat it in the face of the wretched woman, who tortured him more cruelly than the executioners could have done by the greatest torments; for the tyrant, despairing to conquer him by pain, thought to overcome him by pleasure.

This history of the conflict of St. Catherine of Sienna, on the like occasion, is very admirable;— the substance of it is as follows: The wicked spirit had permission from God to assault the purity of this holy virgin with the greatest fury, yet so as not to be allowed to touch her. He presented then all kinds of impure suggestions to her mind; and to move her the more, coming with his companions in the form of men and women, he committed a thousand kinds of immodesties in her sight, adding most filthy language; and although these things were exterior, nevertheless, by means of the senses, they penetrated deep into the heart of the virgin, which as she herself confessed, was filled to the brim with them; so that nothing remained in her, except the pure superior will, which was not shaken. This temptation continued for a long time, till one day our Saviour appearing to her, she said to Him: Where wert thou, my dear Saviour, when my heart was full of so great uncleanness? To which He answered: I was within thy heart, my daughter. But how, she replied, couldst Thou dwell in my heart, where there was so much impurity? is it possible Thou couldst dwell in such an unclean place? To which our Lord replied: Tell me, did these filthy thoughts of thy heart give thee pleasure or sadness, bitterness or delight? The most extreme bitterness and sadness, said she. Who was it then, replied our Saviour, that put this great bitterness and sadness into thy heart but I, who remained concealed in thy soul? Believe me, daughter, had it not been for my presence, these thoughts which surrounded thy will would have doubtless entered in, and with pleasure would have brought death to thy soul; but being present I infused this displeasure into thy heart which enabled thee to reject the temptations as much as it could; but, not being able to do it as much as it would, conceived a greater displeasure and hatred both against the temptation and thyself; and thus, these troubles have proved occasions of great merit to thee, and to a greater increase of thy strength and virtue.

Behold, Philothea, how this fire was covered with ashes, and how the temptation had even entered the heart, and surrounded the will, which, assisted by our Saviour held out to the last, resisting, by her aversion, displeasure, and detestation of the evil suggested, and constantly refusing her consent to the sin which besieged her on every side. Good God! what distress must not a soul that loves God feel, at not knowing whether He is in her or not, and whether the Divine love, for which she fights, is altogether extinguished in her or not! But it is the great perfection of heavenly love to make those who love God suffer and fight for his love, not knowing whether they possess the love for which and by which they fight.

CHAPTER V.

An Encouragement to a soul that is under temptation

Those violent assaults and extraordinary temptations, Philothea, are only permitted by God against those souls which He desires to elevate to the highest degree of Divine love, yet it does not follow that they shall afterwards attain it, for it has often happened that those who have been constant under these assaults, have, for want of faithfully corresponding with the Divine favour, been afterwards overcome by very small temptations. This I tell you, in order that, if you should happen hereafter to be assailed by great temptations you may know that God confers an extraordinary favour on you, when He thus declares his will to make you great in his sight : and that, nevertheless, you must be always humble and fearful, not being able to assure yourself that you can conquer small temptations, even after you have overcome great ones, by any other means than by constant fidelity towards his Divine Majesty.

Therefore, whatever temptation may hereafter assail you, or with whatever delectation they may be accompanied, as long as you refuse your consent, not only to the temptation, but also to the delectation, do not give yourself the trouble, for God is not offended. As, when a man is so far gone in a fit as to show no sign of life, people lay their hands on his heart, and if they feel the least palpitation, judge him to be still alive, and that, by the application of some restorative, he may again recover his strength and senses ; so it sometimes happens that, by the violence of a temptation, our soul seems to have fallen into a fit, so as to have no longer any spiritual life or motion ; but if we desire to know how it is with her, let us lay our hand upon our heart, and consider whether it and our will still retain some palpitation of the spiritual life—that is to say, whether they have done their duty in refusing to consent and yield to the temptation and delectation; for as long as this motion remains, we may rest assured that charity, the life of the soul, remains in us, and that Jesus Christ our Saviour, although concealed, is there present; so by means of the continual exercise of prayer, the sacraments, and confidence in God, we shall again return to a strong, sound, and healthy spiritual life.

CHAPTER VI.

How temptation and delectation may become sinful.

The princess of whom we have before spoken, could not prevent the proposition which was made to her, because, as was assumed, it was made against her will; but had she, on the contrary, given it the least encouragement, or betrayed a willingness to grant her love to him who courted her, doubtless she would then have been guilty in the sight of God, and however she might dissemble it, would certainly deserve both blame and punishment. Thus it sometimes happens that the temptation alone involves us in sin, because we ourselves are the cause of it. For example: I know that when I play I fall easily into violent passion and blasphemy, and that gaming serves me as a temptation to those sins; I sin, therefore, as often as I play, and I am accountable for all the temptations which may come upon me. In like manner, if I know that certain conversations will expose me to the danger of falling into sin, and yet willingly take part in them, I am doubtless guilty for all the temptations I may meet with on such occasions.

When the delectation which proceeds from the temptation can be avoided, it is always a greater or less sin to admit it in proportion as the pleasure we take, or the consent we give to it is of a longer or shorter duration. The young princess, before alluded to, would be highly to blame if, having heard the impure proposal, she took pleasure in it, and let her heart feel satisfaction on so evil a subject; for although she did not consent to the execution of what is proposed to her, she consented, nevertheless, to the interior application of her heart to the evil, by the pleasure she took therein, because it is always criminal to apply either the heart or the body to anything that is immodest, nay, this sin depends so much on the consent of the heart, that without it the application of the body could not be a sin.

Therefore, whenever you are tempted to any sin, consider whether you yourself have not willingly given occasion to your being tempted, for then the temptation itself puts you in a state of sin, on account of the danger into which you have cast yourself: this is to be understood when you could conveniently have avoided the occasion, and could have foreseen, or ought to, the approach of the temptation; but if you have given no occasion to the temptation, it cannot in any way be imputed to you as a sin.

When the delectation which follows temptation might have been avoided, and yet has not, there is always some kind of sin, according to the time one has dwelt upon it, more or less, or according to the pleasure one has taken in it. A woman who has given no occasion to her being courted, and yet takes pleasure therein, is nevertheless to be blamed, if the pleasure she takes originates in no other cause than the courtship. But if, for example, he who sues for her love is an excellent musician, and she should take

pleasure, not in his courtship, but in the harmony and
sweetness of his music, this would be no sin : though
she ought not to continue long in this pleasure, for
fear she should pass from it to a desire to be courted.
In like manner, if anyone should propose to me some
ingenious means of taking revenge of an enemy, and
that I should neither delight in, nor give any consent to the proposed revenge, but only be pleased
with the cleverness of the artful invention ; although
it would be no sin, still I ought not to continue long
amusing myself with this pleasure, for fear lest by
degrees it might carry me to take some delight in
the revenge itself.

One is sometimes surprised by certain symptoms
of pleasure which immediately follow a temptation,
before he is well aware of it. This, at most, can
only be a slight venial sin ; but it becomes greater if,
after we have perceived the evil, we stop some time,
through negligence, to determine whether we should
admit or reject that delectation ; and the sin becomes
still greater if, after being sensible of the delectation, we dwell upon it, through downright negligence,
without having determined to reject it ; but when
we voluntarily, and with full deliberation, resolve to
please ourselves in such delectations, this of itself is
a great sin, provided that the object in which we
take delight is also a great sin. It is a great crime
in a woman to be willing to entertain evil affections,
although she never designs to yield herself up really
to them.

CHAPTER VII.

Remedies against great temptations.

As soon as you perceive that you are tempted,
follow the example of children ; when they see a wolf
or a bear, they at once run to the arms of their

father or mother, or at least they call out to them for help. It is the remedy which our Lord taught, when He said: "Pray, lest you enter into temptation" (Matt. xxvi. 41). If you find, notwithstanding this, that the temptation still continues, or even increases, run in spirit to embrace the holy cross, as if you saw Jesus Christ crucified before you. Protest that you will never consent to the temptation, crave his help against it, and continue still to refuse your consent, as long as the temptation continues.

But in making these protestations and in refusing to consent, look not upon the temptation, but only on our Lord; for if you look upon the temptation, especially whilst it is strong, it may shake your courage. Divert your thoughts to some good and pious reflections, for good thoughts, when they occupy your heart, will chase away every evil temptation and suggestion.

But the great remedy against all temptations, whether great or small, is to lay open your heart to your spiritual director, and communicate its suggestions, feelings, and affections to him; for you must observe, that silence is the first condition that the enemy makes with a soul which he desires to seduce; whereas God, on the other hand, requires that we should make known his inspirations to our superiors and directors.

If after all this, the temptations should still continue to harass and persecute us, we have nothing to do on our part but to continue resolute in our resolution, never to yield our consent; for as a girl can never be married so long as she answers No; so the soul, although she may be ever so long tempted, can never sin so long as she does the same.

Never dispute with your enemy, nor make him any reply but what is similar to that one by which our Saviour confounded him: "Begone, Satan, the Lord thy God shalt thou adore, and Him only shalt thou serve;" for as a chaste wife should never reply to the loose conversation of an immoral man, but quit him abruptly, and at the same instant turn her heart towards her husband, and renew the promise of allegiance which she made to him ; so the devout soul that sees herself assailed by temptation ought not by any means to lose time in answering the enemy, but with all simplicity turn towards Jesus Christ, her Spouse, and renew her protestation of fidelity to Him, and her resolution to remain solely and entirely his for ever.

CHAPTER VIII.

We must resist small temptations.

Although we must fight against great temptations with an invincible courage, and the victory we gain over them may be extremely advantageous, it may happen, nevertheless, that we gain more in fighting manfully against small ones ; for, as great temptations exceed in quality, so the small ones exceed in quantity, for which reason the victory over them may be comparable to that over the greatest. Wolves and bears are without doubt more dangerous than flies, yet the former neither give us so much trouble, nor exercise our patience so much as the latter. It is an easy thing to abstain from murder, but it is extremely difficult to curb all our little bursts of passion, the occasions of which are every moment presenting themselves. It is very easy for a man or a woman to refrain from adultery, but difficult to refrain from glances of the eyes, from giving or receiving favours of love, or from speaking or hearkening to flattering words. It is easy not to admit, visibly or exteriorly, a rival to one's husband or wife, but easy to do so in the heart; it is easy not to steal another man's goods, but difficult not to covet them; it is easy not to bear false witness in judgment, but difficult never to tell a lie; it is easy not to get drunk, but difficult to keep one's self perfectly sober; easy to keep from wishing another man's death, difficult not to desire what may be inconvenient to him; easy to forbear from defaming him, difficult not to despise him. In a word, these lesser temptations of anger, suspicion, jealousy, envy, vain love, levity, vanity, insincerity, affectation, craftiness, and impure thoughts, are continually assailing even those who are the most devout and resolute. We must, therefore, diligently prepare ourselves, my dear Philothea, for this warfare, and rest assured that, for as many victories as we shall gain over these lesser enemies, so many precious stones shall be put into the crown of glory, which God is preparing for us in heaven. Therefore, I say that, in addition to be ever ready to fight courageously against great temptations, we must also constantly and diligently defend ourselves against those that seem weak and trivial.

CHAPTER IX.

What remedies we are to apply against small temptations.

Now as to those lesser temptations of vanity, suspicion, impatience, jealousy, envy, vain love, and such like, which, like flies and gnats, continually hover about us, and sometimes sting us upon the legs, the hands, the cheek, or the nose, as it is impossible to be altogether exempt from being teased by them, the best defence we can make is not to give ourselves much trouble about them; for, although they may tease us, yet they can never hurt us, as long as we continue strongly resolved to dedicate ourselves in earnest to the service of God.

Despise then these petty assaults, without so much as thinking on what they would suggest. Let them buzz and hover here and there, and ever so much about you; pay no more attention to them than you would to flies when they threaten to sting you; but when you perceive that they, in the least, touch your heart, content yourself with quietly removing them, without waiting to contend or dispute with them, and perform some actions of a nature contrary to the temptation, especially acts of the love of God. But you must not continue long, Philothea, in opposing the act of the contrary virtue to the temptation which you feel, for that would be to dispute with it; but after having performed a simple act of the contrary virtue, provided you have had leisure to observe the quality of the temptation, turn your heart gently towards Jesus Christ crucified, and by an act of love, kiss his sacred feet. This is the best means to overcome the enemy, as well in small as in great temptations; for, as the love of God contains within itself the perfection of all the virtues, and is even more excellent than the virtues themselves, so it is also the most sovereign antidote against all kinds of vices; and by accustoming your mind, on these occasions, to have recourse to this remedy, you need not even examine by what kind of temptation it is troubled. Moreover this grand remedy is so terrible to the enemy of our souls, that when once he perceives that his temptations incite us to make acts of divine love, he ceases to tempt us. This is what we have to do against these small and frequent temptations, instead of examining and fighting against them in detail; otherwise we should only give ourselves much trouble and effect very little.

CHAPTER X.

How to fortify our hearts against temptations.

Consider from time to time what passions are most predominant in your soul, and, having discovered them, adopt such a method of thinking, speaking, and acting, as may counteract them. If, for example, you find yourself inclined to vanity, think often on the miseries of human life, what inquietude these vanities will raise in your conscience at the day of your death, how unworthy they are of a generous heart, being nothing but toys, fit only for the amusement of children. Speak also often against vanity, and although it may be to your own prejudice, do not cease to cry it down, for by these means you will engage yourself, even as a matter of honour, to the opposite side; for by declaiming against a thing we bring ourselves to hate it, though at first we may have an affection for it. Exercise works of abjection and humility as much as possible, however great your reluctance may be, since you accustom yourself thus to humility, and weaken your vanity, so that when the temptation comes, you will have less inclination to favour it, and more strength to resist it.

If you are inclined to covetousness, think frequently on the folly of a sin which makes us slaves to that which was only made to serve us, and that at death we must part with all, and leave it in the hands of those who perhaps may squander it, or to whom it may be a cause of damnation. Speak aloud against avarice, and in praise of an utter contempt of the world. Force yourself to give alms, and to neglect some occasions of gain.

Should you be inclined to sensual affections, often think how very dangerous they are, as well to your-

self as to others ; how unworthy a thing it is to employ in an idle pastime the noblest affection of our
soul; and how worthy of blame is such extreme levity
of mind. Speak often in praise of purity and simplicity of heart, and let your actions, to the utmost
of your power, be always conformable to your words,
by avoiding levities in acts or in conversation. In
short, in time of peace, namely, when temptations
to the sin to which you are most inclined, do not
molest you, make several acts of the contrary virtue ;
and if the occasions to practise it do not present
themselves, endeavour to meet them, for by this
means you will strengthen your heart against future
temptations.

CHAPTER XI.

Of Inquietude.

As inquietude is not a single temptation, but a
source from whence many temptations flow upon us,
it is very necessary that I should say something
concerning it. Inquietude or sadness, then, is
nothing else but that grief of mind which we conceive for some evil which we suffer from against our
will, whether it be exterior, as poverty, sickness,
contempt; or interior, as ignorance, dryness of
heart, repugnance to what is good, and temptation.
When the soul, then, perceives that she has some
evil, she becomes sad, is displeased, and with good
reason extremely anxious to rid herself of it; for
everyone naturally desires to embrace good, and fly
from what he apprehends to be evil. If the soul,
for the love of God, wishes to be freed from her
evil, she will seek the means of her deliverance
with patience, meekness, humility, and tranquillity,
expecting it more from the providence of God than
from her own industry or diligence ; but if she seeks

her deliverance from self-love, she will fatigue herself in quest of these means, as if the success depended more on herself than on God. I do not say that she thinks so, but that she hurries herself as if she thought so. Now, if she does not succeed immediately according to her wishes, she falls into disquietude, which, instead of removing, aggravates the evil, and involves her in such extreme anguish and distress, with so great a loss of courage and strength, as to imagine her evil to be beyond remedy. Behold, then, how the sadness, which in the beginning is just, begets inquietude, and inquietude increases the sadness, until it becomes extremely dangerous.

Inquietude is the greatest evil which can befall the soul, sin alone excepted. For as the seditions and internal commotions of any commonwealth prevent it from being able to resist a foreign invasion, so our heart, being troubled within itself, loses the strength to maintain the virtues it had acquired, and the means to resist the temptations of the enemy, who then uses his utmost efforts to fish, as it is said, in troubled waters.

Inquietude proceeds from an inordinate desire of being delivered from the evil we feel, or of acquiring the good we hope for: and yet there is nothing which more increases the evil, and which removes the good further off, than an unquiet mind. Birds remain prisoners in nets, because, finding themselves prisoners, they eagerly flutter and beat about to get loose again, and by that means entangle themselves the more. Whenever, then, you are pressed with a desire to be freed from some evil, or to attain to some good, be careful both to settle your mind in repose and tranquillity, and to compose your judgment and will; and then follow the movements of your desire, using quietly the means which may be most convenient. When I say quietly, I do not mean negligently, but without hurry, trouble, or inquietude; otherwise, instead of obtaining the effect of your desire, you will mar all and embarrass yourself the more.

" My soul is always in my hands, O Lord, and I have not forgotten thy law," said David (Psalm cxviii. 109). Examine frequently in the day, or at least in the morning or evening, whether you have your soul in your hands, or whether some passion or inquietude has not robbed you of it. Consider whether you have your heart at command, or whether it has not escaped out of your hands, to engage itself in some disorderly affection of love, hatred, envy, covetousness, fear, uneasiness, or joy; and if it should have gone astray, seek for it before you do anything else, and bring it quietly back to the presence of God, subjecting all your affections and desires to the obedience and direction of his divine will; for as they who are afraid of losing anything which is precious, hold it fast in their hands, so, in imitation of this great king, we should always say : O my God, my soul is in danger, and therefore I carry it always in my hand, and in this manner I have not forgotten thy holy law.

Permit not your desires, be they ever so trival, to disquiet you, lest afterwards those that are of greater importance should find your heart involved in trouble and disorder. When you perceive inquietude to take possession of your mind, recommend yourself to God, and resolve to do nothing until it is restored to tranquillity, unless it be something that cannot be deferred, and then tempering and moderating the current of your desire as much as possible, do that which is to be done, not according to your desire, but according to your reason.

If you can make known the cause of your inquietude to your spiritual director, or at least to some faithful and devout friend, you shall without doubt presently find ease; for the communicating of the griefs of the heart works the same effect in the soul, as the letting of blood does in the body of him that is in a continual fever; and this is the remedy of remedies. Accordingly, the holy king St. Louis gave this counsel to his son: "If you have any uneasiness in your heart, tell it presently to your confessor, or to some good person, and then you shall be enabled to bear the evil very easy, by the comfort he will give you."

CHAPTER XII.

Of Sadness.

"The sadness that is according to God," says St. Paul, "worketh penance steadfast unto salvation; but the sadness of the world worketh death." (2 Cor. vii.) Sadness, then, may be good or evil, according to its different effects. It is true it produces more evil than good ones, for it has only two that are good, compassion and repentance; but it has six that are evil, namely, anxiety, sloth, indignation, jealousy, envy, and impatience, which caused the wise man to say, "Sadness kills many, and there is no profit in it" (Ecclus. xxx. 25), because for two good streams which flow from the source of sadness there are six very evil ones.

The enemy makes use of sadness to tempt the just; for as he endeavours to make the wicked rejoice in their sins, so he strives to make the good grieve in their good works; and as he can only induce persons to commit evil by making it appear agreeable, so he can only divert us from good by making it appear disagreeable. The prince of darkness is pleased with sadness and melancholy, because he is and shall be sad and melancholy to all eternity; therefore he desires that everyone may be like himself.

17

The sadness which is evil troubles and perplexes the soul, causes inordinate fears, gives a distaste to prayer, stupefies and oppresses the brain, robs the mind of counsel, resolution, judgment, and courage, and destroys its strength. In a word, it is like a severe winter that destroys all the beauty of the country, and kills very many animals; for it takes away all sweetness from the soul, and renders her disabled in all her faculties. If you should at any time be seized with this evil kind of sadness, Philothea, apply the following remedies:—

"Is anyone sad," says St. James, "let him pray." Prayer is a sovereign remedy, for it lifts up the spirit to God, our only joy and consolation. But in praying, let your words and affections, whether interior or exterior, always tend to a lively confidence in the divine goodness; use prayers such as, "O God of mercy, O infinite goodness, O my sweet Saviour, O God of my heart, my joy, and my hope, O my dear Spouse, the well-beloved of my soul," &c.

Oppose vigorously the least inclination to sadness; and although it may seem that all you do at that time is performed with tepidity and sloth, you must nevertheless persevere; for the enemy, who seeks by sadness to make us weary of good works, seeing that we do not cease to do them, but even continue them in spite of his opposition, and that thus they become more meritorious, will cease to trouble you any longer.

Sing spiritual canticles, for the devil, by this means, has often desisted from his operations; witness the evil spirit by which Saul was afflicted, whose violence was repressed by such music. It is also necessary we should employ ourselves in exterior works, and vary them as much as possible, in 'er to divert the soul from the melancholy object, 'o purify and warm the spirits, sadness being a ʠ of a cold and dry character.

Perform external actions of fervour, although you may do them without the least relish : such as embracing the crucifix, pressing it close to your breast, kissing the feet and the hands, lifting up your eyes and your hands to heaven, raising your voice to God, by words of love and confidence, like these : " My beloved is mine, and I am his. My beloved is to me a bouquet of myrrh. My eyes have fainted after Thee, O my God." Say also : " When wilt Thou comfort me? O Jesus, be Thou Jesus to me. Live, sweet Jesus, and my soul shall live. Who shall ever separate me from the love of my God?" and such like.

The moderate use of the discipline is also good against sadness, because this voluntary exterior affliction begets interior consolation, and the soul, feeling pain without, diverts herself from the pain within. But frequent communion is the best remedy, because that heavenly bread strengthens the heart and rejoices the spirit.

Make known all the feelings, affections, and suggestions which proceed from your sadness, humbly and faithfully to your confessor. Seek the conversation of devout persons, and frequent their company as much as you can. In a word, resign yourself into the hands of God, preparing yourself to suffer this troublesome sadness with patience, as a just punishment of your vain joys, and doubt not but God will deliver you from this evil.

CHAPTER XIII.

Of spiritual and sensible consolations, and how we must behave with regard to them.

God continues the existence of this great world in perpetual changes, by which day is always succeeded by night, spring by summer, summer by autumn, autumn by winter, and winter again by spring. Days seldom exactly resemble each other : some are cloudy, others rainy; some dry, others windy; thus causing variety, which adds considerably to the beauty of the universe. It is the same with man, who, according to the saying of old writers, is an epitome of the universe, or another little world, for he never remains long in the one and the same state ; his life flows on upon earth like the waters, floating and undulating in a perpetual diversity of motion, which sometimes lifts him up with hope ; sometimes brings him down with fear, sometimes carries him to the right hand by consolation, sometimes to the left by affliction, and not one of his days, not even one of his hours, is in every respect like another.

Now it is necessary that we should endeavour to preserve an inviolable equality of heart, amidst so great an inequality of occurrences; and that, although all things change around us, we should remain constantly immovable, ever looking and aspiring towards God. Let the ship take what course it will, let it sail towards the east, west, north, or south, or let it be driven by any wind whatsoever, the needle of the compass will never point any other way but towards the bright polar star. Let all be overturned and disturbed, not only around us, but within us, that is to say, let our soul be overwhelmed with sorrow or joy, sweetness or bitterness, peace or trouble, light or darkness, temptation or repose, pleasure or disgust, dryness or tenderness ; whether it be like earth burned by the sun or refreshed by the dew, yet our heart, our spirit, and our superior will, which is our compass, must incessantly tend towards the love of God, its Creator, its Saviour, its only Sovereign Good. "Whether we live or die," says the apostle (Rom.

xiv. 8), "we belong to the Lord." And, "Who shall be able to separate us from the love of God?" No, nothing shall separate us from this love: neither tribulation, nor anguish, nor death, nor life, nor present grief, nor the fear of future accidents, nor the artifices of evil spirits, nor the height of consolations, nor the depth of afflictions, nor tenderness, nor dryness, ought ever to separate us from this holy charity, which is founded in Jesus Christ.

This fixed and absolute resolution never to forsake God, nor to abandon his sweet love, serves as a counterpoise to our souls, to keep them in a holy equilibrium amidst the inequality of the several motions attached to the condition of this life; for as little bees, surprised by a storm in the fields, take up little pieces of gravel, that they may be able to balance themselves in the air, and not be so easily carried away by the wind; so our soul, having, by a strong resolution, firmly embraced the precious love of God, continues constant in the midst of the inconstancy and vicissitudes of consolations and afflictions, whether spiritual or temporal, exterior or interior.

But, besides these general instructions, we have need of some particular rules.

1. I say, therefore, that devotion does not always consist in that sweetness, delight, consolation, or sensible tenderness of heart, which moves us to tears, and gives us a certain agreeable and savoury satisfaction in certain spiritual exercises; no, Philothea, for there are many souls who experience these tendernesses and consolations, and nevertheless are very vicious, and consequently have not a true love of God, much less true devotion. Saul, whilst persecuting David to death, who was fleeing before him in the wilderness of Engaddi, entered alone into a cavern, where David and his people lay concealed;

David, who on that occasion had many opportunities of killing him, spared his life, and did not even put him in bodily fear; but, having suffered him to go out without injury, afterwards called on him to demonstrate to him his innocence, and to convince him that he had been at his mercy. Now, upon that occasion, what did Saul not do to show that his heart was mollified towards David? He called him his child, he wept aloud, he praised him, he acknowledged his goodness, he prayed to God for him, he foretold his future greatness, and he recommended to him his posterity. What greater manifestation could he make of sweetness and tenderness of heart? Nevertheless, his heart was not changed, nor did he cease to persecute David as cruelly as before. In like manner, there are some persons who, on considering the goodness of God and the passion of our Saviour, feel so great a tenderness of heart as to make them sigh, weep, pray, and give thanks in so feeling a manner, that one would think their hearts were possessed with an extraordinary degree of devotion; but when it is put to the trial, we see that as passing showers of a hot summer, which fall in great drops on the earth, but do not sink into it, serve for nothing but to produce mushrooms; so these tender tears falling on a vicious heart, and not penetrating it, are altogether unprofitable; for, notwithstanding all this apparent devotion, these tender souls will not part with a farthing of the ill-gotten riches they possess, nor renounce one of their perverse affections, nor suffer the least temporal inconvenience for the service of our Saviour, over whose sufferings they have but just ceased to weep; so that the good sentiments which they had were no better than certain spiritual mushrooms, and their devotion no better than a delusion of the enemy, who amuses souls with these false consolations, in order

to make them rest contented, lest they should search
any farther for the true and solid devotion which
consists in a constant, resolute, prompt, and active
will, to put into practice whatsover we know to be
pleasing to God. A child will weep tenderly when
it sees its mother pricked by a lancet so as to bleed;
but if its mother, for whom it is weeping, would at the
same time demand the apple or sweetmeats which it
has in its hand, it would by no means part with
them; such is the nature of our tender devotions
when, contemplating the stroke of the lance which
pierced the heart of Jesus Christ crucified, we weep
bitterly. Alas! Philothea, it is well to lament the
painful death and passion of our blessed Redeemer;
but why, then, do we not give Him the apple which
we have in our hands, which He so earnestly asks
for? why do we not give Him our heart, the only apple
of love which our dear Saviour requires of us; why
do we not resign to Him so many affections, delights,
and pleasures, which He wants to pluck out of our
hands, but cannot, because they are the sweetmeats
of which we are more fond than of his heavenly
grace? Ah, Philothea, these are the friendships of
little children, tender indeed, but weak, fantastical,
and of no effect. Devotion, therefore, does not consist in these sensible affections, which sometimes
proceed from a soft nature, susceptible of any im-
pression we have a mind to give it. No; it some-
simes comes from the enemy, who, in order to amuse,
stirs up our imagination to artificial impressions.

2. Yet these tender and delightful affections are
sometimes good and profitable; for they excite the
appetite for piety in the soul, strengthen the spirit,
and add to the promptitude of devotion a holy gaiety
and cheerfulness, which makes our actions more
beautiful and agreeable, even on the exterior. This
relish which one meets with in the things of God,

is that which made David exclaim: "O Lord, how sweet are thy words to my palate! they are sweeter than honey to my mouth. The slightest consolation of devotion that we receive is certainly, in every respect, preferable to the finest recreations of the world. The milk of the heavenly Spouse is sweeter to the soul than the wine of the most delicious pleasures on earth. He that has once tasted it esteems all other consolations no better than gall or wormwood; for, as they that hold the herb *scitique* in their mouth imbibe so excessive a sweetness from it, that they neither feel hunger nor thirst; so they to whom God has given the heavenly manna can neither desire nor relish the consolations of the world, so far, at least, as to fix their affections on them: they are slight foretastes of those everlasting delights which God has in reserve for the souls that seek Him; they are the sweetmeats which He gives to his little children in order to allure them; they are the cordial waters wherewith He strengthens them; and they are also sometimes the earnest of eternal felicities. It is said that Alexander the Great, sailing on the ocean, discovered Arabia Felix by perceiving the fragrant odours which were borne by the wind from thence, and thereupon encouraged both himself and his companions; so we oftentimes receive these sweet consolations on this sea of our mortal life, which, doubtless, must give us a certain foretaste of the delights of that heavenly country to which we tend and aspire.

3. But you will perhaps ask me, since there are sensible consolations which are good, because they come from God, and others unprofitable, dangerous, and even pernicious, that proceed either from nature or from the enemy, how shall I be able to distinguish the one from the other, or know those that are evil or unprofitable from those that are good? It is a

general doctrine, Philothea, with regard to the affections and passions of our souls, that we must know them by their fruits. Our hearts are the trees; the affections and passions are the branches; and their words or actions are the fruit. The heart is good which has good affections, and those affections and passions are good which produce in us good effects and holy actions. If these sweetnesses, tendernesses, and consolations, make us more humble, patient, tractable, charitable, and compassionate towards our neighbour; more fervent in mortifying our concupiscences and evil inclinations; more constant in our exercises; more pliant and submissive to those whom we ought to obey; more sincere and upright in our lives, then, Philothea, they proceed, without doubt, from God. But if these consolations have no sweetness but for ourselves; if they make us inquisitive, harsh, quarrelsome, impatient, obstinate, haughty, presumptuous, and rigorous towards our neighbour; cause us to imagine ourselves to be little saints already, and to disdain to be any longer subject to direction or correction; they are then, beyond all doubt, false and pernicious, for a good tree cannot bring forth bad fruit.

4. Whenever we experience these consolations we must humble ourselves exceedingly before God, and beware of saying: "Oh, how good am I!" No, Philothea, these consolations, as I have already said, cannot make us the better: devotion does not consist in them; but let us say: "O how good is God to such as hope in Him, to the soul that seeks Him!" 1. As he that has sugar in his mouth cannot say that his mouth is sweet, but that the sugar is sweet; so, although this spiritual sweetness is excellent, and though God, who gives it, is most good, yet it does not follow that he who receives it is also good. 2. Let us acknowledge ourselves to be as yet but little children,

who have need of milk; and that these sweetmeats are given to us because our tender and delicate spirits have need of bribes and allurements to entice us to the love of God.   3. Let us afterwards humbly accept of these extraordinary graces and favours, and esteem them, not so much on account of their excellence, as because it is the hand of God which puts them into our hearts, as a mother would do who, the more to please her child, puts the sweetmeats into its mouth with her own hand, one by one; for if the child has understanding. it sets a greater value on the tenderness of his mother than on their sweetness; and thus, Philothea, it is a great matter to taste the sweetness of sensible consolations, but it is infinitely more sweet to consider that it is his most loving and tender hand that puts them, at is were, into our mouth, our heart, our soul, and our spirit. 4. Having thus received them humbly, let us employ them carefully, according to the intention of the donor.   Now to what end, think you, does God give us these sweet consolations? To make us sweet towards everyone, and excite us to love Him.   The mother gives sweetmeats to her child to induce it to kiss her; l et us then embrace our Blessed Saviour, who gives us these sweet things. But to embrace Him is to obey Him, to keep his commandments, do his will, and follow his desires, with a tender obedience and fidelity.   Whenever, therefore, we receive any spiritual consolation, we must be more diligent in doing good and in humbling ourselves. 5. Besides all this, we must, from time to time, renounce those sweet and tender consolations, by withdrawing our heart from them, and love them, because God sends them, and because they excite us to his love, yet it is not these we seek, but God Himself, and his holy love; not the consolations, but the Comforter; not their deliciousness, but the sweet Saviour; not their tenderness, but Him who is the delight of heaven and earth. It is in this manner we ought to dispose ourselves to persevere in the holy love of God, although throughout our whole life we were never to meet with any consolation; and be ready to say, as well from Calvary as upon Thabor: "O Lord, it is good for me to be with Thee," whether Thou art upon the cross or in thy glory. 6. To conclude, I admonish you, that should you experience any great abundance of such consolations, tendernesses, tears, or sweetnesses, you must confer faithfully with your spiritual director, that you may learn how to moderate and behave yourself under them; for it is written: "Hast thou found honey? Eat but as much of it as is sufficient for thee" (Prov. xxv. 16).

CHAPTER XIV.
Of spiritual dryness.

As long as consolations may last, do as I have just now directed you, Philothea. But this fine and agreeable weather will not always continue; for sometimes you shall find yourself so absolutely destitute of all feeling of devotion that your soul shall seem to be a wild, fruitless, barren desert, in which there is no trace of a pathway to find her God, nor any water of grace to refresh her, on account of the dryness which seems to threaten her with total and absolute desolation. Alas! how much does a poor soul in such a state deserve compassion: but especially when this evil is vehement; for then, in imitation of David, she feeds herself with tears night and day, while the enemy, to cast her into despair, mocks her by a thousand suggestions of despondency, saying, Ah, poor wretch, where is thy God? By what path shall thou be able to find

Him? Who can ever restore to thee the joy of his holy grace?

What shall you then do, Philothea? Examine the source from whence this evil has flowed to you: for it is we ourselves that are often the cause of our spiritual dryness.

1. As a mother refuses to give sugar to her child that is subject to worms, so God withholds consolations from us when we take a vain complacency in them, and are subject to the worms of self-conceit and presumption. "O my God, it is good for me that Thou hast humbled me; yes, for before I was humbled, I did offend Thee." (Ps. cxviii.)

2. When we neglect to gather the sweets and delights of the love of God at the proper season, He removes them from us in punishment of our sloth. The Israelites who neglected to gather the manna early in the morning could gather none after sunrise, for it was then all melted away.

3. We sometimes lie on a luxurious bed, like the spouse in the Canticles; the Spouse of our soul comes and knocks at the door of our heart, and invites us to return to our spiritual exercises; but we put them off, because we are unwilling to quit these vain amusements and false satisfactions; for which reason He departs, and permits us to slumber on. But afterwards, when we are desirous to seek Him, it is with great difficulty we find Him: and it is no more than what we have justly deserved, since we have been so unfaithful and disloyal as to have refused the participation of his love, to enjoy the consolations of the world. Ah! if you still keep the flour of Egypt you shall not have the manna of heaven. Bees detest artificial odours; and the sweetnesses of the Holy Spirit are incompatible with the counterfeit delights of the world.

4. The double-dealing and subtlety which we use

in our spiritual communications with our director may also produce dryness, for since you lie to the Holy Ghost, it is no wonder He should refuse you his consolations. If you will not be as sincere and plain as a little child, you shall not then have the sweetmeats of little children.

5. If you have glutted yourself with worldly pleasures, it is no wonder that you should find an unsavoury taste in spiritual delights. Doves that have eaten too much, says the old proverb, find cherries bitter. "He hath filled the hungry with good things," says our Blessed Lady, "and sent the rich empty away" (Luke, ii. 33). They that are glutted with the pleasures of the world are not capable of the delights of the Spirit.

6. If you have been careful to preserve the fruits of the consolations which you have received, you shall receive new ones; for to him that has more shall be given, but he that has not kept, but lost what was given him through his own fault, shall be deprived even of those graces which he had not, but which were prepared for him. Rain refreshes green plants, but it rots and destroys those that have lost their verdure.

There are several causes which occasion our fall from the consolations of devotion into dryness and barrenness of spirit. Let us then examine whether we can find any of them in ourselves; but observe, Philothea, that this examination is not to be made either with inquietude or too much curiosity; but if, after having faithfully considered our conduct, we find the cause of the evil to originate in ourselves, let us thank God for the discovery; for the evil is half cured when the cause of it is known; but if, on the contrary, you can find nothing in particular which may seem to have occasioned this dryness, do not trouble yourself about making any further inquiry, but with all simplicity, do as I shall now advise you.

1. Humble yourself very much before God, by acknowledging your own nothingness and misery. Alas! O Lord, what am I when left to myself but a dry parched ground, which, being rent on every side, has a great thirst for rain, but which, in the meantime, is dispersed by the wind, being reduced to dust. 2. Call upon God, and beg comfort of Him. "Restore unto me, O Lord, the joy of thy salvation. Father, if it be possible, let this chalice pass away from me." Away, O thou barren north wind, that witherest my soul; and blow, O gentle gale of consolations, upon the garden of my heart, that its good affections may diffuse around the odour of sweetness. 3. Go to your confessor, open your soul to him, and follow the advice he gives you, with the utmost simplicity and humility; for God, who is well pleased with obedience, frequently renders the counsels we take from others, but especially from those who are the guides of our soul, profitable, when otherwise there might be no great appearance of success; as He made the waters of Jordan healthful to Namaan, the use of which Eliseus had ordained him, without any appearance of human reason (4 Kings, v. 14). 4. But after all this, there is nothing so profitable and so fruitful in a state of spiritual dryness, as not to suffer our affections to be too strongly fixed upon the desire of being delivered from it. I do not say that we ought not simply to wish for deliverance, but that we should not set our heart upon it, but rather yield ourselves up to the pure mercy and special providence of God, that He may make use of us to serve Him as long as He pleases. In the midst of these thorns and deserts, let us say: "O Father, if it be possible, let this chalice pass away from me;" let us also add, courageously, "yet not my will, but

thine be done!" But here let us stop with as much tranquillity as possible : for God, beholding this holy indifference, will comfort us with many graces and favours; as was the case with Abraham, when he resolved to deprive himself of his son Isaac; God, who contented Himself in seeing him in this disposition of pure resignation, comforted him with a most delightful vision, accompanied by the most consolatory benedictions. We ought, then, under all kinds of afflictions, whether corporal or spiritual, and amidst all distractions or lessenings of sensible devotion, which may happen to us, to say, with Job, from the bottom of our heart, with profound submission, "The Lord gave me consolations, and the Lord has taken them away; his holy name be for ever blessed. For if we continue in this humility, He will restore to us his delightful favours, as He did to Job, who constantly used the like words in all his miseries.

Finally, Philothea, in the midst of our spiritual dryness, let us never lose courage, but wait with patience for the return of consolation. Let us not omit any of our exercises of devotion, but if possible, let us multiply our good works; and not being able to present liquid sweetmeats to our dear Spouse, let us offer Him dry ones; for either is acceptable to Him, provided that the heart which offers them is perfectly fixed in the resolution of loving Him. When the spring is fair, it is said that bees make more honey, and multiply less; but when the spring is cold and cloudy, they multiply more, and make less honey. Thus it happens frequently, Philothea, that the soul, finding herself in the fair spring of spiritual consolations, amuses herself so much in gathering and sucking them, that in the abundance of these sweet delights she produces fewer good works; whilst, on the contrary, in the midst of spiritual dryness, the more destitute she finds herself of the consolations of devotion, the more she multiplies her good works, and enriches herself more and more with the virtues of patience, humility, self-contempt, resignation, and renunciation of self-love.

It is the mistake of many, especially of women, to believe that the service of God, without relish, tenderness of heart, or sensible satisfaction, is less agreeable to his Divine Majesty; for as our actions are like roses, which, when fresh, have more beauty, yet, when dry, have more perfume and sweetness; even so, though our works done with tenderness of heart are more agreeable to ourselves, who regard only our own delight, yet, when performed in the time of dryness, they possess more sweetness, and become more precious in the sight of God. Yes, Philothea, in the time of dryness our will carries us by main force, as it were, to the service of God, and consequently it must be more vigorous and constant than in the time of consolation.

There is not much merit in serving a prince in times of peace, amid the delights of the court; but to serve him amidst the hardships of war, or in troubles and persecutions, is a true mark of constancy and fidelity. Blessed Angela de Foligno says, that the prayer which is most acceptable to God is that which we make by force and constraint, the prayer to which we apply ourselves, not for any relish we find in it, nor by inclination, but purely to please God, to which our will carries us against our inclinations, violently forcing its way through the midst of those clouds of dryness which oppose it. I say the same of all sorts of good works, whether interior or exterior; for the more contradictions we find in doing them, the higher they are esteemed in the sight of God. The less there is of our par-

ticular interest in the pursuit of virtues, the brighter
does the purity of divine love shine forth in them.
A child willingly kisses its mother when she gives
it sugar; but it is a sign of great love if it kisses her
after she has given it wormwood or any other
bitter drink.

CHAPTER XV.

*A confirmation and illustration of what has been
said by a remarkable example.*

To make the whole of this instruction the more
evident, I will here relate an excellent passage from
the history of St. Bernard, as it has been related by
a learned and judicious writer. It is an ordinary
thing, he says, with all that serve God, and are not
as yet experienced in the vicissitudes of spiritual
life, to lose breath and fall into pusillanimity and
sadness when the sweetness of sensible devotion,
together with that agreeable light which invites
them to run forward in the way of God, is withdrawn from them. Persons of understanding assign
the following reason for this, that man's nature
cannot hold out for any length of time without some
kind of delight, either heavenly or earthly. Now,
as souls that are elevated above themselves by
striving after spiritual pleasure easily renounce
visible objects, so when, by the divine disposition,
spiritual joy is withdrawn from them, whilst they
find themselves at the same time deprived of corporal consolations, and are not as yet accustomed
to wait with patience for the return of the true
sun, it seems to them as if they were neither in
heaven nor on earth, and that they shall remain
buried in perpetual night; so that like a little infant deprived of its mother's breast, they languish
and moan, and become uneasy and troublesome to

1

everyone, more especially to themselves. This then happened, in the journey of St. Bernard, to Geoffry of Perrone, who had lately dedicated himself to the service of God. Having suddenly become quite deprived of consolations and filled with interior darkness, he began to remember his worldly friends, his kindred, and the riches he had lately forsaken; by which he was assaulted with so strong a temptation, that, not being able to conceal it in his behaviour, one of his greatest confidants perceived it, and having taken an opportunity, he accosted him with mildness, and said to him in private: What means this, Geoffry? Whence comes it to pass that, contrary to custom, you are so pensive and melancholy? Ah, brother! answered Geoffry, with a deep sigh, I shall never more be joyful whilst I live. The other, moved to pity by these words, went at once with brotherly zeal, and told it to their common father, St. Bernard, who, perceiving the danger, went into the church to pray to God for him: whilst Geoffry in the meantime, being overwhelmed with sadness, and resting his head upon a stone, fell asleep. Shortly after both of them arose, the one from prayer, having obtained the favour he asked for, and the other from sleep, but with so pleasant and serene a countenance, that his friend, surprised at so great and sudden a change, could not refrain from reproaching him in a good-natured manner with the answer he had a little before given him. To this Geoffry replied: If I told you before, that I should never more be joyful, I now assure you that I shall never more be sorrowful.

Such was the result of the temptation of that devout person. But observe in this relation, Philothea—1. That God commonly gives a foretaste of heavenly delight to such as enter into his service, in order to withdraw them from earthly pleasures, and encourage them in the pursuit of his love, as a mother who to allure her infant to her breast puts honey upon it.　2. That, according to the secret design of his providence, He is pleased to withhold from us the milk and honey of his consolation, that, by weaning us in this manner, we may learn to feed on the more dry and solid bread of vigorous devotion, exercised under the trial of distaste and spiritual dryness.　3. That as violent temptations frequently arise amidst these desolating drynesses, we must resolutely fight against them, since they do not proceed from God; but nevertheless, we must patiently suffer them, since God has ordained them for our exercise.　4. That we must never lose courage amidst those interior pains and conflicts, nor say with the good Geoffry, "I shall never more be joyful;" for in the midst of the darkness of the night we must look for the return of the brightness of day; and again, in the fairest spiritual weather, we must not say, I shall never more be sorrowful: for as the wise man says, "In the day of good things we must not be unmindful of evil things" (Eccles. xi. 27.)　We must hope in the midst of afflictions, and fear in the midst of prosperity; and under both circumstances we must always humble ourselves.　5. That it is a sovereign remedy to discover our miseries to some spiritual friend, who may be able to give us comfort.

I think it necessary to observe, Philothea, that in these conflicts, God and our spiritual enemy have contrary designs.　God seeks to conduct us to perfect purity of heart, to an entire renunciation of self-interest in what relates to his service, and to an absolute self-denial; whereas the enemy of our souls endeavours, by these severe conflicts, to discourage us from the practice of prayer, and entice us back to sensual pleasures, that, by thus making troublesome to ourselves as to our neighbours, he may scandalise and disgrace holy devotion. But, provided you observe the lessons I have given you, you shall, amidst these interior afflictions, greatly advance on the way to perfection. I cannot, however, dismiss this important subject without saying a few words more.

It sometimes happens that spiritual dryness proceeds from the indisposition of body, as when, through an excess of watching, labour, or fasting, we find ourselves oppressed by fatigue, drowsiness, lassitude, and such like infirmities, which, though they depend on the body, yet are apt to incommode the spirit also, on account of the intimate connexion that subsists between both. Now, on such occasions, we must never omit to perform several acts of virtue, by using, as much as possible, our spirit and superior will. For although our whole soul seems to be asleep, and overwhelmed with drowsiness and fatigue, yet the actions of our spirit do not cease to be very acceptable to God; and we may say at the same time with the sacred Spouse, "I sleep, but my heart watcheth." (Cant. v. 2). For, as I have observed before, if there is less relish in this manner of performing our spiritual exercises, there is, on the other hand, more merit and virtue. Now, the remedy on such occasions is to recruit the strength and vigour of our body by some kind of lawful recreation. For this reason St. Francis ordained that his religious should use moderation in their labours, so as not to oppress the fervour of their spirits.

As I am speaking of this glorious father, I must not forget to tell you he himself was once assaulted and perplexed with so deep a melancholy of spirit, that he could not help showing it in his behaviour: for if he was disposed to converse with his religious, he was unable; if he withdrew himself from them it was worse; abstinence and corporal mortification oppressed him, and prayer gave him no relief. He continued two years in this state, so that he seemed to be quite abandoned by God; but at length, after he had humbly suffered this violent storm, our Saviour, in an instant, restored him to a happy tranquillity. If, therefore, the greatest servants of God are subject to these shocks, how can we be astonished if they sometimes happen to us?

PART THE FIFTH.

◆

INSTRUCTIONS AND EXERCISES NECESSARY FOR
RENEWING THE SOUL, AND CONFIRMING
HER IN DEVOTION.

CHAPTER I.

*We ought every year to renew our good resolutions by
the following exercises.*

THE first point of these exercises consists in our
being thoroughly sensible of their importance. Human nature easily falls off from its good affections,
on account of the frailty and evil inclinations of the
flesh, which depress the soul, and draw her always
downwards, unless she often raises herself upwards
by continual efforts: just like birds, which will fall
to the ground if they do not keep their wings constantly in motion, so as to sustain their flight. For
this reason, Philothea, you must repeat very often
the good resolutions you have made to serve God,
lest, by neglecting to do so, you should relapse into
your former state, or even into a worse condition;
for spiritual falls always cast us down to a lower
state than that in which we were before we aspired
to devotion.

As there is no watch, be it ever so good, but
must be often wound up, and now and then taken
asunder to remove rust and dust, and have mended
or repaired what may be broken or out of order,
so he that is careful of his soul ought to wind it
up morning and evening by the foregoing exer-

cises, and, at least, once a year take it asunder to examine all its dispositions, in order to repair all its defects.; and as the watchmaker puts fine oil on the wheels and springs, that their motions may be more easy, and the works of the watch less subject to rust, so a devout person, after making this review of his heart, in order to renew it, must anoint it with the graces received in confession and the Holy Eucharist. This exercise will repair your spirit, impaired by time, warm your heart, reanimate your good resolutions, and make your virtues flourish vigorously.

The primitive Christians practised this diligently on the anniversary day of the baptism of our Lord, when, as St. Gregory Nazianzen relates, they renewed those professions and protestations that are usually made in baptism. Let us also, Philothea, seriously dispose ourselves to follow their example. Having, then, for this purpose, chosen the most convenient time, according to the advice of your spiritual father, for a retreat of a few days, meditate on the following points, according to the method I have prescribed in the second part.

CHAPTER II.

Considerations on the favour which God does us in calling us to his service, according to the protestation indicated in the first part.

Consider the points of your protestation :—First, to have forsaken, cast away, detested, and renounced for ever all mortal sin ; secondly, to have dedicated and consecrated your soul, heart, and body, with all their powers and faculties, to the love and service of God ; thirdly, that if you should chance to fall into any sin, you would immediately rise again by the help of God's grace. Are not these just, noble, and generous resolutions? Consider well in your soul, therefore, how holy and reasonable this protestation is, and how much it is to be desired.

2. Consider to whom you have made this protestation; for it is to God. If our word given to men bind us strictly, how much more so those we have given to God "It is to Thee, O Lord," said David, "my heart hath spoken it, my heart hath sent forth this good word. Oh! I will never forget it." (Ps. xliv.)

3. Consider that you made this protestation in the presence of the whole court of heaven. Yes, your patron saint and all that blessed company beheld you, and their breasts heaved with emotions of joy and exultation at your words : they saw, with the eyes of unspeakable love, your heart prostrate at the feet of your Saviour, consecrating itself to his service. As there was a particular joy on that occasion in the heavenly Jerusalem, so there will be now a commemoration of the same, if with a sincere heart you renew your resolutions.

4. Consider by what means you were induced to make your protestation. Ah! how good and gracious was God to you at that time? Oh, tell me sincerely were you not invited to it by the sweet attractions of the Holy Ghost? Were not the ropes wherewith God drew your boat to that blessed haven composed of love and charity? How earnestly did He seek to attract you thereto by the delicious sweetness of his grace in the sacraments, spiritual reading, and prayer. Alas! Philothea, you were asleep whilst God watched : He thought over your soul thoughts of peace, and meditated in your favour meditations of love.

5. Consider that God inspired you with these holy resolutions in the flower of your age. Ah! what a happiness it is to learn so soon that which we cannot know but too late. St. Augustin, having

been called at the age of thirty years, exclaimed: "O ancient beauty! how comes it that I have known thee so late? Alas! I saw thee before, but considered thee not:" and you may well say, O ancient sweetness! why did I not relish thee before? Alas! you did not even then deserve it. However, acknowledging the special favour which God has done you in attracting you to Himself in your youth, say, with David: "Thou hast taught me, O my God, from my youth, and I will for ever declare thy wonderful works." (Ps. xvii. 47.) But if this has happened in your old age, ah! Philothea, what an extraordinary grace, that, after having thus misspent all your former years, God should call you before your death, and stop the course of your misery at a time in which, if it had continued, you must have been miserable for eternity.

6. Consider the effects of this vocation, and comparing what you now are with what you have been, you will doubtless find in yourself a great change for the better. Do you not esteem it a happiness to know how to converse with God by prayer; to be inflamed with a desire to love Him; to have obtained a complete victory over the many passions wherewith you were troubled; to have avoided innumerable sins and perplexities of conscience; and, in fine, to have communicated so much oftener than you would have done, uniting yourself to that sovereign source of never-ending grace? Ah, how great are these favours! We must weigh them, Philothea, with the weights of the sanctuary; it is God's right hand that has done all this: "The right hand of the Lord," says David, "hath exalted me; I shall not die, but live, and shall declare with my heart, with my mouth, and by my actions, the wonderful works of the Lord." (Ps. cxvii.)

After all these considerations, which must, doubt-

less, furnish you with many pious affections, conclude simply with an act of thanksgiving and fervent
prayer, that you may make good use of them : and
so retire with the most profound humility and utmost confidence in God, deferring the making the
effort of your resolutions till after the second point
of this exercise.

CHAPTER III.

*The examination of the soul concerning the advance-
ment of a devout life.*

As the second point of the exercise is somewhat
long, in order to practise it, I must tell you that it
is not necessary you should perform it all at once,
but at different times, taking what regards your
conduct towards God, for one time; what relates to
yourself, for another; what concerns your neighbour, for a third; and the consideration of your
passions, for the fourth. Neither is it expedient
that you should perform it on your knees, except at
the beginning and the end, which comprises the
affections. The other points of the examination you
may perform profitably whilst walking abroad, or
still more profitably in bed, provided you can preserve yourself against drowsiness, and keep thoroughly awake : but then, to do this, you must have
read attentively beforehand. It is necessary, however, to go through the whole of the second point in
three days and two nights at furthest, dedicating
as much time to it on each day and night as you
possibly can; for if this exercise should be deferred
to times far distant from each other, it would lose
its force and make but weak impressions.

After every point of the examination, you must ·
remark those in which you may find that you have

failed ; also in what you are defective, and the nature of the principal disorders you may have discovered, that you may declare them to your confessor, in order to take his advice and acquire resolution and spiritual strength to overcome them; and although on some days, on which you may perform one or other exercise, it is not absolutely necessary to withdraw yourself from all company, yet you must be in some measure retired, especially towards the evening, that you may go sooner to bed, and take that repose of body and mind which is necessary for reflection. You must also in the daytime make frequent aspirations to God, to our Lady, to the angels, and to the whole court of heaven : moreover, all this must be done with a heart fully inflamed with the love of God, and a desire of attaining perfection.

To begin then this examination properly, 1. Place yourself in the presence of God. 2. Invoke the Holy Ghost, begging of Him to enlighten your understanding, that you may gain a perfect knowledge of yourself, crying out with St. Augustin, in the spirit of humility: "O Lord, let me know Thee, and let me know myself;" and with St. Francis: "Lord, who art Thou, and who am I?" Protest that it is not your intention to acquire this knowledge in order to attribute any glory to yourself on the occasion, but that you may rejoice in God : return Him thanks, and glorify his blessed name for all his benefits. Protest, likewise, that if you find, as you fear you shall, that you have made but little or no progress, or even that you have gone backward, be not, nevertheless, by any means dejected, chilled, or overcome by any sort of cowardice or faintheartedness ; but, on the contrary, encourage and animate yourself, humble yourself the more, and apply, with the assistance of divine grace, the proper remedies to your defects. Afterwards consider calmly how you have behaved up to the present hour towards God, your neighbour, and yourself.

CHAPTER IV.

An examination of the state of your soul towards God.

How stands your heart with respect to mortal sin? Are you firmly resolved never to commit it, on any account whatsoever? Has this resolution continued with you from the time of your protestation till the present moment? In this resolution consists the foundation of this spiritual life.

How is your heart disposed with regard to the commandments of God? Do you find them good, sweet, and agreeable? Ah! my child, he whose taste is in good order and whose stomach is sound, loves good meats, and rejects the bad.

How is your heart affected with regard to venial sins? We cannot keep ourselves so pure as not to fall now and then into such sins; but are there none to which you have a particular inclination, or, which would be still worse, are there none to which you bear an affection and love?

How is your heart affected with relation to spiritual exercises? Do you love them? Do you esteem them? Do they not make you uneasy? Are you not disgusted with them? To which of them do you find yourself more or less inclined? To hear the word of God, to read it, to discourse of it, to meditate on it, to aspire to God, to go to confession, to receive spiritual advice, to prepare yourself for communion, to communicate, to restrain your affections; what is there in all this that is repugnant to your heart? and if you find anything to which your heart has less inclination, examine the cause from whence this dislike arises and apply the remedy.

How does your heart stand with regard to God Himself? Does it delight in the remembrance of God? Does this remembrance leave an agreeable sweetness behind it? " Ah!" said David, " I remembered God and was delighted." Do you find a certain propensity in your heart to love God, and a particular satisfaction in relishing that love? Does your heart feel joy in reflecting on the immensity, goodness, or sweetness of God? If the remembrance of God comes to you amidst the occupations and vanities of the world, does it make room for itself? Does it seize upon your heart? Does it seem to you that your heart turns in that direction, and, is it were, runs to meet God? Certainly there are such souls to be found.

Is it not true that a loving wife, as soon as she learns the return of her husband after a long absence, or when she thinks she hears his voice, goes at once to meet him? Nothing keeps her heart from him; she gives up all other thoughts, in order to think on him alone. It is the same with souls that love God well; be they ever so busy, when the remembrance of God comes near them, they lose almost the thought of all things else, for joy to see that this dear remembrance is returned; and this is an extremely good sign.

How is your heart affected towards Jesus Christ? God and man? Are you pleased at being with Him? As bees are pleased with their honey, and wasps with corrupted things, so good souls find their contentment in thinking on Jesus Christ, and feel great love for Him; but the wicked take delight in vanities.

How is your heart affected towards our Blessed Lady, the saints, and your good angel? Do you love them well? Have you a special confidence in their patronage? Are you pleased with their representations, their lives, and their praises?

As to your tongue: how do you speak of God? Does it please you to speak well of Him, according to your condition and ability? Do you love to sing his praises?

As to works: consider whether you take the exterior glory of God to heart, and are emulous of doing something for his honour; for such as love God, love, like David, the adorning of his house.

Can you find that you have forsaken any affection, or renounced anything for the sake of God? for it is a great sign of love, to deprive ourselves of anything in favour of Him whom we love. What, then, have you hitherto forsaken for the love of God?

CHAPTER V.

An examination of our state with regard to ourselves.

How do you love yourself? Do you not love yourself too much for this world? If so, you will desire to live always here, and be very solicitous to establish yourself on this earth; but if you love yourself for heaven, you will desire, or at least be content, to depart from hence at whatsoever hour it shall please the Lord.

Do you regulate well the love you feel for yourself? For it is only the inordinate love of ourselves that will be our ruin. Now, a well-ordered love requires that we should love the soul better than the body; that we should be more solicitous to acquire virtue than any other thing; that we should set a higher estimation on the favour of heaven than on the honour of this low and perishable world. A well-ordered heart will oftener say within itself: "What will the angels say," if I think upon such a thing? than, "What will men say?"

What kind of love have you for your own heart? you not get annoyed at having to serve it in its sickness? Alas! you ought to assist and procure assistance for it, and lay aside all things else, whenever passions torment it.

What do you esteem yourself before God? Doubtless nothing. It is no great humility in a fly to esteem itself nothing in comparison with a mountain; nor for a drop of water to hold itself as nothing in comparison with the sea; nor for a spark of fire to hold itself as nothing when compared with the sun; but humility consists in not esteeming ourselves above others, and in not desiring to be so esteemed by others. How are you disposed in this regard?

As to your tongue; do you not sometimes boast of yourself one way or other? Do you not flatter yourself in speaking of yourself?

As to recreations; do you allow yourself any pleasures contrary to your health? I mean any vain, unprofitable, useless pleasures, or such as are prolonged too much into the night.

CHAPTER VI.

An examination of the state of our soul towards our neighbour.

The love of husband and wife ought to be sweet, calm, strong, constant, and persevering: and this principally because it is agreeable to the ordinance of God. I say the same of the love of our children and near relations, and also of our friends, every-one according to his rank.

But to speak in general, how is your heart affected towards your neighbour? Do you love him from your heart, and for the love of God? To discern this well, you must bring to your mind certain troublesome and intractable people, for it is here we exercise the love of God towards our neighbour; and much more with regard to such as injure us either by their actions or words. Examine well whether your heart is free in their regard, or whether you do not find a greater repugnance to love them.

Are you not apt to speak ill of your neighbours, and especially of such as do not like you? Do you refrain from doing evil to your neighbour, either directly or indirectly? Provided you are a reasonable person, you will easily perceive it.

CHAPTER VII.

An examination of the affections of your soul.

I have considered it my duty to dilate on these points, in the examination of which consists the knowledge of our spiritual advancement; but the examination of sin regards the confession of such as think not seriously of advancing themselves.

Yet we must not examine ourselves upon any of these points otherwise than with calm application, considering in what state our heart has been since our resolution, and what considerable faults against them we have committed.

But to abridge the whole; we must reduce this exercise into an examination into our passions; and if it is troublesome to consider every point so minutely as has been advised, we may examine ourselves as to what we have been, and how we have behaved ourselves in our love to God, our neighbour, and ourselves: in our hatred towards our own and others' sins; for we must desire the extirpation of both: in our desires relating to riches, pleasures, and honours: in our fear of the dangers of sin, and in that of the loss of our worldly goods, for we are apt to fear the one too much and the other too little: in our hope, placing too much reliance on the world and creatures, and too little on God and things eternal: in an inordinate sadness or excessive joy caused by vain or base things . in fine, what affections entangle our heart, what passions possess it, in what it has principally strayed out of the right way; for by the passions we may judge of the state of the soul, by examining them one after the other ; and as he who plays on a stringed instrument, by touching all the strings, finds which are out of tune and brings them into accord either by tightening or loosening them, so if, after having examined all the passions in our soul, we find them little in harmony with the desire we have to glorify God, we may put them in tune by means of his grace and the advice of our spiritual father.

CHAPTER VIII.

Affections to be exercised after this examination.

After having quietly considered each point of the examination into the state of your soul, you must afterwards proceed to the affections in this manner :

1. Return thanks to God for the little amendment you may have found in your life since your resolution, and acknowledge that it has been his mercy alone that has wrought it in and for you.

2. Humble yourself exceedingly before God, acknowledging that if you have not advanced much it has been through your own fault, because you have not faithfully, courageously, and constantly corresponded with the inspirations, lights, and good impulses which He has given you in prayer and at other times.

2. Promise that you will eternally praise Him for the graces by which He has withdrawn you from your evil inclinations by this little amendment.

4. Ask pardon for your unfaithfulness and disloyalty in not corresponding with his graces.

5. Offer Him your heart, to the end that He may make Himself the entire master of it.

6. Beseech of Him to make you faithful to his graces.

7. Invoke the saints, the Blessed Virgin, your guardian angel, your patron, St. Joseph, and the whole court of heaven.

CHAPTER IX.

Considerations suitable for renewing our good purposes.

Having made your examination, and consulted your director on your defects and the proper remedies for them, make use of one of the following considerations every day as a meditation, employing in it the time of your mental prayer, observing the same method as you used in the meditations of the first part, by placing yourself first in the presence of God, and then imploring his grace to establish you in his holy love and service.

CHAPTER X.

The first consideration : the excellence of our soul.

Consider the worth and excellence of your immortal soul, endued with an understanding capable of a knowledge not only of this visible world, but also of the angels, of eternity, of heaven, and of a most high sovereign, and infinitely good God : a soul which, moreover, knows how to live in this visible world. so as to associate herself with the angels in heaven, and to enjoy God for all eternity.

Consider, also, that your soul has a will capable of loving God, and which cannot hate Him in Himself. Examine your heart, and behold how generous it is ; and that, as bees can never stay upon any corrupt thing, but only stop among the flowers, so no creature can ever satisfy your heart, for it can never rest but in God alone. Recall to your remembrance the dearest and strongest affections which have heretofore possessed your heart, and judge in truth, whether, in the midst of them, it was not full of anxious inquietudes, tormenting thoughts, and restless cares.

Our heart, alas! runs eagerly in pursuit of creatures, thinking they will satisfy its desires; but as soon as it has overtaken them, it finds its satisfaction still afar off, God not being willing that our hearts should find any resting-place, even as the dove which went out of Noah's ark could not find one; to the end that it may return to Himself from whom it proceeded. Ah! what natural beauty there is in our heart! Why, then, do we detain it against its will in the service of creatures?

Since then, O my soul! thou art capable of knowing and loving God, why wilt thou amuse thyself with anything less than God? Since thou mayest put in thy claim to eternity, why shouldst thou amuse thyself with transitory moments? It was one of the most grievous reflections of the prodigal son, that he might have fared deliciously at his father's table, whilst he was feeding amongst filthy swine. Since thou art, O my soul, capable of possessing God, woe be to thee if thou contentest thyself with anything less than God.

Elevate your soul cheerfully with this consideration: remind her that she is immortal and worthy of eternity; animate her with courage on this subject.

CHAPTER XI.
The second consideration: the excellence of virtue.
Consider that nothing but virtue and devotion

can make your soul content in this world. Behold how beautiful they are, and draw a comparison between the virtues and their contrary vices. What sweetness in patience, when compared with revenge? In meekness, compared with anger and vexation? In humility. compared with arrogance and ambition? In liberality. compared with covetousness. In charity. in comparison with envy? In sobriety, with revellings? For virtues have this admirable quality. that they delight the soul with an incomparable sweetness and satisfaction after we have exercised them. whereas vices leave the soul exceedingly fatigued and disordered. Why then do we not endeavour to acquire this sweetness?

With respect to the vices, he that has but little of them is uneasy, and he that has much of them is more discontented; but as to the virtues, he that has but a little. has already some contentment, which increases as the virtues themselves increase.

O devout life! how fair, how lovely, how sweet and delightful art thou: thou dost alleviate our tribulations. and dost add sweetness to our consolations: without thee good is evil, and pleasures are full of restlessness, trouble. and deceit. Ah! he that should know thee well might say, with the Samaritan woman: "Lord, give me this water!" an aspiration very frequently used by the holy mother Teresa, and St. Oatherine of Genoa, although upon different occasions.

CHAPTER XII.

The third consideration : the example of the Saints.

Consider the example of the saints in every condition of life; what have they not done to devote themselves entirely to the love and service of God?

Look on the martyrs, invincible in their resolutions; what torments have they not suffered for the faith? But above all, behold that innumerable train of fair and delicate virgins, whiter than lilies in purity, sweeter than roses in charity; some of whom at twelve, others at thirteen, fifteen, twenty, and twenty-five years of age, have endured a thousand kinds of martyrdom, rather than renounce their resolutions, not only in regard to the profession of their faith, but also their protestation of devotion; some dying rather than forsake their virginity; others, rather than desist from consoling their companions-in-torture, comforting the afflicted, and burying the dead. O good God, what constancy have they not shown on these occasions!

Consider the unshaken constancy wherewith so many holy confessors have despised the world. How invincible have they shown themselves in their resolutions, from which nothing could ever divert them: how they embraced them without reserve, and maintained them without exception. Good God! what admirable things does St. Augustin relate of his holy mother, with what constancy did she pursue her design of serving God, both in marriage and widowhood; and St. Jerome also of his dear daughter, Paula, in the midst of so many oppositions, in the midst of such a variety of accidents! What is there that we might not do after such excellent patterns? They were what we are; they served the same God, and practised the same virtues; why should not we also do as much, according to our condition and vocation, in order to preserve our resolution, and the holy protestations we have made to belong to God.

CHAPTER XIII.

The fourth consideration: the love that Jesus Christ bears us.

Consider the incomparable love on account of which Jesus Christ our Lord suffered so much in this world, especially in the garden of Olivet and upon Mount Calvary, for our sake. By all these pains and sufferings He obtained of God the Father the good resolutions and protestations which your heart has made; and by the same means He also obtained for you whatever is necessary to maintain, nourish, strengthen, and fulfil them. O holy resolutions, how precious are ye, since ye are the fruits of the passion of my Saviour! Oh, how tenderly ought my soul cherish ye, having been so dear to my sweet Jesus! Alas! O Saviour of my soul, Thou didst die to purchase for me these resolutions, Oh, grant me thy grace rather to suffer death than to lose them. Observe, Philothea, that it is certain that the Heart of Jesus beheld your heart from the tree of the cross, and by the love which He bore it, obtained for you all the good you ever had or shall ever have. Yes, Philothea, we may all say with the prophet Jeremias: "O Lord, before I had a being, Thou didst behold me, and didst call me by my name;" since the divine goodness did actually prepare for us all the general and particular means of our salvation, and consequently of our resolutions. As a woman before the birth of her infant prepares the cradle, the linen, the swathing clothes, and even a nurse for it, although it is not yet in the world, so our Saviour, who designed to bring you forth to salvation, and make you his child, prepared on his cross all that was necessary for you—your spiritual cradle, your linen, your swathing clothes, and your nurse, all for your happiness; for such are all those graces whereby He seeks to attract your soul and bring it to perfection.

Ah! my God, how deeply ought we to imprint this thy love in our memory! It is impossible that I could have been so tenderly beloved by my Saviour, as that He could think of me in particular, even in all those little occurrences by which He has drawn me to Himself! How much then ought we to love, cherish, and employ all that to our profit! O consoling reflection! the tender heart of Jesus thought on Philothea, loved her, and procured for her a thousand means of salvation, even as many as if it had no other soul in the world to think on. As the sun, shining upon one place of the earth, enlightens it no less than if it shone on no other, so, in the very same manner, is our Lord solicitous for all his dear children, thinking on each of them as if there was no other in the world. "He loved me, and gave Himself up for me," says St. Paul, speaking as of himself alone, and as if Jesus had done nothing for others. O Philothea, let this sacred truth be engraved on your soul, in order to cherish and nourish your resolution, which was so precious to the heart of your Saviour.

CHAPTER XIV.

The fifth consideration: the eternal love of God towards us.

Consider the eternal love which God has had for you; for before our Lord Jesus Christ, as man, suffered on the cross for you, his Divine Majesty, by his omniscience, already foresaw your being, and loved you exceedingly. But when did his love for you begin? Even when He began to be God. But when did He begin to be God? Never; and thus as

He has always been without a beginning or end, so He has loved you from all eternity ; and in consequence of this love has prepared for you those graces and favours. Hence, speaking to you as well as to others, by the prophet Jeremias, ch. xxxi., He says: "I have loved thee with an eternal love, therefore taking pity on thee I have drawn thee to myself :" and amongst other things He caused thee to make firm resolutions to serve Him.

O God, what resolutions are those on which Thou hast thought and meditated from all eternity ! Ah, how dear and precious ought they be to us ! What ought we not suffer rather than forget the smallest portion of them ! no, not even though we were to gain the world ; for the whole world is not worth one soul, and a soul is worth nothing without these resolutions.

CHAPTER XV.

General affections on the preceding considerations, and conclusion of these exercises.

O dear resolutions ! ye are the fair tree of life which God. with his own hand, has planted in the midst of my heart, and which my Saviour desires to water with his Blood, and make it fruitful. I will rather endure a thousand deaths than suffer any wind of prosperity or adversity to pluck thee up. No; neither vanity, delights, riches, nor tribulations, shall ever withdraw me from my design.

Alas ; O Lord, it is Thou thyself who has planted, and eternally preserved in thy fatherly bosom, this fair tree for the garden of my heart. Alas! how many souls are there who have not been favoured in this manner, and how then can I ever sufficiently humble myself beneath thy mercy ?

fair and holy resolutions ! if I keep you, you

will preserve me; if you animate my soul, my soul shall live in you; live then for ever, O resolutions which are eternal in the mercy of God; bide eternally in me, and let me never forsake you.

After these affections you must consider the particular means necessary to maintain your dear resolutions, and determine to be faithful in making good use of them : such as frequent prayer, the sacraments, good works, the amendment of your faults, discovered in the examination, lessening the occasions of evil, and following the advice which may be given you for this purpose.

Afterwards, by way of recruiting your strength, make a thousand protestations that you will persevere in your resolutions; and, as if you he'd your heart, soul, and will in your hands, dedicate, consecrate, sacrifice, and immolate them to God, protesting never to take them back again, but leave them in the hands of his Divine Majesty, in order to follow, on all occasions, his holy ordinances.

Pray to God to renovate you entirely, and that He would give you his blessing, and strengthen this your protestation. Invoke the Blessed Virgin, your patron St. *N. N.*, &c.

In this disposition of heart, go to your spiritual father, and accuse yourself of the principal faults which you may have remarked since your general confession, and receiving absolution in the same manner as the first time, pronounce and sign your protestation before him; and in conclusion, unite your renewed heart to its first principle, your Saviour, in the most holy sacrament of the Eucharist.

CHAPTER XVI.

The sentiments we must preserve after this exercise.

On the day you have made this renovation, and for some days following, you ought frequently to repeat from your heart these fervent words of St. Paul, St. Augustin, and St. Catherine of Genoa: "No, I am no more my own; whether I live, or whether I die, I am my Saviour's. I have no longer anything of me or mine; it is Jesus who lives in me, and all that I can call mine is to be wholly his. O world, thou art always thyself, and I have hitherto been always myself; but from henceforth I will be myself no more. No, we shall be no more ourselves, for we shall have our hearts changed, and the world which has so often deceived us shall be deceived in us; for not perceiving our change but by little and little, it will think that we are still Esaus, but we shall be like unto Jacob.

All these exercises ought to rest in the heart, and when we finish our consideration and meditation, we must turn gently and softly to our ordinary affairs and conversations, lest the balm of our good resolutions should be suddenly spilt; for it must soak and penetrate into all parts of the soul, without either straining the mind or the body.

CHAPTER XVII.

Answer to two objections which may be made to this introduction.

The world perhaps will tell you, Philothea, that these exercises and advices are so numerous, that he who would practise them must apply himself to nothing else. Alas! Philothea, even should we do nothing else, we should do enough, since we should do all that we ought to do in this world. But do you not perceive the stratagem of our enemy? If they were all to be necessarily performed every day, they would then indeed be our whole occupation; but it is not requisite to perform them otherwise than in their proper time and place, as occasions may present themselves. Of the full code of the civil laws, how many ought to be observed? The number must be determined according to circumstances, and no one would contend that all should be practised every day. David was a king occupied with the most difficult affairs, yet he performed many more exercises than I have prescribed to you. St. Louis, a prince admirable in war, peace, and the administration of justice, heard two Masses every day, and said vespers and complin with his chaplain; also made his meditations, visited hospitals every Friday, confessed frequently, and wore haircloth; heard sermons frequently, and held very often spiritual conferences: yet with all this he never met a single occasion for promoting the public good, which he did not lay hold of and diligently put in execution; and his court was more splendid and flourishing than it ever had been in the time of his predecessors. Perform, then, these exercises as I have marked out for you, and God will give you sufficient leisure and strength to perform all the rest of your affairs, even though He should make the sun stand still for you, as He did for Josue. We always do enough when God works with us.

The world will perhaps say that I suppose, almost throughout the whole work, that Philothea has the gift of mental prayer; and yet, everyone has it not; so that this introduction will not serve for all. I have thus presupposed, and it is no less true that everyone has it not; but it is also tr that almost everyone, even the most dull, may have it, provided they have good guides, and are willing to take as much pains to obtain it as it deserves. But even should there be some who have not this gift in the smallest degree, which I think can hardly be the case, a wise spiritual director will easily supply the defect, by teaching them to read, or to hear others read, the considerations included in the meditations, with profound and close attention.

CHAPTER XVIII.

The three last and principal counsels for this introduction.

On the first day of every month repeat the protestation inserted in the first Part,* after your meditation; and at all times protest that you are determined to observe it; saying with David: "No, my God, never will I forget thy justifications, for in them Thou hast given me life." (Ps. cxviii.) When you feel any disorder in your soul, take your protestation in hand, and, prostrate in the spirit of humility, recite it with your whole heart; this will cause you to feel great ease and comfort.

Make an open profession, not that you are devout, but that you desire to become devout. Do not be ashamed to practise those necessary actions which conduct the soul to the love of God. Acknowledge frankly that you would rather die than commit a mortal sin; that you are resolved to frequent the sacraments, and to follow the counsels of your

* Page 38.

director, though it is not necessary to name him, for various reasons ; for this candid profession of our desire to serve God, and to consecrate ourselves entirely to his love, is very acceptable to his Divine Majesty, who would not have us be ashamed either of Him or of his cross. Besides it cuts short many proposals and invitations which the world might make to draw us the contrary way, and obliges us in honour to act according to what we profess. As philosophers profess themselves philosophers that they may be allowed to live like philosophers, so we must profess that we are desirous of devotion, that we may be allowed to live devoutly. If any-one tell you that you may live devoutly without the practice of these counsels and exercises, answer him mildly that, your infirmity being so great, you stand in need of more help and assistance than others.

In fine, Philothea, I conjure you by all that is sacred in heaven and on earth, by the baptism you have received, by the womb which bore Jesus Christ, by the charitable heart wherewith He loved you, and by the bowels of that mercy in which you hope, continue to persevere in this blessed design of leading a devout life. Our days glide away and death is at the gate : "The trumpet sounds the retreat," says St. Gregory Nazianzen, "let every man be ready, for judgment is near." St. Symphorian's mother, seeing him led to martyrdom, cried after him : " My son, remember eternal life ; look up to heaven, and think upon Him who reigns there ; you are approaching quickly the termination of this short course of earthly life." Philothea, I say the same to you : look up to heaven and do not forfeit it for this base earth ! look down to hell, and do not cast yourself into it for transitory toys ! look up to Jesus Christ, and do not renounce Him for the world !

and should the labours of a devout life seem hard to you, sing with St. Francis:

> " Earthly toils are sweet to me,
> Awaiting a blest eternity."

Live, Jesus! to whom with the Father and the Holy Ghost, be all honour and glory, now and for all eternity. Amen.

THE END.

M. H. Gill & Son, Printers, Dublin.